GuadalcanalMarine

Guadal

anal Marine

Kerry L. Lane

Lieutenant Colonel, U.S. Marine Corps (Ret.)

University Press of Mississippi / Jackson

www.upress.state.ms.us

The University Press of Mississippi is a member of the
Association of American University Presses.

12 11 10 09 08 07 06 05 04   4 3 2 1

∞

Library of Congress Cataloging-in-Publication Data

Lane, Kerry.
 Guadalcanal Marine / Kerry L. Lane.
    p. cm.
 Includes bibliographical references and index.
 ISBN 1-57806-664-6 (alk. paper)
   1. Lane, Kerry. 2. United States. Marine Corps. Marines, 1st.
3. United States. Marine Corps—Non-commissioned officers—
Biography. 4. World War, 1939–1945—Regimental histories—
United States. 5. World War, 1939–1945—Personal narratives,
American. 6. World War, 1939–1945—Campaigns—Pacific Area.
I. Title.

 D769.371st .L36   2004
 940.54′265933′092—dc22   2004000520

British Library Cataloging-in-Publication Data available

For Connie, my wife and best friend, who listened to my war story for thirty years and then declared "Enough already. Go write another book!"

Contents

Part II. Cape Gloucester

Introduction

On August 7, 1942, the 1st Marines Division took a momentous step in World War II by landing on Japanese-held soil. The island was Guadalcanal. It was the first of many obscure islands that suddenly become so important that young American men would die to gain control of them. The Battle of Guadalcanal was over a Japanese airstrip being built to deny the use of Allied bases and American convoys to New Zealand and Australia. The Japanese saw Guadalcanal as the fork in the road that meant a victory for them or us.

The Marines first horrifying sight during the landing on Guadalcanal was its own naval fleet steaming away in fear of a Japanese counterattack. When the Marines ashore saw their ships disappear over the horizon, they knew they were being abandoned. It was a terrible feeling to know that they were on that island without any naval or air support. More than half of their supplies, including critical rations and ammunition, were still aboard the departing troop transports and attack cargo ships. Guadalcanal would be the only campaign conducted in the Pacific theater of operation in World War II in which U.S. military forces did not have air and naval superiority.

Seen from offshore at a distance, Guadalcanal looked like a South Sea island of enchantment depicted in the color travelogues. But once the Marines landed, they discovered that Guadalcanal was an island hell. The heat was terrible. There were drenching rains, rats, and insects of every description. Marines were struck down by malaria and dysentery, and their skin broke out in jungle rot. But the worst of all was the enemy. He came out of the jungle at night in wild suicide charges. He fought according to no code an American could understand. He was tricky and deadly.

Marines ashore, mindful of the task, moved inland. Having to contend with the jungle and malaria was bad enough, but they also faced the Japanese, who were told to hang on or die fighting. That's what they did. The Japanese and the men of the 1st Marine Division came out of the jungle at one another, day after day for six months, meeting in hand-to-hand combat, grappling with knives and bayonets, and firing at one another with the small arms of the individual foot soldier, the battle always in shaky balance. The Japanese soldiers fought hard and most died. By the time the last enemy sniper was silenced on Guadalcanal, there were 24,000 dead Japanese. The dead American Marines totaled 1752. This was the first time the Japanese had been defeated on land since the beginning of World War II.

It was at Guadalcanal that the Americans fully realized for the first time what sort of foe they were up against and the kind of place in which they would have to fight. This was no clean, modern campaign decided by advanced technology, no recruiting-poster sort of war. In February 1943, when the Japanese evacuated what was left of their starving men, Tokyo was still 3000 miles away. But when this intimate campaign was over, the men of the 1st Marine Division had proven to themselves, their officers, and the American public that the youth of a democracy can meet and defeat the youth of a nation regimented in fanaticism. In comparing his Marines with the Japanese, Maj. Gen. Alexander A. Vandegrift said, "The Japanese soldier was trained to go to a place, stay there, fight there, and die there. We train our American Marines to go to a place, fight to win, and to live. I can assure you ours is a better way."

As the ultimate sacrifice, the Japanese soldier celebrated the Samurai "death before dishonor" code of *bushido*. Under that code duty is everything, and life is nothing by comparison. These soldiers' eager passion for unconscionably devouring life permanently stained the history of mankind. Their quality of military leadership and tenacity on the battlefield during World War II would fill countless military journals and cemeteries.

After Guadalcanal, the Pacific war that had been moving south toward Australia turned north toward Japan. Having been starved for victory, the United States never again tasted defeat. More simply, after Guadalcanal the Americans were on the offensive and the Japanese were on the defensive.

Following a nine-month sojourn of rest and rehabilitation in and around Melbourne, Australia, and preparation for their next campaign, the men in the 1st Marine Division once again headed off to war and spent the Christmas holiday in harm's way. This time the Marines waded ashore at Cape Gloucester, the green inferno, on the Japanese-held island of New Britain just off the coast of New Guinea.

Photo of Kerry Lane. Courtesy of the author.

Abbreviations and Terms

Adm.	Admiral
AK	cargo ship
APD	destroyer transport
Betty	Mitsubishi G-4 medium bomber (Japanese)
B. Gen.	Brigadier General
Capt.	Captain
Cactus	code name for Guadalcanal
Col.	Colonel
Cpl.	Corporal
F4F	Wildcat, Navy and Marine fighter Grumman
1st Sgt.	First Sergeant
Gen.	General
L. Cdr.	Lieutenant Commander
LCI	landing craft infantry
LST	landing ship tank
Lt.	Lieutenant
Lt. Col.	Lieutenant Colonel
Lt. Gen.	Lieutenant General
Maj.	Major
Maj. Gen.	Major General
M-1	Garand rifle

NCO	Noncommissioned Officer
P-39	Bell Air Cobra fighter (Army Air Force)
Pfc.	Private First Class
Pvt.	Private
R. Adm.	Rear Admiral
S. Sgt.	Staff Sergeant
SBD	Dauntless dive-bomber
Sgt.	Sergeant
Sgt. Maj.	Sergeant Major
USAT	U.S. Army transport
USMC	U.S. Marine Corps
USN	U.S. Navy
V. Adm.	Vice Admiral
Zero	Mitsubishi fighter (Japanese)

Key to Military Map Symbols

SIZE SYMBOLS

•	Squad
• •	Section
• • •	Platoon
I	Company or Battery
I I	Battalion or Squadron
I I I	Regiment or Air Group
x	Brigade
x x	Division or Wing

UNIT SYMBOLS

☐	Basic Unit
∞	Air
LVT	Amphibian Tractor
△	Antiaircraft
• DB	Defense Battalion
E	Engineer
•	Field Artillery
⊠	Infantry
⊠ Para	Parachute
⊠ Prcht	

UNIT SYMBOLS

P	Pioneer
⊠ Rdr	Raider
⊠	Tank

MISCELLANEOUS SYMBOLS

⚑	Command Post
△	Observation Post
/	Boundary (battalion)
┼	Aid Station (battalion)

EXAMPLES

1L • 1DB	1st Sec, L Btry, 1st Def Bn
B ⊠ 5	Co B, 5th Mar Regt
⊠ 1Rdr	1st Rdr Bn
• 11	11th Mar Regt
2 △ 7	OP, 2d Bn, 7th Mar Regt
⊠ 1	CP, 1st Mar Div

Part I   **Guadalcanal**

[1]   **Making of a Marine**

Like so many young men of my generation who were raised during the Great Depression of the 1930s, I joined the military to see the world and to fight, should the nation enter the war that was raging in Europe at that time. To enlist, I had to hitchhike some seventy miles from my family's farm outside Hertford, North Carolina, to the recruiting station in Norfolk, Virginia.

Hitchhiking proved to be quite an experience. I left home early in the morning and returned late at night. There were very few people traveling up U.S. 17 at that time. The ones who stopped to give me a ride were in most incidents only going a short distance of ten to twenty miles. The most difficult part was traveling the twenty blocks by "shanks mare," walking the distance between the city outskirts to downtown Main Street, where the recruiting office was located in the U.S. Post Office building.

I planned to go into the Navy, but the lines for the Marines were shorter. The Navy recruiter warned me I'd get my "A-double-S shot off with that gung-ho group," but I joined anyway and never looked back. The Marine recruiter sitting behind the desk looked very impressive in his dress blue uniform, with gold chevrons and service stripes on his sleeves extending from his wrist to his shoulder blades and with rows of campaign ribbons on his chest. He asked, "What can I do for you, young man?" I replied, "I'm here to join the Marine Corps." Then he asked me how old I was. When I told him that I was 16, he informed me to come back in two years, or one year with my parents' consent.

Undaunted, I returned two days later with my parents' consent signature in hand, and received a waiver based on a date of birth entry penciled in the family Bible in lieu of a birth certificate. Shortly after my arrival, I was taken across the river by ferryboat to Marine Barracks Portsmouth, Virginia, for a physical examination and my swearing in.

The barracks, located in the naval shipyard at Portsmouth, was a magnificent turn-of-the-century edifice. In 1940, the old red brick three-story Colonial structure with huge second-floor balcony was imperially majestic, in a way. It faced an immense drill field and was dominated by a hundred-foot flagpole and a three-inch naval gun saluting battery at the main entrance. That was my first visit to a military installation, and needless to say I stood in awe as I absorbed my new surroundings. I was particularly impressed with the Marines attending the Sea School, who upon graduation would serve with a Marine detachment aboard Navy ships. They all wore the dress blue uniform and looked really sharp on the drill field.

I was also impressed by the old Navy tradition of ringing the ship's bell every hour on the hour. I recall standing on the Marine barracks balcony facing the parade field and watching a Marine orderly, in his Dress D uniform (blue trousers, khaki shirt), march out smartly and ring this large brass ship's bell, then with precision do an about face and march smartly back to the barracks orderly room.

When I first arrived at the Marine barracks, I had an urgent need to relieve myself, so I asked my Marine recruiter escort where I could go to pee. He gave me directions to the men's room. I had not been used to indoor bathrooms. Back home on the farm we would use the outhouse or go behind the barn. I got into the men's room all right, but I was trying to pee in the washbasin and it was too high. Thankfully, I finally got that situation straightened out!

While waiting to take my physical, one of the inductees standing next to me asked, "Aren't you from the country?" I said yes and asked him how he could tell. He said, "I can see the hayseed on your clothes and you look like a country farm boy!" I said, "Now wait just a dad-burn minute. Exactly what's so gosh-darn wrong with being a farm boy is what I'm-a wontin-'t'- know?" Calling someone from the country a farm boy was no insult, but among the highest of compliments, in my opinion.

My pre-enlistment physical examination was an experience I will never forget. First, I was told to piss in a bottle, then drop my skivvies for a "short-arm" inspection. After this very embarrassing experience, I had to stand bare-ass naked in line with other inductees waiting to be examined by a Navy physician.

In the 1940s, all Marine Corps recruits were assigned to one of the Corps' two boot camps. Those enlisting west of the Mississippi River were sent to San Diego, California. Those who joined east of the Mississippi went to Parris Island, South Carolina, an isle whose reputation was just marginally better than Devil's Island. So I was going to the Deep South after all. I'd signed up for four years, or more if the war lasted longer, having sworn that, "I will bear true faith and allegiance to the United States of America; that I will serve them honestly and faithfully against all their enemies whomsoever; and that I will obey the orders of the President of the United States, and the orders of the officers appointed over me, according to the Rules and Articles for the Government of the Army, Navy, and Marine Corps of the United States." In short, I'd put my life in hock for four years to the most fearsome and hazardous of the country's armed forces. I boarded a train with other young men who had done the same. As the train pulled out of the station, it finally dawned on me that I was now on my own, that this was the beginning of a new lifestyle and a new adventure.

There is something about being sixteen years old that is different from any other year in a man's lifetime. It is an uncertain and dangerous time. He is reluctant to turn loose of one's childhood, yet he is more than eager to attain manhood and to prove to the world, and especially to himself, that he is a man and can handle a man's responsibilities. It's a very uncertain age, full of emotional conflicts. I hoped I would do well and make my family proud.

Before I nodded off to sleep on the train, I reflected back to my early childhood for a moment. Like other inductees aboard the train, I grew up during the worse economic downturn in American history. We endured hardships that seem unimaginable by today's standards, and those trials made a lasting impression.

My family was poor, but so was everyone else's in the 1930s and early 40s. The eastern North Carolina region where I lived was mostly agricultural then, and every parent and child had a hand in farm chores. We scrubbed clothes on a washboard and drew water from a well or nearby spring. Light came from kerosene lamps and heat from wood stoves and the fireplace. We slept on corn-shuck mattresses and pillows filled with chicken feathers. Life on our small fifty-acre family farm was tough.

People didn't feel underprivileged or downtrodden because they went bare-footed in the summer and wore clothes made from feed sack material. Everyone had home-made things prior to and during World War II. Even though families like ours were cash poor, we always had something to eat. We ate green vegetables from the garden in the spring and summer and canned fruit and vegetables from a jar during the fall and winter. We made molasses from sugar cane and cornbread from corn grown on the farm. We raised cattle for milk and hogs for meat. We traded eggs for items we couldn't grow, such as coffee, sugar, and baking powder. We all wore hand-me-down clothing, which was just fine with us. At least the shoes were well broken in by the time they reached me, for I was third in line.

My family of eight, including my father, John David Lane, mother, Elsie Jordan Lane, and six children—four boys and two girls—was considered to be a medium-sized family at that time. My oldest brother was named John, next in line was Thomas, then me, my sister Annie Mae, my younger brother Ed, and my baby sister Gail.

All I can remember about my trip south on the train is that we slept and that I awoke trembling with anticipation and apprehension about what awaited me at Parris Island. Despair swept over me as we reached our destination of Yemassee, South Carolina, and heard departing, newly graduated Marines yelling, "You're gonna be sorry!"

Drill instructors wearing Smokey the Bear–style field campaign hats and carrying menacing swagger-sticks came aboard yelling, "Get off this G-- damn train, you bastards!" The command came from somewhere: "Move! Move! Move, you moron! Move out on the double! Move!" Each word was louder. Because few of us at that befogged moment understood what the screaming drill instructors wanted us to do, we bunched together, bumping and jostling one another. This reaction to their commands infuriated them and they shoved us this way and that until we were off the train.

Once we were outside and had formed a line of sorts, drill instructors stared at us as though we were some low and disgusting form of animal life. They spat tobacco juice at our feet and called us shitheads. One of the drill instructors called the roll, demanding, "Yes sir" for each response. Following roll call, we were herded onto open bed trucks and packed off over the causeway to Parris Island, a dismal swampland that was to be our training camp for six of the most miserable weeks of our lives.

It seemed as though I had barely laid down the first night on Parris Island when I was awaken by a corporal shouting: "Alright you shitheads hit the deck. Rise and shine! Be ready to fall out in the company street in five minutes." At Parris Island, the customs of the "boot's" new way of life was flouted at great risk. You were told that there were three ways of doing things: the right way, the wrong way, and the Marine Corps way. The Corps' way was very uncompromising. I soon learned that everything in boot camp is done in double time. You move in place and from place to place at double time.

I distinctly recall John W. Watkins, my senior drill instructor at Parris Island. He was a crusty regular gunnery sergeant, a walking example of spit "n" polish who could recite the Marine Corps manual backwards. He was not a big man, but he had a voice that rang with authority, and he scarred the hell out of me. Gunny Watkins had a neatly trimmed and waxed handlebar mustache. He carried a swagger-stick under his right arm as he strutted around the parade ground like a peacock. Believe me, I drew the wrath of that swagger-stick, which had a shined brass bullet casing on one end and a sharp bullet on the other, on more than one occasion. When we fouled up in close-order drill, and we often did, Sgt. Watkins would make us climb up a large flagpole. When we couldn't climb any further and began to slide down, you guessed it, he would jab us in the ass with the sharp end of that swagger-stick. Another occasion when I met with the swagger-stick was when I failed to correctly recite the eleven General Orders.[1] As a result, I wound up having to walk up and down the street with a scrub bucket over my head, shouting as loud as I could, "I'm a horse's ass from Yemassee, the biggest horse's ass you ever did see!" When I didn't yell loud enough, Gunny Watkins, who was following me, would smack the bucket with his swagger-stick and bellow out, "I can't hear you! Louder, country boy!" And then he would smack me over the head again. Boy, did that make my ears ring!

Sgt. Watkins seldom called me by name. It was always "country boy," "farm boy," or "plow boy." He would say that I walked like I was plowing a field with a mule, that I had two left feet, that I was dumber than dirt, and that I would never make it as a Marine. Well, I proved him wrong on that score. I did become a Marine, and one that I believe even he would be proud of.

One humorous incident I remember from Parris Island is the story about our first pay call and the controversial bucket of toilet articles.

Expecting my promised pay of twenty-one dollars, I was shocked when they handed me the grand sum of one dollar and seventy cents. To my dismay, I learned that after deducting six dollars and forty cents for a life insurance policy, they had taken out money for our bucket of toilet articles that were issued to us when we arrived at Parris Island. The bucket was loaded with items such as soap, combs, toothpaste, shaving cream, razor blades, and a scrub brush. They never said anything to us about having to pay for it later. But pay for it, we did. For all I know, they even charged me for the skin-head-style haircut I got.

The most difficult and unpleasant part of boot camp was the lack of sufficient time or space to complete some of the tasks that were assigned. We had to wash our soiled skivvies, socks, and other apparel in an area with wooden racks on which to scrub. There were about one-half the number of wash racks necessary for everyone to complete their scrubbing in the time allotted. Those of us who were unable to muscle our way to the wash racks would get up in the middle of the night and wash our clothes in the head. We'd wring the clothes out as dry as we could and leave them wadded-up in a bucket under the foot of our bunk until we could hang them out to dry the following morning.

When we were issued our rifle, we were told to treat the weapon as we would treat a wife, with love and gentle care. It was ours to have and hold, to sleep with in the field, to know intimately. We soon learned the rifle was an object of obsession. It was a holy thing, the rifle. It had been given to each of us as a knight of the old must have been given his sword. We were unworthy of it, and we must become worthy. It was placed in our trust, wedded to our lives. It was handed down to us, entrusted to our care, and we were to strive to be fit for it.

Those who gave us our weapons spoke the very word "rifle" with respect. It was to become a part of us. We carried the rifle everywhere. Its 8.6 pounds became our pounds. We learned to handle it easily, gracefully, lovingly, and with abiding affection and respect. But this

Port arms on the march on the drill field at Parris Island in the early 1940s. Note the sun helmets on the troops as they march to the cadence of the drill instructor. Sketch by Vernon H. Bailey. Courtesy of the Naval Art Collection, Naval Historical Center.

respect and love did not come immediately. At first we were new to each other; the rifle was a burden. We did not understand it. We did not know its strength, its reliability, its toughness, its simple effectiveness. We did not know how comforting it would be among enemies, or that we would feel alone and naked without it. In the first days, the rifle was strange to us. Indeed, we were strange to it. God knows, there was never a rifle so good as the Springfield, the U.S. Rifle, .30 caliber, Model 1903. We called it the '03. It was made for fighters who hit what they aimed at. It was made for Marines. Our rifles and we were strangers yet.

We carried many burdens as we marched in the heat. The weight of the rifle was new to our young shoulders, as was the weight of our thick shoes, the web cartridge belt, and bayonet. We marched until our legs cried out. We moved, now at a fast jog, toward our humble double-deck wooden frame barracks and halted in the middle of the street. There we were dismissed.

No matter how beaten down after a long day's workout on the drill field, my first act on returning to our barracks was to clean, oil, and polish the stock of my Springfield '03 rifle to a shiny glow. Over the torturous weeks, I gradually became aware that my rifle was transforming from a symbol of dread into a symbol of pride. I finally came to understand that the Marine and the rifle are one.

Above all, the rifle was a "rifle." Make the mistake of calling it a "gun" and you got humiliated before the entire command. You were forced to stand in the company street in your skivvies, thrusting the rifle upward with one hand and shouting loudly, "This is my rifle," then grabbing your gonads with the other hand, and continuing to shout. "And this is my gun. One is for business and the other is for fun!"

I will never forget our week of weapons orientation. What an ordeal that was! Our time and efforts were focused on snapping in with our rifle (practicing loading, aiming, and firing without live ammunition) and practicing the firing positions: standing offhand, sitting, kneeling, prone-or-else, all in slow and rapid fire. Thank God the snapping in only lasted for a week before we started firing live ammunition. No more squeezing the trigger and hearing a click, I thought.

The .45 caliber pistol, '03 Springfield rifle, light and heavy machine guns, mortars, and many other kinds of weapons were thrown at us that week. I recall being sent into a tent with my '03 rifle and the .45 caliber pistol. We were blindfolded and made to take both apart and put them back together again, without being able to see anything. If we screwed up, we had to do it again and again until we got it right. There was no way that you got off that damned island without completing this phase of the training. We all thought that it was asinine at the time, but it would come in handy later on in combat.

The high point of boot camp was the week on the rifle range. Every possible minute of each hour of the day in that week was spent studying

A blindfolded weapons instructor demonstrates his ability to field strip an M-1917 A1 machine gun at Parris Island in the early 1940s. Courtesy of the Marine Corps Historical Center.

or firing infantry weapons; the main one, of course, was the '03 rifle. This was, indeed, the most important possession of a Marine. A creed ingrained in us was that "Every Marine is a rifleman." No matter where a Marine would go after boot camp, he was considered available to serve as a rifleman at a minute's notice. "This is my rifle, there are many like it but this one is mine," is true whether one is in the infantry or not. In the 1940s, whenever a Marine was reassigned or transferred, he would take his rifle with him.

I recall our weapons instructor emphasizing what it takes to be a rifleman in the Marine Corps. He said, "You must become one with your weapon if you are to survive in combat. Being able to shoot is not enough. Every shot must be where you want it to be, before the enemy can sight in on you. You can gain that expertise only one way: practice, practice, and more practice. Repetition is the only way to improve your skills. The more you fire, the faster you get. This is especially true with the bolt-action '03 rifle."

The rifle range coach at Parris Island convinced me that all I had to do to be a top-notch rifleman was to hold on firmly, take careful aim, relax, and squeeze it off. On Record Day we fired sixty-six shots, all but ten of them rapid-fire at targets 200, 300 and 500 yards away. Each shot was worth a maximum of five points for a bull's eye. Riflemen could qualify in three categories: marksman, sharpshooter, and expert rifleman. The last is very rare, requiring 305 points of a possible 330. I knew I would do well. My rifle was zeroed into perfection. I had steady hands. I could hold my breath indefinitely while steadying the muzzle—a tradition I learned while hunting wild game on the farm in earlier years.

Record Day was clear and windless. I hardly missed anything. My score was 315. Once we shot for record we were Marines. There were a few other skills to be learned, including block-parry-thrust bayonet drills and pistol shooting. But these had no place in the Marine scale of values. The rifle is the Marine's weapon. An expert rifleman's badge brought us five extra dollars a month in pay, not an inconsiderable sum to one earning twenty-one dollars a month. I marched back to the barracks with my chest swelling with pride for having mastered the Springfield rifle. As a result of intensive marksmanship training at Parris Island, a special bond was formed between me and my rifle that would pay dividends on the target range and, later, in combat.

My transformation from a country farm boy to a Marine had been made with difficulty, but my parents had taught me that life was meant to have some hard conditions and that one grows by overcoming those conditions. Now I was a Marine, a member of the greatest fighting force in the world, the United States Marine Corps. I was going to carry on its traditions and wear its uniform with pride.

In our last days of boot camp, we gathered in formation in front of our barracks and marched down to the long familiar parade field for our final inspection. The Marine band, with its majestic beat of drums and the sound of brass instruments, charged the cool morning air with patriotism and lifted our hearts with happiness and pride as our platoon marched along the parade grounds. We were regal yet rigid and precise as we passed in front of the reviewing stand. There is no finer sight than Marine recruits marching in their final parade. Long days of movement together have polished the art, and they are at the peak of perfection.

The platoon had trained day after day under a drill instructor that had been with us from the beginning. The timing was perfect in execution of commands. The heavy shoes struck the parade deck with the unmatched rhythm of hundreds of feet hitting at the same instant. There was a gleam of rifles, bright eyes and tanned faces against the sun. It is always a thrilling sight, and for a Marine there is no other moment like this one.

The final parade was accompanied by sadness and regret, though it marked achievement of a difficult task and offered a future of more exciting and more difficult things. Within a few days, each of us would get our orders, and boot camp would be over. Soon the transfer would break up the platoon to various duty stations.

The end of this training meant much more freedom as we entered into more advanced training at our new duty station. At Parris Island, we had learned the basic fundamentals. Those fundamentals would carry us over many tough spots and guide us in many strange situations. Without boot camp, we would not have been Marines. We knew this and we were proud to have gone through Parris Island.

[2] **Preparing for Combat**

After basic training at Parris Island, I was transferred to Quantico, Virginia, for duty with the 1st Marine Brigade.
Upon reporting to my new command on March 14, 1940, I was
assigned to A Company, 1st Battalion, 5th Marines. My company commander was Capt. William K. Enright, a regular spit-and-polish officer
who distinguished himself in combat in World War II and retired with
the rank of colonel.

The barracks at Quantico, designated by letters, were three-story
red brick buildings with white window sashes and trim, below a roof
of slate. Those substantial buildings were a far cry from the old two-
story wooden-frame barracks we were used to at Parris Island.

When I arrived at A Barracks, breakfast was my first concern. Our
food and drinks were served on china plates and in cups and saucers,
which impressed me. It was a luxury I hadn't enjoyed for some time.
All we had at Parris Island were metal serving trays and canteen cups.
After breakfast, I ambled over to the company office to check in.

The first sergeant's name was Dave Kurner. As I recall our first meeting, I was simultaneously welcomed and admonished. I said, "Pvt.
Lane, reporting for duty, Sir." First Sgt. Kurner immediately responded,
"Don't call me Sir, private. That title is reserved for commissioned
officers in this command. My title is first sergeant and you will address
me as such." Then in a calmer voice he said, "Welcome aboard, Pvt.
Lane. We are glad to have you in the company."

When I left Parris Island I was programmed to salute and say "Sir" to everyone and everything except the cat. I was programmed to call "Atten-shun!" whenever our drill instructor entered the barracks and to respond to questions he might ask with a "Yes, Sir" or "No, Sir." This Sir routine no longer being a requirement for anyone in the enlisted ranks at my new duty station would take some getting used to.

The first sergeant looked old to someone like me, still in my teens. He was dressed in a green uniform with campaign ribbons on his chest and the fourragére[1] of the Croix de Guerre on the left shoulder. He served with the famed 5th Marine Regiment in France during World War I and earned the fourragére for extraordinary bravery. With his snowy hair and amused, patrician smile, "Top" Kurner, made those of lesser rank feel at ease in his presence. He made a few remarks about me going on furlough and the tough training that I would face when I returned. He made a point to emphasize that the regiment I was now part of had an elite tradition and that I should wear the braided fourragére as part of my uniform with pride.

I soon learned that the person in charge of the barracks was the police sergeant, and that as long as we lived in his domain we were at his mercy. He was not a policeman, but he sure did exercise police powers when it came to neatness and decorum in the barracks. If the prerequisite for being a barracks police sergeant was longevity, the sergeant we had in A Barracks was well qualified; he had hash marks on his sleeve up to his elbow, denoting over twenty years of service in the Corps.

My area in the squad bay was a small cubicle, large enough for one iron bunk with steel springs, a double-steel wall locker, and a wooden footlocker. The wall locker was used primarily to store my uniform and accessories, with my combat pack, field marching pack, and steel helmet placed neatly on top. I used the wooden footlocker to secure the rest of my personal gear. The footlocker also doubled as a chair to sit on or as a shoeshine stand. When not in use, I pushed it under the foot of the bunk.

I really liked this outfit. When I wrote home I told my parents I thought I was lucky to be assigned to such an elite regiment, that I was authorized to wear the fourragére as part of my uniform, and that I was proud of it. I was pleased to learn that once I got settled in the barracks, I would be allowed to go on furlough for ten days. I was anxious for my family and friends to see me in my Marine dress blue uniform.

On March 17, three days after reporting for duty ay Quantico, Virginia, I was allowed to check out for my long awaited furlough. The company provided military transportation to the Greyhound bus station in Triangle, Virginia, just outside the main gate. From there I traveled south to Norfolk, Virginia, where I changed to a Trailways bus to my home in Hertford, North Carolina.

The bus stopped in front of the family farm to let me off. As the bus pulled off, I swung the sea bag over my shoulder and headed up the driveway. My mother must have seen me get off the bus. She came running across the yard with her arms wide open to greet me. She was beside herself, crying and hugging me. The past few months had been very difficult for her. I was the only one of her six children who had ever been away from home. It was a happy but emotional moment for both of us. Homecomings are very special occasions, and this one was no exception. Time to enjoy Mom's cooking, go hunting and fishing with my brothers, and visit my grandparents, who were very close to me.

One of the highlights of my furlough was the chance to wear my Marine uniform with the braided fourragére on my shoulder and the expect rifleman's badge on my chest. I walked down the streets of Hertford as proud as a peacock. Another highlight was visiting with my older brother John and his wife, Louise, who had given birth to a baby girl while I was at Parris Island. I was able to see her and hold her in my arms. Her name was Peggy. She was the first grandchild in the Lane family and destined to be spoiled by everyone, especially her proud Uncle Kerry. It was nice to be with my family again, and my

The *"Blue Goose"* in *Guantanamo Bay, Cuba, erected by enlisted men as a recreational center. Courtesy of Jim White.*

time with them passed all too quickly. Little did I know that it would be almost a year before I would see them again.

When I returned to Quantico, I found out that my new duty assignment was to be the company runner. I was provided a small desk and chair in the company office. My primary duty was to deliver messages and run errands for the first sergeant and company commander. As the company runner, I was also the orderly for Capt. Enright. I made sure his boots, Sam Browne belt, and saber were polished and always maintained in good order.

On April 1, 1940, I was transferred to the newly activated 3rd Battalion, 5th Marines and was assigned to I Company. One of the officers who joined the company about the same time I did was Lt. Gordon D. Gayle. Two years out of the U.S. Naval Academy, he was one of the new breed of professional career officers who would later distinguish himself in combat. He retired with the rank of brigadier general.

My duties in I Company were the same as in A Company. Only by this time most of my days were spent out in the field training. I soon learned semaphore, a system of signaling by the use of flags. One of us would stand on a hill with a flag in each hand to signal someone else on another hill. In semaphore signaling, letters of the alphabet are represented by the various positions of the arms.

Shortly after reporting for duty with the newly activated I Company, I observed a group of Marines signing a sheet posted on the company bulletin board. Being inquisitive, I decided to see what was going on. The center of attention was a newly posted notice requesting volunteer's to sign up for submarine duty. This seemed like an exciting adventure, so I added my name to the list. The following morning when the company formed in formation for roll call, the company gunny passed the word for those of us who signed up for submarine duty to fall out and report to the police sergeant. Upon reporting, we were informed that during police call for the next month we would be submerging our hands with a scrub brush into the urinals and toilet commodes located in the barracks head. What a hoax. So much for volunteering!

After a short period with the newly activated 3rd Battalion, 5th Marines, we embarked on a nine-month stay in Guantanamo Bay (Gitmo), Cuba. All we did down there was training, training, and more training. No liberty at all. There was a town across the bay from our campsite at Caravella Point by the name of Caimanera. The sailors could go there, but not the Marines. In those days we always seemed to get the short end of the stick. We did have our own slopchute where you could go get Cuban beer. And when I say slopchute, I mean it. The Blue Goose had a long open pavilion with a palm-covered roof that provided a means of protection from the hot tropical sun. We used to go there in the evening and drink a few fifteen-cent beers, then go back to our tents to sleep it off. The next morning it was back to training again.

It didn't take long for me to find out why the men in I Company called me "Runner" Lane. It was because I ran up and down those damn rocky, brush-covered hills overlooking Guantanamo Bay, Cuba, a hundred times delivering messages during training exercises. When I complained around my buddies, they would laugh and say, "Why don't you learn how to send smoke signals, then you won't have to run so much." Then a couple of the clowns would get up and do a little Indian war dance.

There was a story going around among the enlisted men that Horse Marines[2] patrolled the area, looking out for anyone trying to sneak out of camp. They were the same China Marines that patrolled the Gobi Desert, and if you were spotted, they'd let go with their .45s. Maybe their presence was enough to scare the hell out of us, because I never heard about anyone being shot. I'm not saying that the Corps did this on purpose, but it was one of the ways they had control over us.

I suppose the Corps was looking for a few good men with strong backs in those days. We had a hell of a lot of steel workers, coal miners, and farm boys in our outfit. You had to be strong to carry and maneuver those heavy weapons and equipment. Believe me, it was work! The artillery guns had wooden wheels, not rubber tires, which made it hard to push them around and we didn't have Higgins' landing craft then either. We had Navy motor-sailers, twenty-six feet long, something like a whaling boat. When we practiced landings we didn't dare beach the boats because we were afraid of damaging them. The Navy didn't have much money then and the Marine Corps had even less.

We had to wade in a good deal of the way. Once ashore, Cubans would appear out of nowhere to try to sell us rum and other special favors. We usually end up bivouacking up in the hills, and frequently at night we'd all have a few drinks. A couple of fellows would break out their harmonicas and we would sing loud enough to wake the dead. Few of us could carry a tune and our idea of a scale was that it is to raise or lower our voices. But we liked to bellow out the words. We

Marines go ashore from Navy motor-sailers at Guantanamo Bay, Cuba, in the late fall of 1940. Courtesy of the Marine Corps Historical Center.

sang mostly old sentimental country ballads that were popular at the time such as "Oh Susanna," "Shenandoah," and "Red River Valley." We'd end our songfest with my favorite hymn, "Amazing Grace."

Some of the men got hold of that Cuban rum. They were accustomed to beer, so the rum with its high alcohol content hit them hard. Several got so drunk they were puking their guts out in a nearby straddle trench, a condition common to young men who have just been introduced to the hard stuff.

In the morning, it was "Saddle up, we're moving out." When the company commander came into the campsite, the air would fill with the moans and groans of hung-over Marines. He said, "All right, you men, you had a great time last night. Today, you are going on a ten-mile conditioning march up and over the hills. Get your packs on and prepare to move out." The skipper took off at a gallop and we followed. Peacetime soldiering wasn't all fun and games.

B. Gen. Holland M. "Howlin' Mad" Smith commanded the brigade then and had it as his goal "to keep the fat out of our waist band" during our seven-month stay at Guantanamo Bay. By the time we had completed the landing exercises on the dry, hot, and dusty coastal plains of Culebra, off Puerto Rico in the Caribbean Sea, in February 1941, we were cursing the steaming Caribbean wilderness, the elements, and the day we became Marines.

On November 1, 1940, I was reassigned to the newly formed K Company, 3rd Battalion, 5th Marines, commanded by Capt. Lyman D. Spurlock. A few days later, K Company embarked aboard the battleship USS *Texas* for amphibious exercises on the island of Culebra. On November 25, while aboard the USS *Texas*, I was promoted to the rank of private first class. My warrant was signed and presented to me by the brigade commander, B. Gen. Smith.

Along with my promotion came a new assignment as company scout and a new nickname. I was no longer referred to as "Runner" Lane; the men in the company called me Scout "Hondo" Lane. It seemed that the company gunny had read a book or had seen a movie about a famous Indian scout on the western frontier named Hondo Lane. I suspect the main reason he hung that moniker on me was that the other company scout, a Cherokee Indian from Lumberton, North Carolina, was called "Tonto." I vividly recall his loud command "Scouts Hondo and Tonto, out!" whenever we would head out on patrol.

I seemed to have had a knack for this new assignment. I soon acquired vital basic skills of scouting, patrolling, and map making. Being from a small rural farming community in North Carolina, I had acquired the skills to move quietly through the wooded areas in pursuit of wild game, but I had no background or experience in moving about in dense tropical jungles like we encountered while on maneuvers in the Caribbean. There, we learned to rely on stealth, to read the stars and other signs to find our location in unfamiliar jungle terrain.

On February 1, 1941, one of history's greatest fighting units, the 1st Marine Division, was born. It came into existence by change of designation from a brigade. At that time, the 1st Marine Brigade was composed of the 5th Regiment, the 1st Battalion, 10th Regiment, and the 1st Marine Aircraft Group. The strength of the brigade was approximately 2000 officers and men. Less than two months later, under the command of newly promoted Maj. Gen. Holland M. Smith, the new division's strength had increased to 306 officers and more than 7200 enlisted men. The growth was possible only because the organized reserve of the Marine Corps had been called up for active duty in the fall of 1940 and had begun to arrive at Guantanamo Bay the following January.

My unit, redesignated as K Company, 3rd Battalion, 5th Regiment, 1st Marine Division, participated in landings exercises held on Culebra and the neighboring island of Vieques. We practiced numerous day and night landings. Naval gunfire and reconnaissance missions were conducted to lend reality to the situation. Included in this training were night landings from rubber boats. Submarines were used for our reconnaissance missions. The training emphasized fire control procedures and the capabilities of different types of ammunition, as well as their effect on targets we were expected to encounter during battle.

We returned to our base at Gitmo Bay once the maneuvers were completed. First we made a port call in the beautiful coastal city of Camaguey, Cuba. It was great to go ashore on liberty, our first in months. We found the Cuban people very friendly, and the girls quite attractive. Needless to say, all hands had a good time.

The year 1941 was a time of upheaval and expansion. The newly formed 1st Marine Division was in a state of constant turmoil. By the time we returned from the landing exercises held on Culebra and Vieques, things had already began to move. The 5th Marine Regiment returned to Quantico, Virginia, where it was split into three groups. The 1st Battalion became a special test unit tasked to form what was known as the 1st Separate Battalion, later renamed the 1st Raider Battalion.

The 2nd and 3rd Battalions, 5th Marines were carved up to create a new 1st Battalion and to absorb new recruits and conduct small-unit training. Detachments from the 5th Marines were sent to New River, North Carolina, in late May to erect Tent Camp One that would become their home base until they shipped out for the Pacific in May 1942. In late September 1941, the 5th Marines (less the 1st Battalion), boarded trains for movement to New River.

The 7th Marines activated earlier in Gitmo Bay, Cuba relocated to Parris Island, South Carolina. Along with the arrival of the 7th Marines, the 1st Marines began to form. This was only a temporary move, as it was anticipated that these regiments would shortly relocate to New River, which they did. By late spring, the remaining units of the 1st Marine Division relocated to Parris Island began moving by troop train or truck convoy to their new destination, Tent Camp One, where a great swampy tract of land had been taken over. In due course, it became Camp Lejeune.

In 1941 New River, North Carolina, was a rural coastal area. The closest city was Wilmington, North Carolina. The area was dotted by many small towns, which in some cases had to be relocated when the land was acquired by the government. One such area was Verona, North Carolina: a general store, gasoline pump, and crossroads. It was about ten miles from Tent Camp One and was to become the new home of the 11th Marine (Artillery) Regiment that also had been activated at Guantanamo Bay on March 1, 1941.

Upon arrival at Tent Camp One, Marines were heard to say; "This place is really out in the sticks." The only signs of civilization were a few run-down, uncultivated farms with old dilapidated houses on them, and a couple of small crossroad country stores Marines passed on the way in. The 1st Marine Division's World War II historian described the training area located in the New River area of Onslow County, North Carolina, as "111,170 acres of water, swamp, and plains" inhabited largely by mosquitoes, sand flies, ticks, chiggers, and snakes. During the next several months, Marine units located at the New River, North Carolina, training base participated in landing force exercises. Later, in evaluating the operations, Maj. Gen. Holland M. Smith, who was commanding the Marine Amphibious Forces, Atlantic Fleet, said:

> New River became the largest Marine training base in the United States, and its size, enabled us to give substance to what were only dreams in the restricted area of Culebra and Vieques. . . . For the force landing exercises starting August 4, 1941, the largest of its type held in the United States, 1500 yard beaches were laid out and designated by letters for each assault unit. Across them, we put ashore 16,500 officers and men of the 1st Army Division and the 1st Marine Division, 300 vehicles and 2200 tons of supplies. Forty-two naval vessels and four aircraft carriers participated. Such a high degree of realism was attained that following the seizure of a beachhead, an advance of nine miles inland was made before withdrawal was ordered, a necessary ingredient of a well-balanced training plan.
>
> Marine parachute troops were employed for the first time and 266 landing crafts of different types were used. Analyzing the results, the maneuver was again hampered by a lack of equipment and personnel especially in the field of communications. Initial phases of the landing suffered from shortage of tank lighters and of motor transport ashore. There were other deficiencies that an enterprising "enemy" could have exploited, but in my mind the debut of the Higgins boat, complete with ramp, more than compensated for these deficiencies.
>
> The final plan for the exercise at New River, North Carolina, called for a Marine Parachute company to jump at H plus one hour onto a vital crossroads behind enemy lines, secure it, and then attack the

Marines go ashore from Higgins boats during landing exercises along Onslow Beach at New River, North Carolina, in the summer of 1941. Courtesy of the Marine Corps Historical Center.

rear of enemy forces opposing the landing of the 1st Infantry Division. Capt. Howard's recently formed parachute company would jump on the morning of D plus two in support of an amphibious landing by Lt. Col. Merritt A. Edson's Mobile Landing Group and a Marine tank company. Edson's force (the genesis of the 1st Raider Battalion) would go ashore behind enemy lines, advance inland, destroy the opposing reserve force, and seize control of the important lines of communications. Howard's men would land near Edson's objective and secure the road net and bridges in that vicinity.[3]

For the exercise the parachutists were attached to the 1st Marine Aircraft Wing, which operated from a small airfield at New Bern, North Carolina, just north of the of the Marine base. The landing force executed the operation as planned, but Maj. Gen. Holland Smith was not pleased with the results because for there were far too many artificialities, including the lack of an aggressor force and a shortage of transport planes.

Once the exercise was underway, Smith made one attempt to simulate an enemy force. He arranged for Capt. Williams to re-embark one squad and jump behind the lines of the two divisions, with orders to create as much havoc as possible. Williams' tiny force cut tactical telephone lines, hijacked trucks, blocked roads, and successfully evaded for several hours. One after-action report noted that, "the introduction of paratroops lent realism to the necessity for command post security."

From early spring until late fall in 1941, the training on Onslow Beach was intensive. We made so many landings there that most of us began to feel as if we had counted from eye level every grain of sand on it. The sand was not the only feature we became familiar with during the landing exercise across Onslow Beach. Combat training in the coastal area of North Carolina was defined by the forbidding region itself. The forestland ashore was primarily one of scrub pines and oak, overgrown with vines, briars, and other vegetation and was divided by numerous small creeks and swampy areas. These features placed severe constraints on troop movements as we advanced inland.

So the Marines got to know the North Carolina coastal area. They attacked the invisible enemy. They dug countless foxholes and slept in them, learning how to do it despite the rain, cold, and hunger. We spent our first night ashore in hastily dug fighting positions in the sand dunes just inland off the beach. There was a steady drizzle and a cold wind coming in from the Atlantic Ocean. We sat with our heads on our knees, pulled ponchos around our shoulders, and nodded off to sleep the best we could. I'd never been so damn miserable in my entire life.

At the first streak of dawn we each munched on a can of C-rations, drank a cup of hot coffee, saddled up, and moved out. After several hours of maneuvering through dense woods and pine thickets, we reached our designated bivouac area. We pitched our camp in a God-forsaken hole. It could be reached only by a narrow, rutted logging road.

Our new bivouac site was enclosed by tall pines, scrubby oaks, and thick underbrush and infested by mosquitoes, chiggers, and snakes. This campsite would be our base of operations for the next several days. Here we erected three pyramidal tents, one for the galley, another for the sickbay, and one for the company command post.

A cold rain began to fall as the campsite was divided and subdivided into platoons and squads. Two-man pup tents quickly sprang up in the compound, though not in careful and precise rows. They were staggered to conform to the new emphasis on camouflage and dispersal. As soon as the sick bay was set up and operational, sick call sounded: "All sick, lame, and lazy Marines report for treatment." The company medical corpsman was busy for some time treating blisters, cuts, and insect bites.

Those of us who were able to avoid sick call went limping about in search of loblolly pine straw. It was placed beneath our blanket to provide a cushion and to ward off the dampness seeping up from the ground. I knew all about pine straw because I used to gather it by the wagonloads as a young boy. We used it for livestock bedding on the family farm in North Carolina.

When we completed the task of erecting our tents, we heard the call for chow. It had grown late, and it was in darkness that we finally finished our meal and washed our mess gear. This ended our second day in the field, and we were in the rain and darkness. We had qualified for the ranks of the Glorious Swamp Lagoon Warriors.

We had an uninvited guest come to dinner while we were in bivouac. The unwelcome visitor was a polecat, better known as a skunk. It had entered the campsite foraging for food. His objective was a pup tent occupied by two Yankees from New York and Boston, who didn't understand that this critter demanded a great deal of respect and distance. They made the horrible mistake of frantically yelling and throwing their shoes at the unwelcome invader. The polecat responded by giving them a spray job they would never forget. The two Marines, along with their pup tent and all their belongings were placed in self-imposed exile to a position on the outer-fringe of the camp, safely downwind from the rest of us.

As expected, there was the usual complaining. The men talked about being stuck out in the boonies away from civilization. We had heard that Maj. Gen. Smith didn't want us running home or to go on liberty. When I look back on it, I guess he was right. The men grew proud of being able to take it. Morale went up while we were on maneuvers and in bivouac. The chow was good, and we had plenty of it.

Out in the boondocks at Onslow Beach, local moonshiners sold the Marines jugs of that potent corn whiskey called "white lighting." Navy medical corpsmen and physicians who operated the company and battalion aid stations known as sick bays could always tell when the bootlegger had been around. I had one swig of that corn whiskey and that was one swig too many. The next morning I felt like I'd been kicked by a jackass right between the eyeballs.

The Navy medical personnel were not the only ones who could tell when the moonshiners with their bootleg whiskey had been around. The company gunnery sergeant always seemed to know what was going on. The next day it was "Saddle up, we're going on a ten-mile hike with full marching packs." Most of the time, it seemed like we were running. The company gunny made no bones about his objective, which was to teach us a lesson about drinking moonshine whiskey and to keep us "lean and mean and a well-oiled fighting machine."

By the end of October 1941, we had completed our move from Onslow Beach to the division's isolated tent city in the piney woods of coastal North Carolina. This was back to civilization compared to the living conditions we experienced while on maneuvers off Onslow Beach.

The training at Onslow Beach had toughened us. We had been hardened by the elements and primitive make-do living in the boondocks. We learned from actual field experience, not military textbooks, and the little things that would save us later. We became so familiar with our surroundings that we could sense weather changes and anticipate the rain. Adjusting our minds and bodies conquered the discomforts of wet and cold. Self-reliance was developed to a great degree, and we began to work as a coordinated unit.

All of us had benefited from these exercises, and our training continued after we returned to the tent camp. But first we were authorized a three-day pass to go on liberty in one of the nearby towns. Since my hometown Hertford, North Carolina, was only a short distance away, I elected to go home. I invited one of my Yankee buddies, Sam Russo, who was from Lawrence, Massachusetts, to spend the weekend with me. When it came time for us to depart for our return trip to camp, my mother came out on the front porch to wave good-bye and called out: "Y'all come back now, heah." As we drove off Sam looked at me dumfounded and asked, "What did your mama say?" I laughed and told him that was an old Southern good-bye. "She wants you, Yankee boy, to come back and visit real soon."

Once back in camp, everyone got into the regular training routine. We marched out into the countryside on a two- or three-day field exercise. We pitched our pup tents, dug straddle trenches (open-air field latrines), and ate the Corps' favorite meal for troops in the field: creamed chipped beef on toast, universally known as "SOS," or "shit on a shingle." We learned to eat what was being served: powdered milk, powdered-eggs, dehydrated potatoes, and hardtack biscuits.

These training exercises were designed not only to give us a working knowledge of the mechanics of combat, but also to teach the basic things every Marine should know: How to love the ground, how to use it to advantage, and above all, how to live on it and in it for days at a time without impairment of physical efficiency. Our officers stressed the importance of such things that would make the difference between life and death in combat. They urged us to "train hard so as to fight hard, and to train smart so as to fight smarter."

The weather at Tent City One on the edge of the coastal swamp was bitterly cold. To shore up against the cold, every tent was equipped with a kerosene stove, a smelly, ornery, and often dangerous contraption. The stove often set the tents on fire. They would sometimes cover everything, including sleeping men, with sooty smoke. When that happened, you'd "cough smoke for a week." At first, there were sawdust then wooden-plank decks for the tents, but the cracks were wide and unsealed. Many of us stuffed newspapers, magazines, and comic books into the cracks to seal against the cold air seeping up from the ground.

Shortly after our arrival back at Tent City One, on November 17, 1941, I received my corporal's warrant. This document was presented with much fanfare at a formation of the command. I had witnessed such a ceremony on several occasions while deployed with the brigade in Cuba. The company commander read the warrant as I stood at attention before him in the presence of the entire command. I was presented the precious papers that endowed me with the authority of a noncommissioned officer. In the Marine Corps, the noncommissioned officer is the backbone of the service. Upon him rests the responsibility of getting work done and carrying out commands in the field. NCO ranks carry real authority, which was supported in word and deed by commissioned officers in the 1st Marine Division.

Like most people, I remember what I was doing the day the Japanese attacked Pearl Harbor. Cpl. Jim Campbell, a good buddy of mine, and I had gone back to my hometown of Hertford, North Carolina, for a weekend visit. On Sunday, December 7, 1941, while returning to camp, we decided to stop in New Bern, North Carolina, for a beer. We were sitting at the bar with two Southern girls enjoying the peaceful afternoon, when all of a sudden the bartender at the other end of the bar, who had a radio turned on, hollered, "The Japanese are bombing Pearl Harbor!" I was stunned. I didn't believe that could be true. I listened for a few minutes as more bulletins came over the radio indicating it was a very large raid and serious damage had been done to our Pacific fleet. I realized it was for real when a special bulletin announced that all military personnel were to return to their duty stations immediately. After gaining our composure, we left quickly and returned to camp.

[3]   **Wartime Expansion**

After four months of war, the 1st Marine Division was alerted to its first prospect of action. The Japanese had already pushed the Americans off Corregidor, Bataan, Guam, and Wake Island. The vital Samoa Island in the Pacific appeared to be next on the Japanese invasion list. The Navy called upon the Marines to provide the necessary reinforcements for the meager garrison. In March 1942, headquarters created two brigades for the mission, cutting a regiment and a slice of supporting forces from each of the two Marine divisions. The 7th Marines got the nod at New River, North Carolina, and became the nucleus of the 3rd Brigade. That force initially included Lt. Col. Edson's 1st Raider Battalion, but no paratroopers. In the long run that was a plus for the 1st Parachute Battalion, which remained relatively untouched as the brigade siphoned off much of the best manpower and equipment of the division to bring itself to full readiness.

The division was already reeling from the difficult process of wartime expansion. In the past few months it had absorbed thousands of newly minted Marines, subdivided units to create new ones, given up some of its best assets to field the raiders and parachutists, and built up a base and training areas from the pine forests of New River, North Carolina. The parachutists and the remainder of the division did not have long to wait for their own call to arms. In early April, Marine Corps headquarters alerted the 1st Marine Division that it would begin moving overseas in May.

Part of the division shoved off from Norfolk in May. Some elements, including Companies B and C of the parachutists, took trains to the West Coast and boarded naval transports there on June 19. The rest of the 1st Parachute Battalion was part of a later Norfolk echelon, which set sail for New Zealand on June 10.

On March 23, 1942, at New River, North Carolina, Gen. Vandegrift received his second star and command of the 1st Marine Division. He had already been its assistant commander. He had helped plan and conduct practice amphibious landing across the beaches at Solomon, Maryland, in January and February. But now he had full charge and he poured all his energies into raising the division from about 11,000 to its full strength of 19,000. (Vandegrift relieved Maj. Gen. Philip Torrey, who had assumed command of the division temporarily when Maj. Gen. Smith was elevated to command the Atlantic Fleets 1st Joint Training Force.)

During April 21–30, 1942, before we departed for the Pacific, my unit moved by truck convoy from New River up the coastal highway (U.S. Route 17) to the naval base at Norfolk, Virginia, where we went aboard a Navy ship. From there we sailed up the Chesapeake Bay to Solomon Island, Maryland, where we participated in a number of practice amphibious assault landing operation across the beach near Cove Point.

During this same period, rubber-boat landings were executed at Solomon's Island. Dog Company and the unwanted 81-mm mortar platoon 1st Raider Battalion sailing aboard a converted World War I four-piper destroyer of Transport Division 11 executed rubber-boat landings at Solomon's Island within the Chesapeake Bay. The raiders inflated their rubber boats, climbed down a cargo net, paddled clear of the transports, and staged a mock landing by storming the beach with their bayoneted Springfield rifles held high. The 81-mm mortar platoon went ashore in Higgins boats landing in a second wave.

The amphibious practice landings moved to Solomon, Maryland, were originally scheduled to be conducted at New River's Onslow Beach, but they had to be moved inside the safety of the Chesapeake

Bay because German submarines were sinking Allied ships at will along the Atlantic Coast. In fact, the area off North Carolina was so dangerous it became known as the "Graveyard of the Atlantic." In the first half of 1942, 397 ships were torpedoed and sunk by German U-boats along the treacherous shoals off the North Carolina Outer Banks. Even more tragic, nearly 5000 people lost their lives.

Hoping to prevent America from supplying its hard-pressed European allies, German submarines prowled the waters just off the North Carolina coast, torpedoing just about everything with a pro-peller. So many burning tankers and freighters lit up the night sky that sea lanes offshore received a new nickname, "Torpedo Alley."

The World War II Liberty Ships, the slow plodding ugly ducklings of the sea, manned by Merchant Marines and Navy Armed Guards were hit hard off the east coast. The German U-boat crews called them "fish bait" because they were sinking so many of them, but once they faced convoys with armed escorts fewer of these ships were sunk.

German U-boats would surface offshore at night. Spies and sabo-teurs were put ashore to gather shore-based intelligence to aid U-boats at sea. Coded messages on ship movements were transmitted by electronic means to Adm. Karl Donitz's U-boat wolf pack prowl-ing along the treacherous shoals off the North Carolina Outer Banks. Patriotic citizens living in the coastal area responded to the threat by posting signs with the message: "Loose Lips—Sinks Ships!"

In Tent Camp One near New River, Maj. Gen. Alexander A. Vandegrift assembled the men he was to lead on Guadalcanal. Marine Corps headquarters now began pumping personnel into New River to bring Vandegrift's command to war-time strength. Odd lots arrived daily. They were a motley bunch. Hundreds were young recruits only recently out of boot camp at Parris Island. Others were older. These were the professionals, the old breed. Many had fought in Haiti, Nicaragua, and with other American sailors in bars at liberty ports around the world. They knew they were tough and they knew they were good. There were enough of them to even the division and to impart to the thousands of younger men a share of the unique spirit and skills the older Marines possessed.

The expansion of the Marine Corps ranks was so sudden its recruiting offices were swamped with more applicants than could be accepted. Young men seeking adventure provided by war clamored for an opportunity to fight the Japanese. An unprecedented fire of patriotism swept the nation.

During the period of the 1st Marine Division build-up, I was sent to the Army Combat Engineer School at Fort Belvoir, Virginia, for six weeks. There, I completed an extensive training program involving the use and application of military explosives and demolition techniques in combat.

Upon my return to camp, my new assignment was to the recently formed 1st Pioneer Battalion, commanded by a crusty old mustang colonel by the name of George R. Rowan.[1] The 1st Pioneer Battalion was activated to meet the need for a specialized unit to conduct shore party operations during the initial landing and to provide close combat engineer support for the infantry once ashore. I guess you could say Marine pioneers were the jack-of-all-trades. If a bridge had to be built, we built it. If demolition specialist were needed, we were trained for the job. They called on us when replacements were needed on the front lines. We were a unique outfit that could do and did almost anything, and we were proud of it. Man by man, the newly activated 1st Pioneer Battalion was molded together by rugged training and the sharing of hardships.

Most of the men in my unit, B Company Pioneers, had enlisted in the burst of patriotic fervor following the attack on Pearl Harbor. They came from different backgrounds, different parts of the country. They were farmers, steel workers, coal miners, mountain men, and sons of the South. Some were desperately poor, others from the middle class. It was laughingly said that the farm boys from the Deep South still had manure between their toes. We had several teenage coal miners from the mountains of West Virginia and eastern Pennsylvania in the company; they had learned the value of dedication and perseverance.

The average age of the enlisted personnel was not more than eighteen. About ninety percent of them had enlisted since Pearl Harbor. They referred to themselves as draft dodgers because they volunteered to avoid the draft. I remember one of them telling me stories about hand-digging coal at the Gibson mine outside his hometown of Bentleyville, Pennsylvania, and after working a shift in the mine he would go down to the slate dump and pick burlap bags of coal for the home furnace. Most of them would tell you that they had shoveled many a ton into the coal bin using a number-4 shovel. Anyone that screwed around with these young boys from the hills and hollows of Pennsylvania and West Virginia were apt to get an old-fashioned "butt whooping." They would fight you at the drop of a hat.

They were a fine group of young men, full of the patriotism and enthusiasm that makes good Marines. They needed capable leaders, and they needed more training for combat. The battalion commander was determined they would have both. During the short period allotted the 1st Marine Division before going overseas, they trained hard to sharpen their skills by participating in infantry weapons training during live firing exercises. In my unit, special emphasis was placed on the use and application of military explosives in a combat environment.

The young wartime officers were very much a new breed. By and large, they were young newly commissioned second lieutenants, products of the Reserve Officers Training Command. They were sometimes referred to as "ninety-day-wonders" who had signed on for the duration. Although, they were just out of basic training and had received little or no combat training, they were in most cases exceedingly bright, highly motivated, and eager to get on with the war in order to get on with the peace that would follow. Three of the officers who joined the 1st Pioneer Battalion about the same time as I did were 1st Lt. Warren S. Sivertsen, Lt. William J. Heepe, and Lt. Roy L. Walters.

Shortly after joining the 1st Pioneer Battalion, I was promoted to the rank of sergeant and put in charge of a special assault demolition squad. The word had already been passed through official channels that we would be shipping out soon. Like most of the other Marines at that time, I was impatient to get overseas where the shooting was going on. But first there was a lot of waiting around to be done. Scuttlebutt had us leaving every day, and to practically every spot on the globe.

I received some words of wisdom from Col. Rowan at the time of my promotion. He said, "It is no accident that you wear sergeant chevrons today. You earned them, and while they entitle you to certain privileges, they also place upon you a very definite responsibility. The manner in which you wear them will effect the reputation of your unit. If you wear them well with courage and intelligence, and with due humility, you will enhance our reputation. Reputation in the end is only a by-product of our acts. Reputation, to be real, like respect, must be earned, not demanded."

The promotion to the rank of sergeant is a significant step in the chain of command in the Marine Corps. It is the position between the officers who give the orders and the enlisted men who will carry them out. To obtain this rank and special title of "Sarge" with less than two years of service and at the young age of seventeen was not bad for a country farm boy. I would jokingly be referred to as a "slick arm sergeant" by other more senior sergeants in the command who wore one or more hash marks on their sleeve, each denoting four years service.

After several more weeks of intensive training, the company boarded a train for San Francisco, California, on June 14, 1942. Everyone was excited and apprehensive about what was going to happen next. Only the old timers, who had seen action, knew what was coming. The rest of us were in ignorant bliss. We packed our sea bags with all our excess clothing and personal gear. Each sea bag was tagged with our name, rank, and serial number, and each was stenciled with our company markings and loaded onto trucks after which they were transported to the rail siding and off-loaded on baggage cars. Once our sea bags were

Shoving off to make history. Courtesy of the Marine Corps Historical Center.

loaded, we struggled into combat packs, formed in ranks, slung our rifles over our shoulder, and marched at route step to the rail spur where the long train of Pullman cars awaited our arrival. We piled aboard, found our seats, stowed our rifles and gear on the racks above us, and slumped down on the seats to catch our breath.

Our troop movement was secret. There were no great crowds. No sweethearts or parents to say good-bye to as we looked out the windows, observing the last sights. I felt the familiar jerk of the train, and we began to move slowly away. The band positioned by the trackside struck up the "Marine Corps Hymn" as we made our way out of Tent City One. We glued our faces to the windows and drank in for the last time the sight we knew so well. There was a general belief among the enlisted Marines that with the exception of Quantico, all Marine installations were selected with only one objective in mind: to make the men stationed in them so miserable they would gladly go anywhere in the world just to get away. This was our feeling then, as we watched the tent city fade into the distance.

[4] Shoving off to Make History

Everyone was in high spirits, as though we were headed for a picnic instead of war. We were gung-ho kids at that time. We had lots of guts and were ready to take on the whole world. We were astonished to learn that we would not be traveling on a grimy crowded troop train but rather on a line of first-class Pullman cars with a separate berth for each man and where porters with their faces wreathed in smiles attended to our every need. We ate our meals in a luxurious dining car in which waiters in white jackets served our individual tastes on fancy china and starched white linen tablecloths and napkins. It was a first—and most enjoyable—experience for me, as well as for most of the other Marines on board.

Because rank has its privilege, I exercised my authority and got a lower berth. I quickly dozed off listening to the train wheels making their *clicky-clack* sound as they crossed the rail-ties. Troop trains and mess cars would come later in the war.

The trip to the West Coast took five uneventful days. The monotony was broken with card games, playing pranks on each other, waving, yelling, and whistling at any and all women that we saw from our windows. I had just turned seventeen and was seeing the country for the first time. Our trip was more than a means of moving us from coast to coast; it provided us a portrait of our nation's vastness and beauty. My only regret was that I didn't keep a diary. There are only bits and pieces I can recall. I remember the beauty of the Ozarks with

USAT John Ericsson, *formerly the deluxe Swedish-American Motorliner* Kungsholm.
Courtesy of Forrest Gesswein.

their green forests as far as the eye could see, the Great Plains with
fields of amber grain, the Rockies with their majestic peaks and
valleys, the Colorado River snaking through the Royal Gorge, and our
sweeping ascent from the mountain peaks of Nevada into sunny
California.

At the waterfront in San Francisco, we were surrounded by the
towering majestic hills of Berkeley. The smell of the sea filtered through
the air into the smoke-filled Pullman cars as we pulled into the railroad station. We gathered up our packs and checked to see if we had
everything. With our rifles at sling arms, we filed out of the Pullman
cars to board buses standing by to take us to the Oakland Naval Base,
where we would embark aboard ship.

Upon our arrival at the naval base, the buses pulled onto a long,
covered pier. Towering high above us was a great vessel of the sea, the
USAT *John Ericsson.* The ship was formerly the deluxe Swedish-
American motorliner *Kungsholm.* It had been converted into a troop
transport. She was an impressive sight for the young teen-age Marines

who had never been aboard a large ocean liner before. We gazed in awe at the wide decks high above the pier.

We formed single-file columns on the broad deck of the pier and marched up the gangplank in single file. We then descended deep into the ship's bowels to the troops' berthing compartment, where canvas-laced sleeping racks were stacked twelve high. The racks were so close to one another that it was difficult for a man to turn over. The aisles between the sleeping racks were about thirty inches apart. It seemed like everywhere you turned, there was another Marine bumping into you or you bumping into him. We were packed like sardines in a tin can.

The sign on the compartment door notified us that the door would be closed in case of emergency. This thought did not comfort me. I decided to try and do something about my sleeping arrangements. If I could, I would be sleeping topside on deck once we got underway. After getting our sleeping rack assignment and stowing our gear, our attention was turned to finding our way back to the pier to join working parties loading equipment and supplies into the ship's holds.

Initially, we were so confused by the narrow, twisting passageways and having to duck through hatch combings and climb up and down ladders that for the first few days we needed a guide to find our way from our berthing compartments to the weld deck topside. Nothing tries the patience of a ship's crew more than embarking heavy-laden Marines with little or no shipboard experience. Encumbered with rifle, pack, helmet, cartridge belt, and heavy sea bag, the men struggled to negotiate narrow passageways, often tripping or catching items of equipment on objects projecting from the bulkhead or deck. The sound of steel on steel could occasionally be heard as helmet-clad Marines failed to duck low enough when going through a hatch between the ship's compartments, often leaving the Marine sprawled on his backside in the passageway and with a stiff neck.

Invariably, the physical exertion and ship's heat below deck caused the men to break out in sweat, soaking their uniforms and causing even more discomfort. Tempers grew short, as crewmembers and working parties tried to push their way through the packed berthing spaces. Barely organized confusion reigned, yet somehow or other the troops were embarked and supplies loaded and stowed in the ship's holds.

We faced not only a new environment but also an entirely new jargon: "deck" for floor, "overhead" for ceiling, "ladder" for stairway, "passageway" for hallway, "hatch" for door, and "head" for toilet. We learned to follow Navy etiquette: when arriving or departing the ship, salute the colors and then the officer of the deck, then say. "Request permission to come aboard (or depart) the ship, Sir." We learned about taking Navy showers and other traditions about whose origin we neither knew nor cared. Fresh water was a premium aboard ship, so taking a shower was a challenge. The line for the shower was always long, and water was cut off sometimes unexpectedly. When that happened, the fuming bather was left covered with soap. We were told that there would be no more freshwater showers once we got under way.

It was several days before we passed under the Golden Gate Bridge and headed out to sea. Before that, I had a few nights out on the town, shore patrol duty, and my first assignment as sergeant of the guard. There were many memorable incidents during our stay in the City by the Bay. I remember rides on the cable car trolley, a lobster dinner at Fisherman's Wharf, and, while on shore patrol duty, breaking up fights between drunken sailors and Marines.

The incident I'll never forget involved B. Gen. William H. Rupertus, the assistant commanding general of the 1st Marine Division. The general was returning to the ship, and as he passed the guard gate his aide-de-camp called out, "Turn out the guard!" I didn't know what the hell he meant. But, there is an old adage in the Corps: "When in doubt, salute." So that's what I did. The general returned my salute and continued up the ship's gangplank. A short time later his aide-de-camp came back ashore and asked me why I didn't turn out the guard in accordance with military protocol. When I explained that this was my first experience as sergeant of the guard and had not been instructed in the matters of protocol, he accepted my explanation and simply said, "Carry on sergeant." I saluted him and responded, "Aye, aye, Sir." He returned my salute and went back aboard ship.

Our ship left the morning of June 22, 1942. It was a miserable, rainy day. The men lined the rails to see the Golden Gate Bridge slip astern. For nearly every one of us, it was our first trip outside the United States. A sense of homesickness set in, complete with a realization that this might be the last time we would ever see these sights. I hoped that I would fight well and make my family and country proud.

The officers aboard would long remember the marvelous time they had during their brief stay in San Francisco, especially drinking cocktails and socializing with the young ladies in the Sky Room at the top of the Mark Hopkins Hotel. The twelfth-floor Sky Room commands a panoramic view of San Francisco Bay. As for the enlisted Marines, our hangout was mostly at bars and nightclubs along Market Street and in Chinatown, an exotic section of San Francisco filled with wondrous sights, sounds, and beautiful Asian girls.

All of us, I believe, were glad to be leaving for the battlefront. It was pleasant to stand on the rolling deck with the blue panel of the moving sea to our portside. There we could see two others in our fleet of transports, the *Barnett* and *Elliott* rolling over the long swells, nosing into the white surf. However, the good feeling didn't last very long for me. I suddenly became aware that the ship was rolling and pitching and, like most Marines aboard, felt some queasiness as the ship plowed through the choppy bay. Alcatraz fell to our starboard side as the Oakland and San Francisco skyline faded into the distance.

The ship began to pitch and roll as it hit the open Pacific. I watched the California coastline recede as the *John Ericsson* and the rest of the nine-ship convoy began zigzagging to evade enemy submarines. A vertical movement made the entire ship's surface rise and fall in relation to the fixed land, which appeared and disappeared with the ship's

Troops on the portside watch the San Francisco skyline fade in the distance. Courtesy of the Marine Corps Historical Center.

motion. The Marines along the rails viewed the oddity of the big rolling ground swells that caused the ship to pitch and roll, all in a steady rhythm. Within a short time, sections of the ship's railing were lined with dozen of Marines emptying their stomachs into the sea. The deck and sides of the ship caught much of their effort.

I was really a bit smug about their distress because I felt fine except for some queasiness, a natural reaction to choppy seas, and then I saw a member of my assault demolition squad make a frantic dash from middeck to the rail. His bulging eyes popped open to the size of ping-pong balls and his inflated cheeks looked like two small balloons about to burst. Before he could reach the rail, out spewed vomit. That undid me, and within seconds I joined the growing host of those feeding the fishes. After several days at sea, most of the men found their sea legs.

Our convoy escort included one light cruiser and two destroyers that were submarine-chasers. They could be seen patrolling on the horizon. Behind us were months of boot camp and arduous stateside training. Ahead of us lay a voyage to a foreign land and amphibious maneuvers on island beaches. The division was not to be committed to combat until the end of the year—at least that's what we thought at the time. For most, the immediate challenge was how to go about dating the girls we would meet upon arriving at our destination.

As might be expected, there was much conjecture about where we were going. Some said Hawaii, New Zealand, Australia, or even the Aleutians in Alaska, but the most credible scuttlebutt, as we sailed out across the Pacific, was that it would be some island in the South Pacific.

In the tight quarters aboard ship, a Marine got to know a lot about the young men around him, their personalities, their worries, and their ways. Most of us were still in our teens, and most were away from home for the first time. We were all cruising into war. That makes a bond develop pretty quickly. I recall my long talks with Pfc. Ed Swierk, who was idealistic about serving his country in the war and filled with plans for the future. He spoke constantly about his wonderful family back home in Woonsocket, Rhode Island, and what he wanted to do with a family of his own once the war was over.

The *John Ericsson* bristled with the collective irritation of the approximately 5000 enlisted men aboard; we were crowded. We didn't mind it too much while we were on deck, where the air was cool and fresh, but the sleeping compartments below deck were something else. Due to poor ventilation, the odor was overwhelming, making sleep impossible for many others and me. At times the below-deck heads reeked like open cesspools.

To avoid the stench, and because we felt safer above the water level, many of us stayed on deck during the day and slept there at night. In bad weather, we were forced below. This sort of shipboard life required us to place our green woolen blankets in a selected spot and to guard that spot constantly. To leave it meant someone else would take over. It was common practice for squads and other small units to stick together, so there was always someone there to protect the selected spot. In this way, positions in the endless chow lines could be kept without fear of real-estate seizure.

Eventually, so many Marines were sleeping topside that anybody trying to move about in the dark was bound to step on somebody. The yelling and cussing of Marines became part of the night. Navy personnel constantly harassed the Marines on deck. All during the day, orders for "Sweepers, man your brooms!" and "Sweep all decks fore an aft!" were announced over the ship's loudspeakers. This meant we had to pick up our blankets and other gear as brooms swept, quite often followed by saltwater wash-downs from high-pressure hoses used in the deck-cleaning process.

Most Marines became accustomed to getting wet, either by frequent rainsqualls or water hoses, and thought nothing of it. At night, you just rolled up in a blanket and went to sleep on the steel deck, using your life jacket as a pillow. The deck was hard and I was soft. Try as I might, I couldn't get much sleep while we were underway.

As our great ship of the sea continued a zigzagging course across the Pacific, the days and nights seemed endless. We passed the time during the day by playing cards, writing letters, and reading books. The paperbacks were passed around until they fell apart. The favorite pastime for members of my squad, other than writing and reading, were the games cribbage and pinochle.

At night, talking relieved the boredom. We talked about life aboard a ship that was a steel sweatbox below deck and the crowded conditions topside. You had to stand in line just to get a place to sit down. There was much talk about sex. Of course, everyone would exaggerate his prowess with women. In fact, we talked more about girls than God, country, or the Japanese.

Most of the card games were played topside. If you made out okay in a topside game, you usually went below deck to the head, where the big game was held. None of the penny ante stuff down there. They played with folding money for high stakes. That's where Cpl. Warren D. "Ace" Hartwig from B Company Pioneers played.

Except for the man-over-board and fire drills, I don't think that card game ever stopped. Most of the players hardly ever went above deck. They even cut the pot for a galley swabbie to bring them their chow and for a Marine to stand in the ship store's pogey-bait (candy, soft drinks, peanuts) line with their purchase order. Even when there was a submarine scare and the water was cut off, the game went on. It stunk like an overloaded two-holer, but they'd stay there, wiping sweat, holding their noses, and crouching on their helmets or sitting on life jackets and grunting, "Hit me," or "The bank pays eighteen."

As the days and nights stretched into weeks, many of the men aboard ship began to get a short fuse. They would fly off the handle with little or no provocation. They were openly beating their gums over the stench and heat below deck, of drinking lukewarm coffee that the swabbie mess-man handed you like he wanted to charge you for it. There was more and more bitching about the chow being served in the ships galley and the crowded conditions topside.

The criticism of the food was well founded. The longer we were aboard, the worse it got. Only two meals were served during the greater part of the passage, and one of these often consisted of soup or soup and bread. Most of the men complained about the continuous lines for each meal, the watery soup, and having to eat bread hardtack left over from World War I. The bread was about a half-inch thick and very hard. The only way it could be eaten was to soak it in soup or water. We stood up in the ships mess to eat. There were no seats, and if the ship started to roll, most of our food would slide off our mess trays and end up on the nearest Marine. The meals weren't worth struggling over, though we usually went to see what was being served. At least we could get a canteen cup of coffee to take up on deck.

Another criticism was the shortage of fresh water. There was just enough for drinking and for use in the ships galley. No freshwater showers were allowed while we were at sea. The fresh water was turned on for about fifteen minutes each morning, just long enough to brush your teeth and shave. You could take a saltwater shower if you could get to one, and if you could find a bar of special saltwater soap; the ordinary brand, which most brought aboard, would smear and could not be used. All of the men carried canteens with them and filled them up with fresh water whenever the opportunity presented itself.

All sergeants aboard the *John Ericsson* were placed on the guard roster and stood duty as junior officer of the day. I soon found out that the duty was not onerous, that the colonel commanding (with delegated captain's mast authority) had some definite requirements, which were not to be treated lightly. One was to be present in the ship's mess at all meals and attest to the fact that the vittles were not only fit for human consumption, but also sufficient in quantity and quality. Another was to validate tranquility in the ship's mess and the long waiting lines in the passageway outside. All these were to be duly noted in the ship's log book presented to the commanding officer the following morning.

On one occasion I overslept and was late reporting for duty. This dereliction of duty resulted in my appearance at captain's mast. Col. Rowan was not one for mincing words when it came to disciplinary action. As I stood at attention before him, he stared at me for a moment and said, "Sergeant, you are out of uniform. You are now a corporal."

Luckily for me, my company commander, Capt. Walter H. Stephens, was present at the time and asked to speak on my behalf. He told Col. Rowan that I was one of his best sergeants and that he would need me in the upcoming campaign. He also emphasized the fact that I had an exemplary record and should be given a second chance. His recommendation was that I be given a verbal reprimand rather than a reduction in rank. After some hesitancy, the colonel reversed his decision and I retained my sergeant rank.

Afterwards, Capt. Stephens passed along some words of wisdom. He said, "A trained Marine can overcome anything, so clean the dust off and stand tall!" He also said: "You will stand tall because it is expected of you. You are one of the few NCOs in my command that has extensive infantry training and I will rely heavily on your leadership ability and knowledge of infantry weapons when we get in combat." Capt. Stephens, unlike the other company officers, was a trained '03 infantry officer.

Asked later by a member of my squad what infraction caused me to appear at captain's mast, I said, "I don't want to talk about it." It was not one of my proudest moments. But, I tell you what, that colonel put the fear of God into me. A lesson was learned that would serve me well throughout my military career.

As I reflect back on this event, I realize I got off easy compared to other Marines who appeared at captain's mast aboard ship and received the most dreaded sentence of P&P ("piss and punk"), that is, bread and water. Those who got it were sealed in a one-man privy for seventy-two hours. Quit apart from the diet, such confinement in a dark hot stuffy ship's brig cell deep in the bow of the ship was both cruel and unusual punishment. The sentence of P&P was most often awarded for missing ship, fighting, or insubordination.

As our convoy sailed across the Pacific the timetable of war was changing. One of the darkest chapters in American history was still unfolding. On July 1, as the *John Ericsson* crossed the equator, Gen. Vandegrift, who was already in New Zealand, was notified he was to lead an assault on Guadalcanal. This operation, code name Watchtower, was top-secret information and not shared with the troops.

At the time, Gen. Vandegrift was immersed in the problems of reorganizing his scattered Marine units into an amphibious force capable of fighting the victorious Japanese army in the Pacific. He was taken by surprise when orders came to take his Marines to the Solomon Islands. Feeling there was not enough time for such a large-scale and dangerous undertaking, he asked for an extension. He was granted a mere seven days additional time to prepare for the amphibious assault. At the time, the 1st Marine Division was scattered over half the Pacific Ocean.

One regiment, the 7th Marines, his best-trained and best-equipped unit, was on garrison duty in the Samoan Islands. Another, the 5th Marines, had just gone into its encampments outside Wellington, New Zealand. The remaining rifle regiment, the 1st Marines, was still at sea and would not arrive in Wellington until July 11; its youthful, recently recruited troops were particularly in need of further training. The whole division needed training to operate as a unit and to test newly received weapons and equipment.

The rest of the reinforced division's major units were getting ready to embark. The 1st Raider Battalion was on New Caledonia, and the 3rd Defense Battalion was at Pearl Harbor. The 2nd Marines of the 2nd Marine Division, a unit that would replace the 1st Division's 7th Marines stationed in British Samoa, was loading out from San Diego and would sail under the formidable protection of the aircraft carrier *Wasp.* This great ship had been rushed from the Atlantic to the Pacific to escort this borrowed regiment to the 1st Marine Division's rendezvous in the Fiji Islands. All three infantry regiments of the landing force had battalions of artillery attached, from the 11th Marines, and in case of the 2nd Marines its reinforcing 75-mm howitzers were attached from the 2nd Division's 10th Marines.

Upon crossing the equator on the first day of July, the Marines aboard the USAT *John Ericsson* observed the ancient rites of initiation. The first-timers aboard were transformed from "pollywogs" into "shellbacks." The shellbacks, the "old salts of the sea," gathered up the pollywogs, those of us who had never crossed the equator, and horseplay continued unabated throughout the day.

One of the initiations into King Neptune's Court took place on a greased deck where butt-naked Marines had to crawl through a line of Marines wielding belts. Another one was the infamous man-overboard barber-chair event. I'll never forget that one! On the main deck, a ten-foot wide, six-foot deep saltwater pool had been built. Then a barber's chair was placed three decks directly above it. A few select Marines were blindfolded and led to the barber chair while being told that they were going to get a haircut. As soon as they sat down in the chair, it was flipped back and they fell over backwards, thirty feet into the pool. As they were going over, everyone yelled, "Man overboard." I'm still amazed that no one was killed or seriously hurt during this stunt.

Officers were targeted for special treatment: Lt. Col. Roy L. Walters, now retired and living in Top Sail Beach, North Carolina, shares his recollections of crossing the equator on July 1, 1942: "I was a lieutenant in B Company Pioneers, one of the 300 plus officers on board the *John Ericsson*. For many of us the initiation into King Neptune's Court was easy, compared to what others had to tolerate. My initiation into the court was having half of my well-developed moustache shaved off. I was upset until I heard what was happing with other pollywogs on board." Stanley L. Rich, then a lieutenant in A Company Pioneer's related, "I had to stand guard in full winter field equipment, including a twenty-one-pound Browning automatic rifle and steel helmet, out on deck in the broiling tropic sun, minus my pants, to the delight of the enlisted men aboard."

My baptism included the rites of initiation in which, as a first-timer aboard, I was required to kneel down before this character dressed as King Neptune the God of the Sea and honor him by kissing the rings on his fingers and toes. The initiation also included a good old-fashioned ass paddling as I ran a gauntlet of veteran shell-backs with nothing on but my skivvies. Those wooden paddles really left their mark. I couldn't sit for days without pain. Along with the other Marines aboard, I took our hazing good-naturedly.

At the day's end, we were all awarded a very fancy certificate that announced to the world that we were now bona fide members of the Order of the Deep and admitted to the realm of King Neptune's

Certificate "To all the Travelers of the seven seas" presented to Roy L. Walters while aboard the John Ericsson, *July 1, 1942. Courtesy of Lt. Col. Roy L. Walters.*

Court. Most now considered themselves to be old salts of the sea, with a fancy certificate to prove it.

In the early morning hours of July 11, 1942, the coastline of New Zealand appeared on the horizon. As we lined the rails, we watched with hungry eyes to make out details too far to be distinguished. The mountains grew larger and details of the coast began to grow on the horizon as we moved closer to our destination.

Here's how it looked: Wellington, New Zealand, as it was seen by many Marines.
Courtesy of the Marine Corps Historical Center.

Everything was different that day. The sailors in the crew of our transport, USAT *John Ericsson*, were as nice as pie, as if they had not been tormenting us for weeks with comments like, "You can't stand there, Marine!" and "Pick up your gear and move your ass, Marine!" And worse.

The *John Ericsson* slowed to a crawl. A small pilot boat came alongside. The pilot climbed the Jacob's rope ladder up her high freeboard and headed for the bridge. Under his skilled hands the ship nosed carefully into a narrow channel, feeling our way through a tight-harbor entrance. The first sight of Wellington after the ship swung around the headlands was reminiscent of San Francisco' majestic hills climbing to the sky.

As we entered Wellington's beautiful harbor, we saw a great round of deep blue water girded by an amphitheater of sloping green hills.

We gazed upward at a towering snow-capped mountain with its mid-slopes lush with green pastures that were dotted with grazing sheep. We marveled at the unique architecture of the white homes nestled at the base of the mountain that extended out to form a rim around the harbor. The houses had the most beautiful tile rooftops I had ever seen. Some were blue, others green, yellow, and red. It was a picturesque sight I'll never forget.

Everyone was on deck at this point. The rails were crowded, and vantage points were at a premium. This was the first foreign land most of us had ever seen. We were anxious to dock, and watched with great excitement as we waited to disembark.

As our ship came alongside, I saw one of my buddies, Cpl. Jim Campbell, in the crowd of Marines standing on the pier waving at us. Jim was from Georgia, and we had become fast friends while serving together in the 5th Marines before I was reassigned to the pioneers. Over the crowd noise I could hear him saying something about not unpacking. I learned later that he was trying to tell me that the word had been changed and that we were supposed to reload and head out for combat. Jim had arrived in New Zealand ahead of us on a Sunday, June 21, aboard the *Wakefield*. This was the last time I would see Jim alive. He was killed during the Battle of Guadalcanal.

In my first letter home upon our arrival in New Zealand, I wrote:

Today is a great day; at last we sailed in to the New Zealand port of Wellington after a long and dangerous sea voyage from San Francisco, California. There was always the prospect of sudden death, with the Japanese submarines hunting our troop convoy.

Now I know something about heavy seas. There were times when I began to wonder if our troop transport was going to capsize as it wallowed in the heavy seas. Marines caught up on deck during the storm would grab and hold on to anything stationary to keep from being washed overboard. It was pretty scary for a few days.

We experienced another scary incident when our ship, the USAT *John Ericsson*, stopped dead in the water. Here we were sitting like a "dead duck" in the middle of the Pacific Ocean, thousands of miles from the nearest land. We were told that the ship's loss of power was due to a broken propeller shaft, and that efforts were underway to repair the shaft. In the meantime all hands were to wear their life jackets at all times and to muster on deck for abandon-ship drills. Needless to say, we were apprehensive at first, but felt much better when we saw a Navy destroyer sub-chaser steaming toward us to provide protection against a possible Japanese submarine attack.

The broken propeller shaft was replaced within four hours and we were underway once again. It was a relief to learn that the Navy destroyer sub-chasers would remain on station as our escort for the remainder of the voyage.

I am unable to tell you how long we will be in New Zealand or where we will be going next. All troop movements are very secret in time of war and for good reasons. I will write as soon as I am allowed to. In the meantime, keep me in your prayers.

Word was passed over the ship's loudspeaker for B Company Pioneers to muster on deck. We formed in ranks expecting to get the word to load-up and disembark, but Frank Cotrufo, the company first sergeant, had other news for us, "At ease, men. Orders are for all units to reduce their equipment and supplies to those items that are actually required to live and fight." One-third of the supplies had to be left behind. To make the amphibious assault, the cargo that had been loaded in San Francisco, California, would have to be reconfigured into a combat load. We weren't combat-loaded because we had thought that we were going to disembark here and train for six months or more. Everything had been changed with new orders.

First Sgt. Frank Cotrufo continued by telling us: "To further complicate matter, the Wellington dockworkers are on strike and so you

Marines are going to do the hoisting and hauling yourselves.[1] We are going to unload these ships and then reload them for combat. That's going to be a lot of work. We haven't much time. We'll be working in around-the-clock shifts to complete this task in nine days. Your sea bags are going to stay here. If there is anything in them you want to take with you, you had better get it out. Store the gear you want to leave behind in the sea bags, and it will be here when you get back, or shipped to wherever we go next. We're authorized liberty tonight, after shifts are assigned. Be here for your assigned shifts. When you are off shift, you are to be either sleeping or on liberty. Sign out as to what you are doing. Get your gear ready now. Take your sea bags down the gangplank and stack them on the pier. They will be taken to the warehouse for storage. Dismissed."

The usual excited and ill-founded rumors of an early liberty immediately became the main, if not the only topic of conversation. Later that night as working parties were posted on the bulletin boards in the troop berthing compartments, the realization set in that first there was a great deal of work to be done. The changeover from administrative loading of the various unit equipment and supplies to combat loading were positioned to come off the ship first with the assault troops. Combat gear and equipment desperately needed ashore, such as weapons, ammunition, and rations, were given top priority. This round-the-clock toil in the chilly winter rain had a very real benefit. The grumbling Marines softened by the long ocean voyage were whipped back into shape.

Loading problems made it seem almost impossible for Gen. Vandegrift to meet an August 1 deadline for D-Day. His first order of business would be to reconfigure the amphibious shipping, which had been administrative in nature, to combat load configuration. The 1st Marines, their attached units, weapons, ammunition, equipment, and supplies would have to be unloaded from the ships that ferried them across the Pacific, then reloaded aboard attack transports and combat cargo ships, according to the intricate pattern of combat loading.

At this early stage of the Pacific campaign, there was not enough shipping available to simultaneously transport the division's personnel and heavy equipment. As a consequence, most of the division's heaviest ordnance had to be left behind in New Zealand. Limited ship space and time meant the division's big guns, a 155-mm howitzer battalion, and all the motor transport battalion's two-and-half-ton trucks would not be reloaded. Col. Pedro A. del Valle, commanding the 11th Marines, was unhappy at the loss of his heavy 155-mm howitzers and equally distressed that essential sound and flash-ranging equipment necessary for effecting counter-battery fire was being left behind.

Because there were not enough ships available, individual and organization equipment was cut to the bone. Failing to make the cuts in the battle for shipping space were canvas tents, all spare clothing, bedding rolls, and supplies necessary to support the reinforced division beyond sixty days. Ten-day supplies of ammunition for each of the division's weapons would remain in New Zealand. Left behind were office supplies, equipment, and unit muster rolls and pay clerks. Cpl. John Fencyk and Cpl. Frank Pawli from B Company remained behind. They would become part of the rear echelon in Wellington.

In addition, the Marines had none of the specialized clothing and equipment characteristic of later Pacific campaigns. They lacked insect repellent and mosquito netting, despite the fact that they would be landing on a tropical island where fleas, leaches, sand flies and malaria-bearing mosquitoes bit every inch of exposed flesh.

It was winter in that part of the world, and on the miserably cold wind-swept pier the division working parties labored in eight-hour shifts around the clock to carry out the unloading and reloading of the ships. It rained almost continuously, soaking cardboard containers and bags of rations, and causing the contents to spill over the

The dock scene at Wellington, New Zealand, was one of complete disarray. Some ships were being loaded, some unloaded, some were being loaded and unloaded at the same time. Courtesy of the Marine Corps Historical Center.

wharf. Some supplies disintegrated, labels washed off, and crates were jumbled in complete disarray.

Gen. Vandegrift described the dock site in language notable for moderation, calling it "an unparalleled logistics problem." The enlisted men, who worked in shifts, described it in less elegant terms as a "mucked-up mess." Despite the confusion, the men of the 1st Marine Division once again accomplished the almost impossible, and they were ready to join the mightiest task force ever assembled up to that time, which consisted of eighty-nine ships and 16,000 U.S. Marines.

The Marines didn't get to see much of New Zealand because they worked steadily for eleven days to off-load and reload ships. When they could get to town, they amused themselves by scrawling obscene references to New Zealand dockworkers on the wall of hotel and restaurant lavatories. "All wharfees are bastards" is possibly the most restrained of the recorded graffiti. Needless to say, there was a great feeling of dislike for the striking New Zealand dockworkers.

The few times the men in my unit got to go ashore, we would just walk around, go to a restaurant, or take in a movie. Some of the men, especially the fast workers, would get dates with the local girls. The people were friendly and very glad to see the Marines arrive. The war was real in this part of the world, and our presence provided them with a sense of security.

Liberty in Wellington was enjoyable. The girls were pretty and eager to date the Marines, for there was a shortage of young men there at that time. Since the outbreak of World War II, in September 1939, many of their countrymen of the same age shipped out with the 2nd New Zealand Kiwi Division to fight the Germans in North Africa and the Balkans.

The restaurants and hotels in Wellington served excellent meals, which broke the monotony of shipboard menus. Steak and eggs, a local specialty, rapidly became a favorite with the Marines. Milk bars, serving ice-cream sodas and milk shakes, were numerous and popular.

The movie theaters in Wellington were also popular with the Marines, both those with or without dates. At the beginning of each show, the lights dimmed, a picture of King George VI of England came on the screen, and the British national anthem was played. Every one of us would stand to show respect.

The Marines and the New Zealand girls realized quite rapidly that words and phrases had different meanings in their two cultures. The Marines soon learned that the word "bloody" was not to be used in polite company in New Zealand. On their part, the girls learned not to use the word "screwed" as slang for "paid."

On July 22, eleven days following the arrival of the 1st Marine Division from San Francisco, the troop ships moved out of the harbor at Wellington, where we had unloaded and reloaded for a combat mission under the most severe, exhausting, and frustrating work schedule. We finally headed north to our eventual destination: Guadalcanal.

Lost in their thoughts, the men lined the rails and watched the now-familiar hills grow smaller as the troop transports exited from the harbor in columns. To and from the houses dotting the hills, worried eyes peered and thoughts flowed from ship to shore and back again, seeking some sort of final communication. The Marines were on their way to war.

In direct command of the amphibious landing force was R. Adm. Richmond K. Turner (known as "Terrible Turner" because of his volcanic temper), who until recently had held down a desk job in Washington, D.C. Marine officers serving on his staff aboard the flagship *McCawley* and in command positions ashore found him to be stubborn and more concerned about the Navy than the Marines aboard ship.

On July 22, the same date we sailed out of the Wellington harbor, the 1st Raiders came out of the boondocks and returned to Noumea. There they embarked aboard destroyer transport ships (APDs), their old standbys the old high-speed destroyer transports, with which they had made so many cold-weather landings along the Atlantic Coast. The sailors made them welcome. Lt. Col. Merritt A. Edson established his flag on board the USS *Little* (APD-4).

These outdated, World War I flush-deck destroyers were converted into transports by removing two boilers and using the empty space for

*R. Adm. Richmond K. Turner, USN, and Maj. Gen. Alexander A. Vandegrift, USMC,
on the flag bridge of USS* McCawley *during the Guadalcanal operation, July–August
1942. Courtesy of the U.S. National Archives.*

troop compartments. Although they were short on creature comfort
and cargo space, these ships were fast enough to keep up with a combat task force and could provide their own naval gunfire support. The
raiders had plenty of experience on the smaller, rough-riding APDs.

The convoy of ships, with its outriding protective screen of carriers,
reached Koro, one of the Fiji Islands, on July 28, 1942. My group,
B Company Pioneers, was aboard the attack cargo ship USS *Alchiba*
(AK-23). It was loaded with men and material. We were aboard a real
Navy ship for a change. It was clean, the chow was good, we had plenty
of fresh water, and it was not too crowded. It was great compared to
the Merchant Ship *John Ericsson.*

The 1st Parachute Battalion had boarded the USS *Haywood* on July 18 and sailed in convoy to Koro Island, where the entire invasion force conducted landing rehearsals on July 28 and 30. These went poorly, since the Navy boat crews and most of the 1st Marine Division were too green. The parachute battalion was better trained than most of the division, but this was its very first experience as a unit in conducting a sea-borne landing. There is no indication that planners gave any thought to using their airborne capability, though in all likelihood that was due to the lack of transport aircraft or the inability of available planes to make a round-trip flight from New Zealand to the Solomons.

After several days at sea, Transdivision 12, *Calhoun*, *Gregory*, *Little*, and *McKean*, joined up with an enormous task force in the Fiji Islands for preinvasion maneuvers. The amphibious task force branched off for a rehearsal landing at Koro. All went well at first. Higgins boats towed strings of inflatable landing rafts as usual, but then the Navy boat commander misread the distance to the beach and cast off the towlines way too far at sea. The raiders had to paddle forever; it was supposed to be a night landing but they didn't reach shore until morning. Gen. Vandergrift would later call the rehearsal a "disaster." Lt. Col. Edson would only shake his head in disgust at the chaos. He also had some unprintable words for that Navy boat commander. Thank God the Fijis weren't in Japanese hands. If that had been the case, we would have been slaughtered.

In truth, the raiders' tactical mobility was restricted to the destroyer transports and a bunch of inflatable rubber boats, none of whose outboard motors reliably worked in salt water. Adm. Turner's decision to rule out a night landing on Tulagi by the raiders had the effect of increasing the demand for Higgins boats, which already were in short supply. Going ashore in rubber boats during a daylight assault across coral reefs would have been disastrous.

Because of the coral damage to our boats during the first landing, our orders for the second day were changed. We climbed down the nets into the Higgins boats, made a pass at the island, turned around, and came back to the ship. After our second day in the Fijis, the rehearsal was called off and the troop transports rendezvoused with the remainder of the task force. At sunset on July 31, the entire task force under the command of V. Adm. Frank J. Fletcher left the Koro area and set a course for the Solomon Islands. The 1st Marine Division was shoving off to make history. As the convoy left the Koro area and the men were told where they were going, they asked themselves, "Where the hell is Guadalcanal?"

The Joint Chief of Staff in Washington, D.C., gave the order to "Occupy and defend Tulagi and adjacent positions (Guadalcanal and Florida Islands and the Santa Cruz Islands) in order to deny these areas to the enemy and to provide United States bases in preparation for future offensive action." The order was to be carried out by the 1st Marine Division, under the command of Maj. Gen. Alexander A. Vandegrift. It was issued in June 1942, and was based on the position of the United States that the protection of our lines of communications to Australia and New Zealand was absolutely critical.

For more than a week, the eighty-nine ships of Task Force 61 steamed through the blue waters of the South Pacific toward Guadalcanal, an island few of us had ever heard of a few days earlier. Radio transmitters were silent. Planes from the three aircraft carriers scouted for Japanese submarines that might spot the naval armada. Aboard the flagships, admirals and generals expressed satisfaction over the lucky weather: low-scudding clouds and tropical downpours shielded the fleet from the threat of prying eyes.

Aboard the troop transports, 16,000 members of the 1st Marine Division were looking for a tough fight. They knew little about the target, less about their opponent. The maps available were shoddy at best. The information on these maps was based on outdated hydrographic charts, information provided by former residents who had been running plantations on the island, missionaries, and captains of

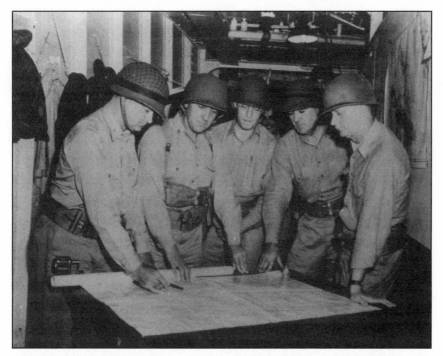

Five high-ranking Marine officers shown at a staff meeting on a transport (left to right): Maj. Gen. Alexander A. Vandegrift, Lt. Col. Gerald C. Thomas, Lt. Col. Randolph McC. Pate, Col. Frank B. Goettge, and Col. William C. James. Courtesy of the Marine Corps Historical Center.

trading ships who had sailed in the waters around Guadalcanal. The maps were hand-drawn, and some of the information was incorrect. But as haphazard as the maps were, they were the only information available.

At a briefing for platoon leaders in the ships wardroom during the approach to Guadalcanal, Lt. Col. William E. Maxwell, commanding officer of a battalion of assault troops presided: "This is going to be a difficult matter, with rivers to cross, kunai grass four to five feet tall, and drainage ditches filled with alligators and snakes, but it can be done, and we've got to lead the way. It's the first time in history we've ever had a huge expedition of this kind accompanied by transports.

It's of worldwide importance. You'd be surprised to know how many people all over the world are following this. You cannot fail them."

Many of the Marines aboard ships, discouraged by the long sea voyage, had given up the daily routine of stripping down and reassembling their rifles, but I was not one of them. I had worked too hard at boot camp mastering the tricky feat to neglect it, especially now that we were headed for combat. Every morning after chow in the ship's galley, I would find a quiet spot on the open deck topside where I diligently tended to my '03 Springfield. In inclement weather, where we were forced below deck, I would locate a spot in the troops berthing compartment where I could do it. This weapons cleaning was required by each member of my squad. I inspected their rifles daily to make sure they were clean and operating properly.

When not otherwise occupied tending to our weapons or listening to a somber know-your-enemy lecture from officers who, by and large, had seen no more combat than the men had—that is to say, none at all—some of the Marines played high-stakes poker below deck in the ships head. Others got together for a usually off-key songfest, singing such favorites as "My Momma Done Told Me," "Sentimental Journey," and "I'll be Seeing You."

The weather was on the side of the Marines. During the final days of the approach to the Solomons, the sky was generally overcast, with a low ceiling and an occasional rainsquall, weather ideal for landing. As each day passed we realized our transport was taking us closer and closer to where we were going to meet the Japanese. The men started to get edgy. Most of us had never been in combat and didn't know what to expect. We knew that we were about to fight an enemy who had been smacking the hell out of everyone else in the Pacific. It was an awesome moment for the young Marines.

On board his command ship, Gen. Vandegrift wrote to his wife, "Tomorrow morning at dawn we land in the first major offensive of the war. Our plans have been made and God grant that our judgment has been sound. We have rehearsed the plans. The officers and the men are keen and ready to go. Way before you read this you will have heard of it. Whatever happens you'll know that I did my best. Let us hope that best will be good enough."

Col. Clifton B. Cates, commanding the 1st Marine Regiment, had a message for his men: "We are fighting for a just cause, there is no doubt about that. It is rights and freedom. We have enjoyed the many advantages given to us under our form of government, and with the help of God, we will guarantee that the same liberty and freedom for our loved ones and to the people of America for generations to come."

It was still dark at 0400 hours on August 7, 1942, when the amphibious task force separated into two groups as it approached Savo Island, the Tulagi Group Yoke passing to the left and the Guadalcanal Group X-ray passing to the right. All elements of the group arrived in position at about 0630 and made ready for the landing.

The Marines were roused from a fitful sleep by the announcement over the ship's loudspeaker that breakfast would be served at 0430 hours. "Now hear this! Now hear this! You are going to have steak and eggs for breakfast. Good luck, Marines."

After we had a hearty breakfast and passed a normally humorous conversation, we returned to our troop compartment to make final preparations to go ashore. We all knew what we had to do. Packs were checked for the last time to make sure they were filled with rations and other essential items. Weapons were given a final inspection to ensure they were clean, oiled, and operating properly.

General quarters were sounded over the ship's loudspeaker at 0530. First, the shrill whistle of the boatswain's pipe, then the bugle sounded the call for general quarters. It's difficult to describe the sound, but it's enough to make the hair stand up on the back of your neck and goose pimples to break out all over your body. Your adrenalin starts pumping and all your training for this day comes into focus.

The entire naval task force had moved up during the night. When dawn came, our ship formed in the line of battle. It was a sight I'll never forget. As far as I could see were ships. Battleships, cruisers,

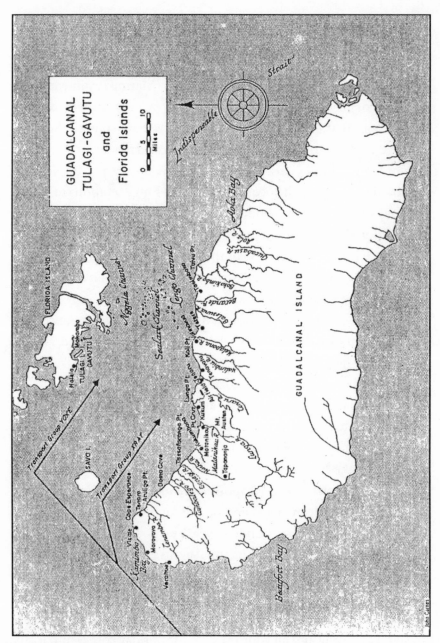

Map of Guadalcanal, Tulagi-Gavutu, and the Florida Islands. Courtesy of the Marine Corps Historical Center.

destroyers, troop transports, combat supply ships. Our aircraft carriers were off a distance over the horizon. It was a good feeling to know that we were not alone, that our Navy was with us on this one.

As the ships slipped through the channel on either side of the rugged Savo Island, which split Sealark Channel near its western end, heavy clouds and dense rain blanketed the task force. The rain and clouds that had cloaked our naval armada for most of the previous twenty-four hours had now withdrawn to reveal a quarter moon rising to the northeast and silhouetting the islands. On the deck of the troop transports, nervous Marines laden with rifles and packs lined the rails to watch the transports slide along Guadalcanal nearly opposite Kukum Beach. There was no sign of life ashore yet. The ship's crew made ready to lower the landing boats as we lined the starboard rail, straining our eyes toward the high, irregular dark mass that lay beyond our accompanying cruiser and destroyer screening force. The sky was still dark, but the rugged black mountain stood distinct against the lighter sky.

The only sounds we heard were the swish of water as our ship's bow cut through the choppy waves and the slight noises of men moving about on the forward deck. Suddenly, from our debarkation station on deck, I saw a greenish yellow flash of light coming from a cruiser on the starboard; it had opened fire. The first shot came from the heavy cruiser USS *Quincy*, which led the line of ships and sent a salvo of 8-inch shells screaming toward the beach. Almost immediately, other cruisers joined her as salvo after salvo raked Lunga Point, code-named Beach Red. That was the designated landing point for the main assault. We watched the shells grow white hot as they neared the shore. It was the most awesome sight I'd witnessed up to that point.

One can only imagine how the Japanese must have felt when they awoke to the fury of our attack. They were on the receiving end and had not expected it. We had achieved complete tactical surprise, thanks to the bad weather of the previous few days. Fires, particularly those from oil storage dumps, roared skyward in vivid orange flames.

Coconut palm trees came crashing down or were quickly defoliated. Then, with the quick tropical dawn came dive-bombers and fighters off the fleet carriers, working over targets of opportunity. As we waited to go over the side, we were impressed by our air and naval gunfire support. We were witness to the work of the most powerful amphibious attack force ever assembled up to that time. As naval gunfire and bombs splintered coconut trees and fragments of steel tore viciously into the earth, ships heaved to off Beach Red and ships' crews commenced to swing out and lower landing craft. Over the ship's bullhorn came the word, "Land the landing force," and they did.

The Battle of Guadalcanal had begun.

[5] Guadalcanal, Their Finest Hour

At 0740 hours, August 7, the eager men of Gen. Alexander A. Vandegrift's 1st Marine Division went ashore on the north coast of Guadalcanal and onto the smaller islands of Tulagi, Gavutu, and Tanambogo. Two naval task forces and other naval units gave their support. The 1st Raider Battalion, under Lt. Col. Merritt A. Edson, reinforced by the 2nd Battalion of the 5th Marines, landed on Tulagi. The 1st Parachute Battalion landed on Gavutu. Gen. Vandegrift was in personal command of the forces landing on Guadalcanal while the assistant division commander, B. Gen. William H. Rupertus, was in general command of the landings on the smaller islands.

There was light resistance when the bulk of the division took part in the Guadalcanal landing made on Beach Red, about four miles east of Lunga Point. It was spearheaded by the 1st and 3rd Battalions of the 5th Marines abreast, and followed by the 1st Marines in column of battalions. By 0930, the assault forces were ashore. Lacking opposition, two battalions of Col. Hunt's 5th Marines, swiftly established a 2000-yard-wide beachhead. Afterwards, they would proceed along the coast, securing that flank.

The 1st Marines, who landed later in the morning, would pass through the 5th Marines, move inland through the jungle, and secure Mount Austen, reportedly only a short distance away. Col. Cates' 1st Marines did not get very far the first day, the tempo of their advance slowed as they trudged through six-foot-high kunai grass toting

The Beach Red landing. Marines coming ashore are part of the initial waves. After crossing the beach, they moved inland to establish a beachhead. Courtesy of the U.S. National Archives.

weapons and ammunition under a blistering hot tropical sun and then into a jungle so thick that the vegetation seemed to block the air. Now came the realization that intelligence concerning the terrain on Guadalcanal was faulty. Mount Austen was by no means a short way off, nor was it the "grassy knoll" as described. It fact, it was the most prominent terrain feature in the area, more than six miles away and well outside the planned perimeter.

Progress was slow. The Ilu (soon to be referred to as the Tenaru River) turned out to be deep, with high banks. The 5th Marines walked across on a sandbar at the beach, but the 1st Marines advancing further inland had to wait for the engineers to throw up a one-way traffic bridge, whose midstream support consisted of two amphibious tractors.

With the pace of the 1st Marines slowed by horrendous heat, tropical growth, and tall kunai grass, Gen. Vandegrift realized that Mount

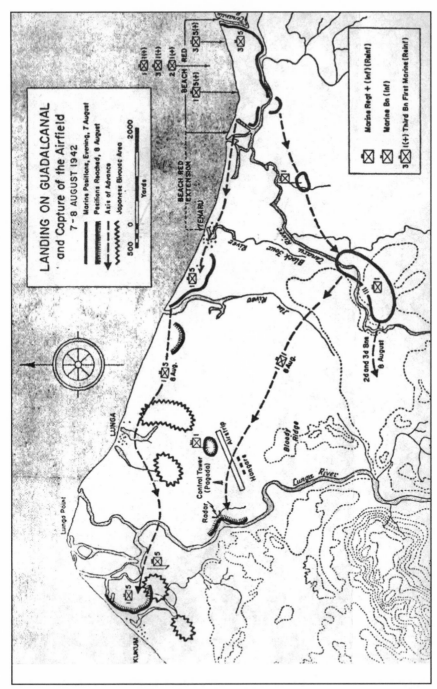

Landing on Guadalcanal and capture of the airfield, August 7–8, 1942. Courtesy of the Marine Corps Historical Center.

This bridge, hastily constructed and supported by amphibious tractors, was heavily used during the early phases of the campaign. Courtesy of the Marine Corps Historical Center.

Austen would not be reached that day; so he changed his plans accordingly. He ordered Cates to halt, consolidate, and dig in for the night. The halt was sorely needed. The men that had been cooped up in the steaming holds of overcrowed transports for two weeks were in deplorable physical condition. Burdened with excessively heavy packs and extra ammunition, blasted by the heat and humidity, short of water and salt tablets, they were in no condition to press forward, much less fight. Fortunately, Cates' Marines did not encounter any Japanese on their first day ashore.

The progress of the 5th Marines was no more satisfactory. In spite of the repeated exhortation from the regimental commander, his 1st Battalion advanced westward at an exasperatingly slow rate. Through the remainder of the afternoon, the landing continued unopposed. At 1600 hours, Gen. Vandegrift moved his headquarters ashore, while expressing extreme frustration at the tortoise-like progress of the landing force. By nightfall the prong of the Marine advance moving along the coast would make it only as far as the Ilu River, still more than 1000 yards from the airfield. A second prong became mired deep in the jungle.

Now that Mount Austen was no longer a primary objective, Vandegrift ordered the airfield to be taken and a defensive perimeter set up. The beachhead would be held temporarily to protect the off-loading of supplies until they could be moved into the perimeter. The next day, August 8, therefore began with a westward advance by all Marine forces on Guadalcanal. The original objective had been changed out of necessity, but the airfield remained the primary objective.

Meanwhile reports of the fighting on Tulagi and its neighboring islands reached the division command post on Guadalcanal, which was set up in a grove of tall coconut palms. Gen. Vandegrift and the remainder of his division headquarters staff came ashore, having spent most of the first day aboard the flagship *McCawley* trying to keep in touch with proceedings on both Guadalcanal and Tulagi, which were separated by twenty miles of water.

B. Gen. Rupertus, commander of the Tulagi landing force, sent a message saying there had been fierce fighting on his side of the water, and heavy casualties among the 1st Raider and Parachute Battalions. He asked for reinforcements. Vandergrift persuaded Adm. Kelly Turner to release one battalion of the 2nd Marines. That regiment had been earmarked for a later landing on Ndeni in the Santa Cruz Islands—one of the Joint Chiefs' specified objectives in their directive for Task One. To the general's surprise and satisfaction, Turner released two battalions. Gen. Vandegrift must have wondered how long the Marines' honeymoon on Guadalcanal would last.

The first night on Guadalcanal was scary. We were in new and threatening surroundings and we had all heard many stories of Japanese combat prowess. Because they were frustrated by their inability to vent pent-up hostility during the day, the troops were easily rattled and were firing at imaginary targets rather than the enemy. At every unfamiliar sound, jittery men opened fire. Every time one Marine would pull the trigger another down the line would also fire into the dark.

At 0930 hours on August 8, the advance on the airfield, the principal objective, began with a pincer movement. The 1st and 3rd Battalion, 5th Marines and A Company, 1st Tank Battalion advanced cautiously westward along the beach toward the Lunga River. At the same time, the 1st Marines, no longer focused on the original target of Mount Austen, moved from their night perimeter, swung west, and crossed the southern edge of the airfield.

Contact with small groups of Japanese began to occur as the Marines closed in on the airfield. Well-built defensive positions consisting of trenches and anti-aircraft emplacements were discovered deserted. The airfield, nearly 3600 feet long and in its last stages of construction, was defended by a small group of Japanese, who were attacked and killed. The attack on the airfield was a complete success. By 1600 hours, the 1st Marines captured the airfield and that night occupied the Line of the Lunga. The airfield that would be named Henderson Field, in honor of Maj. Lofton Henderson, a Marine flying hero who was killed at Midway, was firmly in Marine hands. Now all that remained was to hold on to it. As events would prove, that would take some doing.

Meanwhile, the 5th Marine Regiment continued its cautious advance to the west. By midday, the advancing Marines had laid their hands on several Japanese prisoners who, during interrogation by division intelligence personnel revealed that what few Japanese that were there had fled to the western end of the island. With this news, the 5th was given the word to contract its front and to move westward quickly, faster than it had been moving, astride the road to Kukum, and to seize the village and installations there before nightfall. The 1st and 3rd

As the Marines moved through the Lunga area south of the airfield, they captured stocks of Japanese equipment and foodstuffs. This particular building, which housed a vast quantity of rice, was captured in the first few days. Courtesy of the U.S. National Archives.

Battalion crossed the Lunga River by midday and continued their advance toward the main Japanese encampment at Kukum Beach.

Advance patrols did not reach their objective until midafternoon. Clearly the defenders had hauled-ass in a hurry; the Marines found a litter of uniforms, equipment, and food. In the course of its attack that afternoon, the 5th Marines overran a Japanese headquarters, which consisted of several huts outfitted with large mosquito netting, blankets, pillows, bedrolls, and shelter halves. Open bottles of Japanese sake and wooden bowls half-filled with recently cooked rice testified to the hasty departure of the previous occupants. Later, the advancing Marines found large stores of wormy rice, which they then spurned but which they did not, fortunately, destroy. That rice would one day stand between them and starvation.

Today some sixty years later, I still have vivid memories of the Guadalcanal landing. I remember the fear and apprehension I felt as I readied my assault demolition squad to disembark. Nobody knew what was going to happen to us that day. Paled by inactivity in the ship's hold, the Marines were dripping wet with perspiration. Their utility uniforms clung to them like a second skin. They clambered over the ship's rail, descending clumsily down unsteady cargo nets clinging with desperately clutching hands to the coarse ropes. The movement of the ship banged them mercilessly against the steel hull as they descended into Higgins boats bobbing alongside the ship. The first men down grabbed opposite sides of the net to help steady it for those that followed. The word was passed. "Keep your helmets on," and "Keep your head down" in the landing craft. "Try to keep your weapon dry."

We crouched beneath the gunwales while the loaded Higgins boats churned to the assembly area, forming rings and circling, finally spreading out in a broad line with hulls down and frothing white wake creaming out behind us as we sped inland toward the palm-fringed shores of Guadalcanal and the enemy. Every Marine gripped his weapon, tensed for the expected fight at the water's edge. We ran aground before beaching and had to climb over the side and wade ashore in waist deep water, with our '03 Springfield bolt-action rifles held high overhead. Thank God, we met no enemy resistance. We would have been like sitting ducks in water. If the enemy had been well entrenched and had put up a serious fight on the beach, the casualties would surely have been horrendous for us.

Like most of the other Marines that waded ashore on the Island of Guadalcanal during the early morning hours of August 7, 1942, I carried several personal items in a small waterproof pouch tucked inside the webbing straps of my helmet liner. One of the items was a small American flag. Another item was a pocket-sized Bible with a marker at the verse from Joshua 1:9: "Be strong and courageous! Do not be afraid or discouraged, for the Lord your God is with you wherever you go."

Marines descending clumsily from cargo nets into Higgins boats.
Courtesy of the Marine Historical Center.

Reading this verse prior to the landing and during some of the darkest hours of combat on Guadalcanal provided me great courage and comfort.

The landing was easy, nothing else was. During a combat landing you just sweat every thing out. You wait for the signal to move forward, to attack. It's a time of just waiting, waiting, and wondering if you are going to survive . . . how will you respond. Will you be brave in death or will you be a coward?

Immediately after assault troops cleared the beachhead and moved inland, supplies and equipment—inviting targets for enemy bombers—began to litter the beach. Courtesy of the Marine Corps Historical Center.

Once ashore on Beach Red, we advanced inland through the quiet, shell-shredded palms that fringed the landing beach area until we reached our designated position on the perimeter, where we would dig in and establish our base of operations. For the next twenty-four hours, B Company Pioneers (minus the 2nd Platoon still aboard the USS *Alchiba*) assisted in clearing supplies and equipment from the beach during the day and manned fighting positions on the beachhead at night.

The silence that first night ashore was scary. The absence of opposition was worrisome. The Japanese had fled to the west, spooked by the air bombardment, the preassault naval gunfire, and the large armada of American ships standing offshore. Surely they were there, somewhere in the impenetrable blackness, and it would only be a matter of time before they launched a counterattack. Meanwhile, the only thing we could do was hunker down in our hastily dug fighting positions and wait.

Despite the successful landing and the fact that the Marines ashore were encountering little or no resistance, Gen. Vandegrift found himself in the most dangerous of positions. There was no quick way for him to determine how many Japanese troops were on Guadalcanal, and no way to know when or where they would strike.

Across Sealark Channel, the enemy was not imaginary. The landings on the smaller islands to the north met with considerable opposition, and desperate fighting continued for two days. The Japanese on Tulagi, Gavutu, and Tanambogo were special elite units of the 3rd Kure Special Naval Force the ground combat arm of the Imperial Navy. Member of this Japanese defensive force called *rikusentai* had no intention of giving up what they held without a vicious, no-surrender battle. The several hundred rikusentai defending Talagi would make it a tough nut to crack. The island's reefs and coral heads would limit any landing to light forces.

The D-Day assaults on Tulagi succeeded despite a complicated, five-phased landing plan, the inexperience of the invasion force, and a significant shortage of landing craft. Adm. Kelly Turner's decision to rule out a night landing on Tulagi by the 1st Raiders had the effect of increasing the demand for Higgins boats. Landing by rubber boats in a daylight assault would have been suicidal. The raiders would go ashore in rampless Higgins boats. During the landing operation, a steady stream of Higgins boats shuttled between the shores of Tulagi and the destroyer transport task force offshore.

Tulagi was attacked at 0800 hours, according to schedule. The first to see action was Lt. Col. Merritt "Red Mike" Edson's 1st Raiders debarking from destroyer transports standing offshore. They, too, had suffered from lack of exercise and crowded quarters, but unlike the troops who were to land on Guadalcanal an hour later they were stripped down to minimum equipment for combat. Edson expected a tough

fight. "Don't worry about the food," he said to his company commanders. "There's plenty there. Japs eat, too. All you have to do is get it."

At Tulagi not a single landing craft of the first wave was able to set
its passengers directly ashore. When coral outcroppings grounded the
boats some distance offshore, the troops made a clumsy exit over the
gunwales and began to make their way to the beach through water
ranging from waist to armpit level. Many of them, especially those in
the weapon's company, who were carrying heavy machine guns, 60-
mm mortar tubes, and base plates floundered and went under. Some
of their less burden buddies pulled them up by the stacking swivel (a
technique Marines use in the field to stack a number of rifles leaning
against each other, attached by barrel swivels, in a cone shape stack to
keep them off the ground), and together they struggled shoreward.

The assaulting 1st Raiders, led by Baker and Dog Companies,
landed abreast across Beach Blue on the south coast and moved inland
toward the ridge that ran lengthwise through the island. They were
followed directly by the other two rifle companies Able and Charlie,
and the remnants of Easy Company (whose machine-gun platoons
were attached to the rifle companies). The leading units climbed the
silent steep ridge to their front, wheeled to the right and sped toward
the enemy defense forces concentrated in the southeastern end of the
little boot-shaped island.

On their heels, one hour later at 0900, Edson's backup, Lt. Col.
Harold E. Rosecrans' 2nd Battalion, 5th Marines, came ashore. These
Marines used the same Higgins boats in a second wave, across the
same landing beach, and experienced the same problems of wading
ashore. The men in the 81-mm mortar platoon of the heavy weapons
company faced an even greater challenge as they struggled to wade
ashore with their heavier weapons. Once ashore, Rosecrans' 2nd
Battalion, 5th Marines initially drove through to the northern shore
cleaning its sector of enemy, then reversed directions to reinforce the
raiders later in the fight.

Meanwhile the enemy defense forces, concentrated in the southeastern third of the island, realized that an all-out assault was underway. Between 0725 and 0749 hours, the Japanese Talagi Communication Base notified the 5th Air Flotilla at Rabaul that Tulagi was under bombardment, that the landing had begun, and that the senders were destroying all equipment immediately. At 0800 the Japanese messages said shells were falling near the radio installation. Ten minutes later, the final message went out.[1]

All went well on Tulagi until the 1st Raiders reached the Phase One Line that ran from the wharf along the eastern nose of the ridge, about half the distance of the two-mile-long Tulagi Island. The real battle began there. The Tulagi defenders were veteran rikusentai, too professional to panic at the surprise landing over their one undefended beach. They now were determined to inflict pain on the Marine invaders coming ashore.

By that time, Col. Edson, commanding the 1st Raider Battalion, was ashore and ready to begin a coordinated attack to the southeast. Confronting him was the more thickly settled portion of the island, where British governmental activities had centered. Fighting in this area would continue throughout the first day.

Some resistance was encountered almost immediately by the raiders but was systematically overcome as they drove down the ridgeback of the island until they ran into a shovel-shaped ravine with three steep sides. Here they met the stiffest Japanese resistance. The walls of the ravines surrounded a flat space that the British in peacetime had used as a cricket field. Now the Japanese had dug innumerable large caves into the limestone walls of the ravine. From the narrow mouths of these dugouts they fired rifles, automatic rifles, and machine guns. There was continuous crossfire across the ravine.

By the time the 1st Raiders reached this area, it was dusk and they halted for the night. But the Japanese were organizing for a counterattack. Few would get any real sleep that night. The Japanese launched several attacks, ranging from platoon-sized to a handful of stealthy infiltrators. With further action against the pockets impossible at this time, all battalion elements went into position for the night.

During Edson's sweep down the island, G Company of the 2nd Battalion, 5th Marines, moved its 81-mm mortar section down a trail along the ridgeline to support the battalion under attack. Not long afterwards, Col. Rosecrans' relocated his command post closer to the action. The 2nd Battalion occupied positions behind the raider lines and supported Edson's Marines by fire as they repulsed a series of attacks.

Meanwhile, Col. Edson established his command post in The Residency, the fancy former home of the British resident commissioner. The house over looked the Tulagi Harbor. The house also provided a view across a hill that overlooked the Japanese final position, a ravine on the island's southern tip. That is where the 1st Raiders dug in for the night. Edson positioned his four rifle companies roughly on line, north to south. He also moved his heavy weapons company up from the beach to help in the center, where between midnight and 0530 hours, the enemy had launched five separate small-scale attacks against the command post. The attacks were repulsed. Also turned back were efforts on the part of two enemy groups to skirt the beach flank.

At 2230, the Japanese counterattacked. They broke through between C Company and A Company. C Company was temporarily cut off from Edson's defensive perimeter. The Japanese worked their way along the ridge, coming within fifty to seventy-five yards of Col. Edson's command post. The Japanese used hand grenades, rifles, and machine-gun fire. The 1st Raiders suffered quite a few casualties as they fought hard to hold the enemy back. One machine-gun company lost fifty percent of its noncommissioned officers. Finally, the enemy was thrown back.

The first night on Tulagi turned out to be indicative of the many future nights in the Pacific War. Four separate attacks were launched by the Japanese to dislodge the 1st Raiders from their position. Throughout the night, Japanese swarming from hillside caves staged several fierce counterattacks, during which some infiltrated behind the raider lines. When morning came, the bodies of dead Japanese lay yards from the Marine lines. The pockets of the infiltrators were soon wiped out.

A unit's first night in combat is usually one the survivors would rather forget, but few battalions had more peacetime training than Edson's 1st Raiders. With few exceptions, they maintained superb fire discipline throughout Tulagi's first night. So did Edson's backup, the 2nd Battalion, 5th Marines. Unfortunately, there was little that training could have done to prepare the men for the rampant fog of war, the confusion that attended the wild counterattacks.

At dawn on the second day ashore, the Marine raiders resumed the offensive and encountered stiff pockets of resistance. The fighting around Hill 281, with its man-made cave complex, was the most intense in the entire battle on Tulagi. The Japanese, taking advantage of the caves, dug positions into the base of the hill. From the hill they brought fire to bear on the 1st Raiders. Bringing up reinforcements, two companies of the 2nd Battalion, 5th Marines moved up to assist in the sweep of the southeastern part of the island. Companies E and F passed through Dog Company. The 1st Raider Battalion attacked down the forward slope of Hill 281 and swung right toward the enemy pocket in the ravine.

Marines, flanking this troublesome terrain feature on three sides, laid down a heavy mortar concentration from the 60-mm weapons of the 1st Raiders and the 2nd Battalion 81s. By midafternoon the preparation was complete, and the raiders and 2nd Battalion, 5th Marines pushed through the ravine to wipe out the remaining resistance. That ended organized opposition on the island, and Tulagi was secured by nightfall of August 8.

Col. Edson effectively deployed fresh troops of the 2nd Battalion, 5th Marines throughout the second day. He made such encouraging progress that by sunset he radioed Gen. Vandegrift that all organized resistance on Tulagi had ended. For several days, however, individual Japanese and small groups continued to be flushed from hiding places and hunted down by patrolling Marines.

The Japanese on Tulagi held out for two days of brave, but bitter fighting. Some died in a suicide charge across what had been the cricket ground for the British administration of the Solomons. Others who were holed up in deep caves in the hills back from the shore pounded the approaching Marines with a heavy barrage of machine-gun fire until they were killed by high explosives tossed into the caves.

The shooting and the blasting abruptly ceased late in the afternoon. The wounded and dead were carried up, and the survivors of the grim death-squad emerged. "Killed all the yellow slant-eyed bastards," one returning raider announced aloud to no one in particular.

He didn't look happy, nor did the others who made it back. They were too beat, too tired, too drained to feel any glow of victory. Four wounded and unconscious Japanese were dragged out of caves. The rest were dead: shot, bayonetted, blasted by grenades or explosive charges. Rooted out. Rubbed out. Nobody seemed to know—or care—how many Japanese were killed. Nor could they learn of their own losses in dead and wounded.

"It's over, guys," the grim platoon leader told his men. That does it. Tonight we'll be going back aboard the destroyer-transports. Not one of the taut faces broke out in a smile. Not one uttered a prayer of thanks. Some cursed. Very bitter curses. They were past relief. They were spent.

That gory scenario was to be carried out again and again over the ensuing days and weeks as the Marines on the other islands, slowly, tenaciously overcame Japanese who refused to give up. The Japanese accepted death rather than surrender in shame, as they had been indoctrinated by their military creed. Japanese officers at times committed *hari-kari* with their swords rather than accept defeat. It was their code to live and to die by.

For the first time American troops had encountered Japanese troops strongly dug in their defensive positions. They learned that, in such a posture, the enemy would fight to the death. The 1st Raider Battalion's victory against a tough and well-fortified foe on Tulagi thus came at a considerable cost. While killing all but three of Tulagi's approximately 500 defenders, the raiders had sustained 38 killed and 55 wounded themselves. The 2nd Battalion, 5th Marines, Edson's backup, suffered 56 killed and wounded.

In the three landings made on D-Day, the only trouble getting ashore occurred at Gavutu. That was mainly because there were insufficient boats available to land the 1st Parachute Battalion simultaneously with everyone else. As a result, the rikusentai on Gavutu had plenty of warning to prepare fields of fire from their cave-emplaced machine guns. The parachutists stepped into a buzz saw. Their fight for the twin islands of Gavutu and Tanambogo took three full days and proved extremely costly.

The para-Marine had the toughest mission in many respects. With a grand total of eight small infantry platoons, they had just 361 Marines, much less than half the manpower of other line battalions. More importantly, they lacked the punch of heavy mortars and machine guns and had fewer of the light versions of these weapons, too. Even their high proportion of individual automatic weapons would not help much; many of these were the unreliable Reising submachine gun. The late hour of their attack also sacrificed any element of surprise, though planners assumed that naval and aerial firepower would suppress Japanese defenders. Nor was terrain in their favor.

The coral reef surrounding the islets meant that the only suitable landing site was the boat basin on the northeast cost of Gavutu, but that point was subject to flanking fire from defenders on Tanambogo. In addition, a steep coral hill dominated the flat coastal area of each inlet. Finally, despite a rule of thumb that the attackers should outnumber defenders by three to one in an amphibious assault, they were going up against a significantly larger force. The parachutists' only advantage was their high level of training and spirit.

Plans had called for the landing force to strike the northeast coast after an approach from the east. Because Tanambogo lies northwest of Gavutu, the assault force faced the possibility of flanking fire from that island as well as frontal resistance from the main objective. Opposition from both islands had been expected from the terrain dominating the flat beach.

Naval gunfire and close air support by SBD Douglas dive-bombers from the USS *Wasp* were expected to neutralize most enemy emplacements on these hills, but the fire plan did not reckon with the coral caves. Caves of this magnitude and strategic locations became serious obstacles for the 1st Parachute Battalion on Gavutu at about the same time the 1st Raider Battalion began encountering them on Tulagi.

Surprise, one of the most critical elements in any amphibious landing, was impossible. There was not sufficient landing craft for simultaneous landings, and the hour of assault was established in Gen. Vandegrift's Operation Order as H plus four hours. So four hours after the raiders landed on Tulagi, the 1st Parachute Battalion made its frontal assault in the face of fire from an alerted garrison that was supported by fires from a flanking position.

The 1st Parachute Battalion aboard the USS *Heywood* landed near noon in three waves and went into the harbor inlet of Gavutu. The thoroughness with which the anti-aircraft cruiser *San Juan* had carried out her fire support mission, and the intensity of the *Wasp*'s dive-bombers' caused heavy damage to enemy installations. However, this destruction actually worked to the disadvantage of the 1st Parachute Battalion in one instance. This unit intended to land on a seaplane ramp, from which the beach could be easily reached, but the ramp had been reduced to an unusable mass of rubble.

When the landing wave commanders saw that the ramp was destroyed, they altered course slightly to the north. Consequently, the

The dock where the Marines landed at Gavutu. It was covered by machine-gun firefrom the hill beyond and from Tanambogo. Courtesy of the Marine Corps University Archives.

landing craft became even more vulnerable to flanking fire from Tanambogo. Despite heavy casualties, the parachutists took the northeastern portion of the island and its dominating hill. To secure the island of Gavutu, they knew the adjoining island of Tanambogo would first have to be taken to stop its flanking fire that they knew was delaying the operation.

When para-Marines were forced to go ashore on the exposed area adjoining the ramp, they were easy targets for the defenders of an exceedingly steep hill. The Japanese, secure in their positions, opened fire on the second and third waves, pinning down the first parachutists ashore. Twenty minutes into the battle, Maj. Robert H. Williams, the battalion commander who led the first wave ashore and was leading his men up Hill 148, took a bullet in the lungs that put him out of action. Enemy fire drove off attempts to pull him to safety. Twenty-two para-Marines were killed in the withering fire.

Command was passed to Maj. Charles A. Miller, who established the command post and aid station in a partially demolished building near the dock area. Around 1400 hours he called for an air strike against Tanambogo, and half an hour later he radioed for reinforcements. While the parachutists awaited this assistance, B Company and a few men from A Company continued to attack Hill 148 from its eastern flank. The parachutists got their 60-mm mortars into action, too, and used them against Japanese positions on the upper slope of Hill 148. By 1430, the eastern half of the island was secure, but enemy fire from Tanambogo kept the parachutists from overrunning the western side of the island.

In the course of the afternoon, the Navy responded to Miller's call for support. Dive-bombers worked over Tanambogo, and then two destroyers closed on the island and thoroughly shelled it. In the midst of this action, one pilot mistakenly dropped his ordnance on Gavutu's hilltop and inflicted several casualties on B Company. By 1800 hours, the battalion succeeded in raising the American flag at the summit of Hill 148 and physically occupying the remainder of Gavutu. With the suppression of fire from Tanambogo and the cover of night, the parachutists collected their casualties, to include Maj. Williams, and began evacuating the wounded to the transports offshore.[2]

Despite heavy casualties, the parachutists took the northeastern portion of the island, and its dominating hill, but to secure Gavutu, Tanambogo would have to be taken to stop its flanking fire, which was delaying the operation. Reinforcements were requested to undertake this phase of the operation.

Not being informed as to the number of reinforcements needed for Tanambogo, and with the bulk of his forces tied up on Tulagi, B. Gen. Rupertus attached B Company, 1st Battalion, 2nd Marines to the 1st Parachute Battalion.

Earlier in the day at 0740, twenty minutes before H hour, this company under the command of Capt. Edward J. Crane landed on

Florida Island near Haleta. His mission was to occupy a point of land on Florida Island that commanded Beach Blue, the invasion beach where the main assault was to land on Tulagi a few minutes later. The landing to protect the left flank of the Tulagi force was unopposed, although enemy troops had been reported in position there on July 25. Capt. Crane, his company reinforced by the 4th Machine-gun Platoon of D Company and twenty-five men from Headquarters Company, reached his objective within forty minutes. The 252 officers and men went ashore in eight landing boats. They were guided to their objective by one of the several Australians on detached duty with the division.

While the covering force had deployed inland from its Florida beach, the remainder of the 1st Battalion, 2nd Marines, under the command of Lt. Col. Robert E. Hill, made a similar security landing at Florida's Halavo Peninsula near Gavutu and Tanambogo. The craft drew some fire from Gavutu, but there were no casualties and no enemy encountered on the peninsula. These Marines later returned to their ship.

As Capt. Crane's reinforced company prepared to go back aboard ship after their unopposed landing on Florida Island, he received radio orders to go over to Tanambogo and execute a landing there. The Japanese, driven from Gavutu across a connecting causeway, were making a stand.

The Tanambogo landing, which the Marines delayed until after sunset on D-Day, produced its own special disaster. Just as the men came ashore, one of the shells fired during the preassault, soften-up phase hit a fuel dump on the islet. Instead of the cover of darkness the attackers had hoped for, they were brightly silhouetted in the flaming oil as they were raked by fire from the hills. Several Navy Higgins boats got hung up on the coral reefs as they tried to land. Only two reached the shore. The landing party pulled out under heavy fire. With no reinforcements to assist them, the attacking Marines were

A view of Tanambogo from the top of Gavutu. It was on this island that the worst fighting occurred. The Japanese were well dug in and had plenty of ammunition. Courtesy of the Marine Corps University Archives.

forced to withdraw under the most difficult conditions. They made it back to the ship before midnight.

On August 8, the 3rd Battalion, 2nd Marines, supported by tanks from the 2nd Tank Battalion, and with air and naval gunfire support, made an amphibious landing on Tanambogo. Once a beachhead was established, reinforcements crossed the causeway, and by 2300 hours two-thirds of the island was completely secured. After a lot of fighting during the night, the 3rd Battalion succeeded in getting a lodgment on Tanambogo. It took them two days to clear out the islet's cave defense.

In midafternoon of August 9, B. Gen. Rupertus informed the division commander that the Northern Tulagi Group had taken all objectives. They were in a real fight from the first day of the landing. The assault force captured Tulagi the next day, but the Japanese were dug in nearby on the tiny islands of Gavutu and Tanambogo. They were inside deep, reinforced dugouts and caves. As a forerunner to similar action elsewhere, the Japanese preferred to hide, fight, and die in those deep caverns. The defending Japanese lost 1420 killed, wounded, and captured. Possibly a hundred or more escaped to adjacent Florida Island.

All attempts to induce the defenders to surrender were answered with lead; the Japanese refused to ask for quarters. Gen. Vandegrift described the scene: "Tulagi-Gavutu-Tanambogo as a storming operation decided by the extermination of one another of the adversaries engaged. Soldierly behavior was manifest wherever the enemy was encountered and there was an unflinching willingness to accept the hazards of close and sanguinary combat."

The hard-won success of Edson's battle-minded forces at Tulagi, Gavutu, and Tanambogo caused the division commander to proclaim that the enemy "was driven from everyplace they held by the resolute attack of men who were not afraid to die." While victory did not crown every endeavor, the Marines fought with singular savagery against some of the most experienced jungle fighters in the Japanese empire.

The few Japanese taken alive on Tulagi, Gavutu and Tanambogo— twenty-three were captured, of whom only three surrendered—proved as instructive to the Americans as the Japanese tactic of holing up in caves. They learned that to all but a few Japanese soldiers, death was preferable to what was viewed in the Japanese code as eternal dishonor.

Tulagi and its two tiny neighbor islands introduced the kind of combat that would characterize much of the war that was to come: a costly assault against heavily dug-in Japanese troops determined to fight to the last man. An estimated 750 to 800 Japanese were present on these islands at the time of the Marines landing. An intelligence summary gives seventy as the approximate number of survivors who escaped to Florida Island. The mopping up on Florida went on for several weeks. The taking of the three islands cost the Marines 144 dead or missing and 194 wounded. Immediately after organized resistance ceased and the isolated defending groups were rounded up or wiped out, Tulagi and its satellite islands were organized for defense against counterattacks. The 1st Parachute Battalion, depleted by its experience on Gavutu, moved from that island at 1700 hours on August 9 to Tulagi, where it went into position in the government building area. The 2nd Battalion, 5th Marines occupied the southeastern sector of the island, while two battalions of the 2nd Marines took over the defense mission in the northwest. The 1st Battalion occupied the extreme end of the island, while the 2nd Battalion established positions at Sasapi. The 3rd Battalion, 2nd Marines, took over the occupation and defense of Gavutu, Tanambogo, and Makambo.

Both sides learned important lessons from the vicious fighting in the Tulagi group. General area bombardment by naval shells and bombs were not effective against cave defenses. To give effective support, ships should move in close and pound specific targets. For their part, the Japanese learned to dig even deeper. During the rest of the war U.S. forces assaulting islands in the central Pacific would find formidable emplacements; they would also find the same do-or-die spirit.

In the meantime, something had been fouled up with the unloading of our transports and supply ships standing off Guadalcanal. Most of our troops were ashore, but a hell of a lot of our supplies and equipment were still on the ships. Finally, the supplies and equipment, inviting targets for enemy bombers, began to litter the beach. Marine support units assigned to do the job were too small and too scattered. The trucks needed to move supplies from the beach to inland supply points were not reloaded in New Zealand.

The first resistance to our landing came from the air. Around 1315 hours on August 7, we heard a dull, throbbing roar that grew louder every second. Planes—many planes—approached from the northwest. As the twenty-seven twin-engine Mitsubishi bombers appeared west of Savo Island, we saw them flying in a wide and stately V-formation, like a flock of Canada wild geese, flying south for the winter.

"Dogfight" (Combat in the Air). Drawing by Capt. Donald L. Dickson. Courtesy of the U.S. National Archives.

Fortunately for us, the two-engine Mitsubishi "Betty" bombers had been fitted with bombs for a raid on an allied airfield at Milne Bay on New Guinea's southeast coast when they received urgent orders to head for Guadalcanal and "drive back the American invasion forces at any cost." They had zoomed off without exchanging the bomb load for torpedoes that would have been more effective against the ships moving at high speed.

From the beach we watched in awe as Grumman Wildcat fighters from our carrier screening force poured down on the enemy bombers, and a few minutes later, our ships opened fire. Here and there, Japanese planes spiraled down, trailing smoke. The enemy planes that did manage to get through were shaken and their bombing was wild. Rattled, the bomber pilots released their payloads while still four miles up, targeting the ships just south of Savo Island. At least sixteen Japanese planes were lost, a sobering statistic for the generally overconfident enemy. In return they scored only one hit, on the destroyer *Mugford*, whose afterdeck house and two stern 5-inch guns were destroyed.

An hour later, someone told me that another air raid was due in about ten minutes. This was the first I had heard of it. I rushed down to the beach to watch the show, and what a show it was. I didn't see the Japanese planes at first, but a sky full of flak from our transports told me they were there. Then I saw them, a flight of twenty-three twin-engine Japanese torpedo bombers came on their first air strike, heading straight for the off-loading ships. They were skimming the water, some only twenty or thirty feet high, aiming straight for the transports. The ships were moving, circling at high speed, and the warship screen threw up a devastating curtain of fire. We watched as many of the Japanese planes exploded in the sea.

Anti-aircraft fire from the ships was terrific. Japanese planes plunged in flames—one, two, three—so many I lost count. There was so much smoke and flame in the transport area that I thought surely many of our ships must have been hit. But as the flames and smoke lifted I saw that apparently only one ship was burning. That was the troop transport ship *George F. Elliott*. The big ship was set hopelessly afire. She was scuttled at dawn the next morning, put to rest in a body of water that would soon be known as "Iron Bottom Sound." Scores of ships would join her there. Much of the 2nd Battalion, 1st Marines equipment was still aboard the *Elliott*.

In the torpedo-plane attack the Japanese lost, by their own admission, seventeen Betty bombers. Quite possibly the toll was more. Our

Japanese Mitsubishi "Betty" Bombers come in low to attack U.S. transports. Courtesy of the Marine Corps Historical Center.

surface ships brought most of them down with intense anti-aircraft fire. Carrier fighters played a critical role in this particular engagement. The day before, eleven fighters were lost while intercepting the two raiding formations coordinating the attack with their torpedo planes. Eight Japanese dive-bombers did penetrate the American screen. They dropped their bombs from 20,000 feet or more to escape anti-aircraft fire. They were not very accurate. They concentrated on the ships in the channel, hitting and damaging a number of them and sinking the destroyer *Jarvis* (DD 393). In their battles to turn back the attacking planes, the carrier fighter squadrons lost twenty-one Wildcats on August 7–8. Then, the air and naval operation that began so favorably for the Americans went terribly wrong.

Shortly before 2300 hours on August 8, Gen. Vandegrift left the island and sped by small boat to the flagship *McCawley* to confer with R. Adm. Turner, commander of the amphibious force. Turner had three pieces of bad news to report. The first was that a large Japanese naval force had been sighted en route from Rabaul. The second was that V. Adm. Frank Jack Fletcher, commander of the entire Task Force 61, was removing his three carriers *Enterprise*, *Saratoga*, and *Wasp* from the scene. The third piece of news was related to the second. Turner, now deprived of the carriers' air cover, felt compelled to leave the area, not to return at 0600 the next morning, even though some 1400 Marines had not been debarked and more than half of Vandegrift's supplies and equipment was still in the ships' holds.

Gen. Vandegrift was stunned at Fletcher's decision to depart. Privately, he felt the admiral was "running away." But the decision had been made. All he could do then was to hurry and keep his troops unloading through the night, and hope the Marines could get by for the few days it was expected to take for the carriers to refuel and return. But even as Vandegrift was leaving the flagship *McCawley* about midnight, the stage was being set for a sea battle that would deprive the Marines of their lifeline for much longer than a few days.[3]

Allied search planes had sighted a large Japanese surface force headed our way. The approaching surface force had five heavy cruisers and two light cruisers. That was not by any means an overwhelming force, but large enough to cause great concern for both R. Adm. Turner and V. Adm. Fletcher, the Task Force commander.

After receiving the warning about the approaching Japanese surface force, R. Adm. Turner positioned his screening force, two destroyers northwest off Savo Island, which was to maintain radar watch on the channel. He then positioned his two cruisers, the *Australia* and *Canberra*, along with two destroyers, the *Bagley* and *Patterson*, to patrol between Savo Island and Cape Esperance. Three additional cruisers, *Vincennes*, *Astoria*, and *Quincy*, were to patrol between Savo and Florida Islands. Two other cruisers and two destroyers guarded the transports.

Meanwhile, the Japanese surface force approached Savo Island undetected. Shortly before arriving they launched floatplanes that flew over the American and Australian ships. The ships did not fire. It was assumed the planes were American because they were flying with their recognition lights on. About 0145 hours on August 9, the planes began to drop flares to illuminate our ships. At the same time, the Japanese naval forces miraculously slipped past the radar picket destroyers.

V. Adm. Gunichi Mikawa, one of the Japanese Navy's boldest tacticians, had arrived. In a remarkable combination of audacity and plain good luck, his cruisers and destroyers had burst through every barrier protecting the Guadalcanal landing area. Now "the fox was in the chicken house." In the ensuing night naval engagement, which developed into a wild melee, the Japanese scored a major victory.

In a brief but devastating night attack, V. Adm. Mikawa's flagship *Chokai* fired the first spread of torpedoes and the admiral ordered all forces to the attack. Soon the waters teemed with "Long Lance" torpedoes speeding toward their unsuspecting targets. The attack ravaged Adm. Turner's screening force, guarding the shipping off Guadalcanal. The heavy cruiser *Chicago* had her bow blown off, the Australian heavy cruiser *Canberra* was turned into a blazing wreck, and the American heavy cruisers *Quincy*, *Astoria*, and *Vincennes* were sunk in a stunning, one-sided victory. This engagement, known as the Battle of Savo Island, was a humiliating defeat. It was the worst whipping ever suffered by the U.S. Navy in wartime.

The Japanese had achieved the element of surprise and had defeated the American force in detail. The battle started with a series of mistakes by the Allied forces, but ended with V. Adm. Mikawa making the most serious mistake of all: not sinking the troop transports and combat cargo ships that still had more than half of the Marines supplies and equipment aboard. Had he done so, he would have effectively curtailed operation in the area.

Not wishing to press his luck, believing that American carriers were still in the area and that their planes would find him in the morning,

Mikawa ignored the now unprotected transports and sped homeward. Behind him he left 1023 Australian and American sailors dead and another 709 wounded, burned, and exhausted men floating in the oil-covered, shark-infested waters of Iron Bottom Sound. No other navy had so prepared itself for night battle. V. Adm. Mikawa thought, remembering one of the Japanese Navy's favorite sayings: "The Americans built things well, but their blue eyes are no match for our dark eyes in night actions."

Night battle doctrine was highly developed in the Imperial Japanese Navy. The ships' captains were skilled veterans, the crew superbly trained. Their high-speed, oxygen-fueled, 24-inch Long Lance torpedoes could carry 1000-pound warheads more than twenty miles and leave no telltale trace on the surface. These far outclassed the American torpedoes, which had a range of less than eight miles without leaving a telltale wake when fired. That gave the Japanese naval forces a formidable advantage in a surface battle.

The margin of V. Adm. Mikawa's victory against a superior force was stunning. Four heavy cruisers were sunk, against minor damage to the cruisers *Chokia* and *Tenryu*. However, the Japanese triumph was to be marred somewhat the next day when a lone American submarine torpedoed and sank the heavy cruiser *Kako* as it sailed for Rabaul.

For the ordinary seaman on V. Adm. Mikawa's flagship *Chokia*, the victorious mood was laced with sadness. Thirty-four of their shipmates had died and forty-eight lay wounded. These casualties occurred when one of the few salvos fired by Quincy's main battery landed near the flag bridge of *Chokia*, destroying her operations room. It was at this time that V. Adm. Mikawa made his decision to break off the action and retire.

In his radio report to the commander-in-chief, Japans' Combined Fleet, V. Adm. Mikawa listed five heavy cruisers and four destroyers sunk and other ships damaged. He stated that two carriers had withdrawn. This somewhat exaggerated the toll exacted, but Mikawa and his

men nevertheless deserved
the congratulatory message
awaiting them upon their
arrival at Rabaul.[4]

The night of August
8–9 could not have been
a good one for Adm.
Turner. From his flagship
McCauley, anchored with
the other transports off
Guadalcanal, he could see
the distance aircraft flares
and the flashes of gunfire,
so he knew that a battle
was raging, but could dis-
cern neither the disposition
nor its results. Neverthe-

*V. Adm. Gunichi Mikawa, Imperial Japanese
Navy. Courtesy of the Naval Historical Center.*

less, he faced a critical decision. V. Adm. Fletcher's carriers had
already been withdrawn out of range. The troop transports and combat
cargo ships in the slot between Guadalcanal and Tulagi were now
without protection. Left without air cover and loss of most of his
cruiser screening force, Adm. Turner had a difficult choice to make.
Should he continue off-loading the ships that still had more than half
of the Marines supplies and equipment aboard, or should he haul-ass
out of the area and head for a safe haven port at New Caledonia? He
chose the latter.

At dusk on August 9, the remaining warships, transports, and
combat cargo ships weighed anchor and steamed out of Iron Bottom
Sound. For the next eleven days, as the Marines rushed to complete
the airstrip, the underequipped forces on Guadalcanal and Tulagi
would be without air cover or naval support. Marines ashore were
locked in a life-and-death struggle to survive.

Sixty years later, Pfc. Salvatore J. "Sam" Russo from Lawrence, Massachusetts, who had a ringside seat aboard the *Alchiba* during the disastrous Savo Island Battle, related a graphic account of this horrifying experience:

> I still have vivid memories of being stranded aboard ship, while most of my unit B Company Pioneers was ashore. Here I was up on deck watching our ships being blasted out of the water by enemy torpedoes and naval gunfire and there wasn't a damn thing I could do about it. I never felt so helpless in my entire life. . . . The ships crew were all at their assigned battle stations, but not the Marine pioneers aboard, we were simply passengers. All we could do was stand by and watch the disastrous sea battle unfold.
>
> I recall a brief but very serious conversation with Cpl. George Cincala, my squad leader, as we attempted to seek some protection by hunkering down behind a deck cargo hatch cover. I said: "George; I don't know what to do." He said, "Just pray, that's all you can do." I said, "George don't leave me." He replied, "Don't leave me either. I don't want to die alone." Somehow we endured that terrible night when all hell broke loose in Sealark Channel, off Tulagi.
>
> As dawn broke we could see the *Astoria* floating around in circles. The word was that the *Alchiba* was going to try and tow the heavily damaged cruiser to New Caledonia, providing the ships damage control team was able to get the fires under control, but before we could come along side and attach a tow cable, the ship's ammunition magazine exploded and she went to the bottom. I could see sailors in the water getting stuck in the ship screw by the whirlpool suction phenomena as she went under bow first.
>
> By 1830 on 9 August, the whole force was gone. Eighteen transports escorted by what was left of the screening force, ended up in New Caledonia. Soon after our arrival, we embarked aboard the troop transport ship *Hunter Leggett*. What a fiasco that turned out to

A Japanese torpedo beached on Guadalcanal. Courtesy of the Marine Corps Historical Center.

be, because the ship was going back to the States, so we had to get off and embark aboard another ship the USS *Fomalhaut*. After several delays, we finally made it back to Guadalcanal.

Late in the afternoon, while the *Fomalhaut* was off-loading some much needed supplies and the stranded pioneer platoon, a Japanese submarine let loose a torpedo at her. She hightailed it out of there. The torpedo missed the *Fomalhaut* and skidded up on the sandy beach south of Lunga Point. There it lay for several days, the object of much curiosity exercised at a respectful distance, until it was disarmed by a demolition team headed by Sgt. Kerry Lane.

I vividly recall our second night ashore. We were still bivouacked in the coconut grove just west of the Tenaru about 200 yards from the beach, where we stretched out on our ponchos and blankets close to our gun positions, hoping to spend the night in comparative peace. Although no Japanese disturbed us, rest was nearly impossible. At about 2300 hours a tropical drizzle began to fall. We wrapped ourselves in ponchos in an effort to keep as dry as possible. But the ponchos were not as effective as they should have been. We slowly became wetter and wetter. The rain stopped and started up again. Lightning and thunder were almost continuous. I finally managed to fall asleep. What a blessing it was! We were all exhausted. None of us had slept for the past twenty-four hours; we caught only catnaps at odd moments.

Marines awoke some time between midnight and dawn and stood quietly watching while a great sea battle flashed and roared near Savo Island. Vibrations from exploding shells and muzzle blasts shook the ground. Watching from a distance, we had no idea what was happening. Perhaps it was just as well. Our morale would not have been helped had we known we were watching our ships being sunk. While we didn't know the outcome of the sea battle, we could be thankful that the Japanese ships didn't get in to shell us or to land troops.

After washing our faces in the sea, we ate a breakfast of pineapple slices and hardtack. We used canned fuel to heat water in our canteen cups. Although the coffee wasn't the best known to mankind, it was brown and it was hot. Coffee at breakfast is a boost to morale in battle. It was usually all we had. It warmed the bones after a night of damp cold. Not long after our coffee, the Navy's after-action report filtered down to the troops on the line. We were shocked to learn that the Japanese had kicked the hell out of our naval forces.

The next thing we knew, the Marines ashore were orphans. After the cruisers went down, the Navy pulled the troop transports and supply ships out, taking much of our food and ammunition with them. Still in their holds was more than half of the Marines' food supply, most of our barbed wire and sandbags. Also gone was all of the heavy-earth moving equipment, except for one bulldozer that somehow reached shore.

As the last of the ships disappeared on the afternoon of August 9, the Marines needed no one to remind them that they were now alone. With the carriers gone, Japanese planes raided every day around noon: "Tojo Time" is what the Marines began to call it. Adm. Turner's transports had left, and no one knew when his ships would be able to return. Almost daily, a Japanese cruiser or destroyer appeared in plain view of the cursing Marines, but out of range of our guns, and shelled the exposed four-mile expanse of the Lunga Point beachhead. The threat of a Japanese counterattack took on a new urgency.

[6]   **Stranded**

As we watched our ships sail eastward, we knew that there would be no reinforcements. We were very much on our own. Any amphibious operation requires ships and air support. Now the Japanese could reinforce their land forces, bomb us by air, and pound us from the sea. We had just 10,000 men on Guadalcanal and fewer than 6000 on Tulagi. Each man had an average of five units of ammunition for his weapon, or a five-day supply. Food was short. It soon became apparent that without air or sea protection, the 1st Marine Division was going to see some rugged duty on Guadalcanal. The Marines ashore felt like they were being abandoned.

Marine combat correspondent George McMillan described our feelings of being forsaken:

> The feeling of expendability is difficult to define. It is loneliness. It is the feeling of being abandoned. It is something more, too. It is as if events over which you have no control have put a ridiculous low price tag on your life. . . . If there was any doubt that the Navy really left, the doubt was completely dispelled when the Division went on short rations, the chow was cut down to two meals per day.
>
> The Marines found themselves surrounded by the enemy. The Japanese already on Guadalcanal could now move around our perimeter. With command of the seas, the Japanese Navy could bring in as many supplies and reinforcements as they elected to send.

Having been ashore only a few days, we had no field fortification and no fixed defenses to oppose a Japanese landing. If they decided to land outside of our perimeter, there was very little we could do to stop them. We had no air support.[1]

When word got around Guadalcanal that the Navy had taken off and left us, the feeling of expendability became a factor in the battle. I know I had that feeling, and I believe a lot of others felt the same way, that we'd never get off that damned island alive. Nobody said that out loud at the time—mostly for fear that if we did it would come true.

We did talk an awful lot about Bataan. In fact, the word was we faced the nightmarish prospect that Guadalcanal might become another Bataan. Gen. Vandegrift's staff drew up contingency plans to fight a guerrilla war in the hills and jungles of the island.

The division's morale was affected by the fact that V. Adm. Frank J. Fletcher was forced to withdraw his fleet from the area with many ships not yet unloaded and holding more than half of the division's supplies needed ashore. Adding to the Marines uneasiness at seeing their naval support disappear below the horizon was the fact that they had been under almost constant enemy attack, beginning shortly after their landing on Guadalcanal.

In an effort to counter the adverse influence on morale of the day and night attacks, Vandegrift began making tours of the division perimeter every morning, to talk to as many of his Marines as possible, and to keep a personal eye on the command. As he noted in his memoir *Once a Marine*, "By August 11, the full impact of the vanished transports was permeating the command, so again I called a conference of my staff and command officers, I ended the conference by posing with this fine group of officers, a morale device that worked because they thought if I went to the trouble of having a picture taken, then I obviously planned to enjoy it in future years."

Marine commanders on Guadalcanal four days after the landing. The photograph includes almost all the senior officers who led the 1st Marine Division ashore. Courtesy of the Marine Corps Historical Center.

The following day, August 12, Gen. Vandegrift sent his message to Adm. Turner, "Essential that vessels containing food arrive here earliest possible date—from rations on hand and consumed to date estimate about twelve days rations landed Guadalcanal. Further lost due to weather and handling reduced this to ten days. No opportunity should be lost to forward rations to this command."

Marines were so poorly supplied at first that they had to subsist partly on captured rations. When our meals were cut down to two per day, those abandoned Japanese stores came in handy. The rice wasn't too bad, but you needed a strong stomach to eat the canned fish stew. After I opened a can and looked at the chopped up fish heads mixed with cabbage sprouts and other mysterious ingredients, I just couldn't eat it.

Lousy diet or not, we had a job to do. The first objective of the operation was to secure the airfield on Guadalcanal. Gen. Vandegrift's Marines had quickly done this without any serious opposition. The captured Japanese landing strip was basically a piece of jungle stripped of vegetation and leveled out to a small but passable degree.

We needed to extend the runway and fill deep bomb craters. The latter was to be a never-ending job. The airstrip was, of course, one of the main Japanese targets, and our planes could not land in craters.

Much still had to be done to prepare the landing strip for the American planes that would be coming. The engineers used incredible improvisation to overcome monumental difficulties. Fill dirt in measured quantities was loaded in captured Japanese trucks and kept on the edge of the airfield to be dumped and packed in craters. Captured Japanese equipment was kept working and repaired by the ingenious mechanics in the 1st Engineer Battalion. Several trucks and road rollers stood where the Japanese had left them.

Henderson Field, an airfield the Japanese had been developing, was completed by the Americans and served as a base for supporting air for the remainder of the fighting in the Solomon Islands and the other island campaigns that would follow. If that field had been completed and remained in the hands of the enemy, the fighters and bombers operating from it could have exacted a terrible toll on U.S. forces and perhaps severed the supply line to New Zealand and Australia.

After three days on the island, Marines held a strip of coconut plantation and strand of beach about seven miles long, while the Japanese surrounding them controlled the balance of the ninety-two-mile-long island and the skies overhead. Concluding that the American Navy had been driven from the Solomon's, Japanese cruisers and submarines boldly patrolled the waters between Guadalcanal and Tulagi during the night.

The Japanese goal was to drive the Marines off Guadalcanal. They would do this by running troops ashore by night destroyers slipping up the slot between the Solomon Islands. The Marines dubbed this operation the "Tokyo Express." The hold we had on that little island was shaky as hell.

Gen. Vandegrift realized his precarious position as he prepared to make a stand against assaults from sea or jungle. He felt the Japanese were going to attempt to overwhelm our beachhead and attack at night, as was their custom. Pulling us into a tight perimeter around the airfield, bound by the Tenaru River on the east and the Matanikau River on the west, Vandegrift's orders were to "Dig in and hold."

Marines were going to hold a perimeter roughly 7500 yards wide from east to west and penetrating inland about 3500 yards. It would be bound on its eastern and right flank by the Tenaru River and on the west by a high ridge above a small coastal village called Kukum, east of the Mataniukau River. Its northern seawall front would be the most heavily fortified, because it was here that Vandegrift expected the Japanese to counterattack.

The 1st Marines were to hold the Tenaru and the beach line west to the Lunga River. The 5th Marines set up on a high hill that commanded the beach and would cover the stretch from the Lunga west to Kukum. Vandergrift would hold his tank company and one battalion from the 1st Marine Regiment in reserve.

Although his front looked solid, Gen. Vandegrift had cause to worry. One risky element of his defensive scheme was the heavily jungled inland flank (the landward side of the perimeter). Lacking rifle battalions, Vandegrift moved support battalions to positions south of the airstrip to provide a deterrent should enemy forces attack in this direction. Particularly worrisome was a narrow, grassy ridge only 1700 yards south of the airfield. The ridge provided an ideal approach to the airstrip. The general countered this danger by posting elements of the 1st Engineer Battalion near the ridge and assigning the battalion a security mission to patrol it during the night.

Another avenue of possible enemy exploitation was down the Lunga River, fordable throughout its upper reaches. The division countered this threat by positioning the 1st Pioneer Battalion on both side of the river. Those Marines were to defend an area of dense jungle between the Lunga and a ridgeline south of the airstrip.

The amphibious tractor battalion was positioned along the upper reaches of the Lunga to the rear of the 5th Marines. The battalion

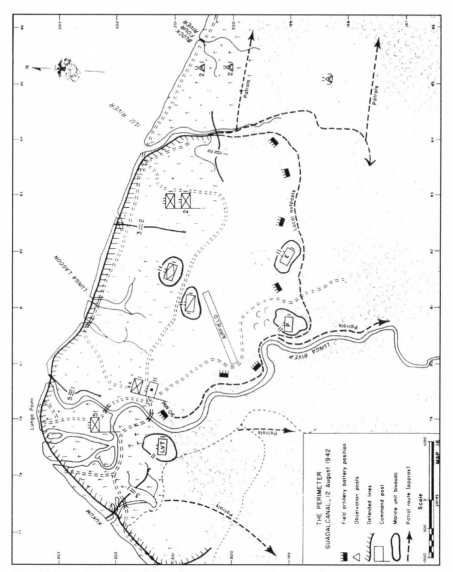

Map of the perimeter, Guadalcanal, August 12, 1942. Courtesy of the Marine Corps Historical Center.

played a key role in repositioning ammunition and supplies forward during daylight hours and manning fighting positions on the inland flank perimeter at night. The 11th Marines (Artillery) Regiment, commanded by Col. Pedro del Valle, thirty-two guns in all were grouped south of the runway in such a way as to bring their mass of fire to bear upon any given sector within range.

By midafternoon on August 10, three days after wading ashore, my unit—B Company Pioneers, committed as part of the division's combat reserve—received orders to work our way over to our new position on the inland jungle perimeter. The distance was not great, but our progress was slow. Gasping in humid heat, bathed in a stream of sweat, and burdened with packs and ammunition loads that were too heavy, the pioneers blundered through a field of kunai grass that grew taller than a man's head and cut off any cooling breeze. The razor-sharp kunai easily sliced the skin, sometimes causing severe swelling, if not treated. Once we reached the uncompleted airstrip, the company swung south through the dense jungle.

The terrain around the airfield was virtually impenetrable. Except for the established trails, we had to hack our own roads. Marines of B Company Pioneers found this to be a most difficult task because our bulldozers and other earth-clearing equipment were still aboard the departing ships, now anchored in the safe harbor of New Caledonia.

The jungle of the Solomons was a rainforest. No air stirred there, and the humidity was beyond the imagination of anyone who had not lived in it. Rot lay just under the exotic lushness. The ground was porous with decaying vegetation, emitting a sour, unpleasant odor. Dampness thick and heavy was everywhere. Malaria-bearing mosquitoes, as well as dengue and a dozen lesser-known fevers threatened from the broad deep swamps, which were slowly drained by sluggish rivers containing giant crocodiles.[2]

Through this steaming wonderland, Marines of B Company Pioneers moved toward their new bivouac area, hacking their way through the underbrush. There was no determined opposition, only a few scattered snipers. The squad wielded large, single-edged bolo knives to cut a trail. Squads were rotated every half hour. One of the men questioned why the trail had to be so wide. I replied that Col. Rowan, the battalion commander, rides in a jeep while we walk. It was late in the afternoon by the time we arrived at our assigned position on the division's inner perimeter. Thus began the jungle warfare, a horrible nightmare that lasted for the next six months.

The heavy jungle flank south of the airfield we were assigned to defend was laced with huge kanaris trees, with giant roots and heavy branches covered with tangled vines. The jungle floor was covered with brush, and there was a stench of wet, decaying vegetation. Adding to the misery of the malaria-ridden mosquitoes were rats, scorpions, and large green lizards. In this hot, humid terrain, the pioneers went about the difficult task of clearing the floor of the bivouac site and setting up perimeter defenses for the night.

We didn't have enough troops to establish a defensive line across the entire perimeter that extended from the north spur of a T-shaped ridge south of the airfield to the Lunga River. So each company in the 1st Pioneer Battalion was assigned an interior sector that it was to hold. Therefore, an all-around defensive cordon augmented by a network of observation posts was established. From this position, we were to mount daily aggressive patrols.

Late in the afternoon, we hurriedly set up our weapons. Our fighting holes were dug long and wide enough to stretch out in, and to make a bed with our ponchos. These hastily dug holes would protect us from small-arms fire and bombs, if the bombs didn't hit too close. We also dug straddle-trenches, "gotta-go" outdoor privies.

By that late hour we were tired and hungry, but there were no hot meals that day. We had to make do with landing rations that we carried in our packs and a cup of coffee. The landing ration, chocolate bars fortified with mysterious elements known only to the War

Department, were hard slabs guarantee to contain enough food value to provide energy for a day or two. Ordinarily, it took about two days to eat one of these chocolate bars, as they were slightly bitter and served only to kill the appetite, rather than satisfy it. We also had hardtack biscuits that some swore were surplus from WWI. Marines with sharp and especially strong teeth could eat the hardtack biscuits without too much difficulty, but others had to break them with a combat knife or bayonet handle.

As the sun began to set on the western horizon in the tropics, there was little twilight. Darkness was soon upon us. Out at sea we saw a signal flare to the east. I began moving up and down the line to check on my men in their fighting holes and machine-gun pit. I reported to the first sergeant as to their readiness to defend our assigned position on the perimeter.

It was hot and humid, and in the stillness we could hear the buzzing of the mosquitoes around our ears. Our foxholes were the nightly rendezvous point for island mosquitoes. They came in all sizes, mostly big. First their scouts came. They would leave after a few minutes and come back with squadrons of dive-bombers that were better shots than their Japanese allies. Because we had no mosquito netting, we attempted to escape by bedding down wrapped up in our ponchos, with only our noses protruding. But the night was hot, and perspiration would roll off us in torrents. When we would partly uncover, the mosquitoes would swoop down upon us in vast multitudes. They chewed us clear beneath our underwear and socks. We would make a few desperate and vain slaps, and again retire behind our ponchos for another night of misery. One was not apt to be bright-eyed and bushy-tailed after a night of fighting mosquitoes in damp, soggy foxholes.

The nights were extremely unsettled during the first weeks. The first night on the line brought out the evidence of nervousness among members of my twelve-man squad. We could sense the Japanese everywhere. Surely, each one by now had triangulated on our exposed posterior as we lay in hastily dug fighting holes, and they were homing in to do a little bayonet stabbing in the spot where the sun don't shine. Marines were firing at anything that moved. If land creatures were heard scurrying through the brush, they were shot at. If birds called or rustled amid the trees, they were also the target of someone's rifle or machine-gun fire. The men were nervous and uncertain.

We learned quickly that mistakes could mean the difference between life and death. Better fire-discipline was the new order of the day. He had to conserve ammunition. I told my men, "You'll need all you've got. Don't waste any. Our supply is limited. Don't fire unless you are engaged." To emphasize this point even more forcefully, I said, "You'd better sharpen up your bayonets because very little ammunition was unloaded and when that's gone we will be forced to resort to cold steel."

We were handicapped at Guadalcanal because we didn't have maps or high-tech intelligence advances of the sort available to Marines in later wars. The way we overcame this handicap was to constantly patrol our sector of the island. Daily patrols told us where the enemy was, his probable routes of approach to our lines, his strengths and his weaknesses. Even when our patrols didn't find any sign of the enemy, the negative information was valuable. It told us where he was not; so then we knew we could move our own forces accordingly.

Few patrols during the first week made any hard contacts. The inexperienced, often sleepless Marine pioneers were overly cautious. In time, we became more confident. Later, when patrols were able to penetrate deeper into the rainforest, we began capturing some of the Japanese who had hauled ass into the jungle on D-Day, which increased our confidence. Shooting at shadows and noises subsided. The men became better rested, and they were generally more alert and aggressive.

The following account of C Company, 1st Pioneer Battalion's action on the fifth day ashore draws on recollections of pioneers who were there. In a personal interview with Commissioned Warrant

Patrols such as this one were sent out to gather intelligence on the Japanese. In the early days of the campaign, these patrols proved invaluable. This particular patrol is shown with a captured Japanese soldier, who might provide intelligence on Japanese forces in the area. Courtesy of the U.S. National Archives.

Officer Edward J. Schroeder, who was the company first sergeant at the time, he told me:

> As the company was preparing to move to the Lunga perimeter on August 11, Marines on outpost duty were confronted by a stocky black man with pink hair, cloth puttees wrapped above his bare feet, and a large Union Jack flag pulled about his shoulders. Capt. Halstead Ellison, C Company commander, was called out to deal with this strange, haughty islander whose responses to questions were in pidgin, a polyglot most Marines had not yet come to understand. Ellison called division headquarters to ask that a British liaison officer be sent to help with the interrogation.

Coastwatcher Capt. W. F. Martin Clemens, British Solomon Islands Defense Force, poses with some of his constabulary. Courtesy of the Marine Corps Historical Center.

Capt. Charles Widdy, who managed the Lever Brothers Plantation at Lunga Point before the Japanese arrived, quickly learned that the islander was Jacob Vouza, a Guadalcanal native who had served for many years in the police patrol on neighboring Malaita. Vouza had retired as a sergeant major just before the war, and later volunteered his services to the British District Office at Aola Bay when the Japanese invaded Tulagi.

He had just completed a long hike from the hills behind Aola Bay to bring a message from his boss, Capt. Clemens, who wanted to bring his force of islanders to Lunga Point to serve as the core of a native scout force. On instructions from division headquarters, Widdy handed Vouza a hastily scrawled message to take back to Clemens. The Pioneers were ordered to maintain their position on the Tenaru.

According to division intelligence reports, Martin Clemens left Vungana Village on the morning of August 14 and marched downhill through the rainforest toward the Lunga perimeter with sixty constables, clerks, and bearers. The party was crossing a wide kunai grass plain on the morning of August 15 when a bearer saw an airplane high overhead. Their optimism got the better of their caution, for they were nearing the safety of American lines. Everyone, including Clemens, dropped his meager bundle and frantically waved to catch the attention of the pilot. Food and ammunition packed in stout wicker baskets were parachuted by a Japanese pilot, who no doubt was searching for stragglers from the Marine landing. Without yet realizing its source, Clemens sent scouts to retrieve the supplies.

From his position on the Tenaru, Capt. Ellison watched the parachutes blossom and deduced that the Japanese were dropping parachutists to go up against the Clemens party. He grabbed his rifle and helmet and jumped aboard his vehicle with a couple of volunteers to lend a helping hand. Minutes later they were filling the vehicle with the green wicker baskets and billowing parachutes.

Each wicker basket recovered contained 810 rounds of .25-caliber ammunition, various types of concentrated food, canned meat, and some candy. All the contents were in a rubber bag within the basket case. As the Marines pulled out, a thoroughly shaken Clemens emerged from his hiding place and reorganized his party for the final lap into Volonava Village, the rendezvous point designated in Capt. Charles Widdy's letter.

The native inhabitants on Guadalcanal were very friendly and provided assistance while we were fighting the Japanese. The ones trained by the Australians as constabularies had the ability to live off the jungle and were able to recognize what was taking place there, primarily through their sense of smell. After a lifetime in the dense rainforest, they had highly developed olfactory glands and could determine who was in the jungle by just sniffing the air. Because of this ability, we used

*A parachute drop, a little Japanese basket containing ammunition
and food. Japanese airmen meant this drop and three others for
their troops on Guadalcanal, but they fell within our lines. Courtesy
of the Marine Corps University Archives.*

them almost like bloodhounds. The Australians had incorporated the
best of them into their coast-watchers, the radio-equipped intelligence network that provided invaluable information about Japanese
movement in the Guadalcanal area.

The local natives were stocky black men with long bushy hair. Their
loyalty earned the complete admiration and respect of the Marines on

Guadalcanal. Most of the native men in the island constabulary and coast-watchers were fluent in pidgin English and had gained a basic level of English that enabled them to converse comfortably with the American Marines who understood the polyglot.

Five days after landing on Guadalcanal, the already underfed Marines were so low on provisions that they were reduced to two skimpy meals a day, at times no more than bags of rice captured from the enemy. Four weeks of savage fighting was carried on with that meager diet before the normal, unappetizing but belly-filling three chow calls a day could be restored.

During that cruel month, a crescendo of calls went out for my demolition team to provide some fresh fish to supplement our meager diet. We accomplished this task by throwing grenades and blocks of TNT into the nearest river. The concussion would kill the fish and bring them up to the surface. The pioneers had one up on their fellow Marines in other units because we had ready access to what few explosives were available on the island. Killing the fish was the easy part. Retrieving them from the crocodile-infested Lunga River was another story. It was hazardous duty!

On August 12–13, Lt. Col. Frank D. Goettge, the division intelligence officer, led a patrol of twenty-five men to follow up on a captured Japanese naval warrant officer's report that some of his fellow mates at a garrison located between the Matanikau River and Kokumbona were wandering aimlessly through the jungle without food and that some of them might surrender. The boats got away from the perimeter at about 1800 hours and landed at an undetermined point west of the Matanikau shortly after midnight. The Japanese, instead of surrendering, attacked the patrol upon landing.

The patrol was virtually annihilated on the beach. Col. Goettge was the first to be felled by enemy fire. One by one members of the patrol were killed or wounded. Only three members, Platoon Sgt. Frank L. Few, Sgt. Charles C. Arndt, and Cpl. Joseph Spaulding, managed to escape. They made their way out of a doomed pocket by swimming or crawling across the rough coral along the shore until they reached our lines, a distance of some three miles. Imprinted in the mind of one of the three survivors was the memory of Japanese sabers flashing in the moonlight while stabbing and beheading wounded Marines as they lay dying in the sand. For the first time, the Marines on Guadalcanal had some measure of the ruthless and savagery of the foe they faced.

The Goettge patrol was an unmitigated disaster. It cost the division's intelligence section, and that of a regiment, some of their best men, to no purpose. For a small party with an ill-defined mission, most untrained in patrolling skills, to land at night at the very spot where the small enemy garrison was assumed to be concentrated was professionally embarrassing, quite apart from the unnecessary human cost. The only good to come from the Goettge disaster was it hardened our resolve to continue the fight until every one of those Jap sons of bitches was annihilated. Patrols that had been cautious to the point of timidity now turned aggressive. Marines who would one day dread recurrent combat were openly hoping for battle. From then on there would be no quarter.

On the island, each man made a personal note of it, "Sabers flashing in the early morning light." Putting down the Japanese soldier as a treacherous and fanatical enemy, fixing once and for all in his mind the phrase that was never to lose its validity among the men of the 1st Marine Division: "The only good Jap is a dead Jap." The Marines would have their revenge.

Two later patrols from the 5th Marines tried to cross the Matanikau and reach the area where the Goettge group had been struck down, but the patrols were turned back by heavy enemy fire at the river's mouth. Still later, on August 18 and 19, three companies from the 5th Marines undertook a three-pronged attack on the area. One group crossed the river about a mile from the mouth. One went by boat to land at Point Cruz. The third tried unsuccessfully to force a crossing at the sandbar where the Matanikau joins the sea. About sixty-five Japanese were killed. Among the Marines there were nineteen casualties, including four dead.

By August 13, working parties had cleared the landing beaches of supplies and engineers had completed the runway to a length of 2600 feet. By the 18th, it had been extended to 3778 feet. Captured Japanese equipment made both tasks possible. Japanese trucks helped haul things from the landing beaches to dumps. Without Japanese road rollers and earth-moving equipment, the airstrip could not have been so quickly completed. Little Marine engineering equipment had been landed. Without Japanese rice bags of woven straw, gun emplacements could not have been built, for sandbags had not been landed either.

On August 17 and 18, Guadalcanal was shelled from the sea, and on both days Japanese Betty bombers dropped delayed-action bombs that burst sporadically under the runway. Those bombs complicated the task of the engineers, who suffered casualties after each raid as they struggled to repair the strip to receive the planes that were to arrive a few days later.

After our second week ashore, we were loosely holding the beach line between the Tenaru on our east and the Matanikau River on our west. Our perimeter curved along the banks of these rivers for about 1500 yards, with special units scattered throughout the inland perimeter.

Responding to reports of Japanese movements in the Matanikau area, three companies of the 5th Marines attacked toward Kokumbona, in what was later identified as the first Battle of the Matanikau. They destroyed a Japanese base camp, killing sixty-two. Our own casualties numbered sixteen. There was action on the east as well. Capt. Charles Brush and his men from the 1st Marines were patrolling toward Koli Point when they encountered a detachment of Japanese Special Naval

Landing Force. The Brush patrol killed thirty-one of them and returned with eight casualties. The Japanese were a rear echelon, and we would hear from the remainder of the detachment shortly.

As these events were occurring, the 1st Pioneer Battalion continued to patrol along the Lunga River, an inner perimeter established to defend the prize of Guadalcanal—its nearly completed airfield. Lt. Col. William "Bill" Heepe, a lieutenant at the time and now retired, recalled one humorous incident that occurred during the early stages of the Guadalcanal campaign while B Company Pioneers was deployed along the Lunga River:

One day when we were bivouacked in the rainforest on the inland side of Henderson Field and near the Lunga, Lt. Teddy Hansen of A Company decided to build a head along side the road over which Col. Rowan's jeep traveled when approaching the battalion command post. Teddy had apparently scrounged some lumber and built quite an over-sizeable structure for a combat-zone privy. He had spent most of the day building it, and in the evening when Col. Rowan, the "Screaming Eagle," returned, he stopped the jeep abreast the head which Teddy was shingling. I happened to be near by and heard Col. Rowan say to Teddy: "Lieutenant, just what in the hell do you think you are building?" To which Lt. Hansen replied: "It's a shithouse, Sir." The colonel, somewhat angered and who probably had in mind that Teddy's shithouse could be seen at 20,000 feet by a Japanese bombardier because it was out in the open, replied, "Shithouse hell. It looks like a hotel."

Col. Rowan's favorite remarks at other times (he was a scorner of wet-behind-the-ears lieutenants) was that lieutenants don't have sense enough to pour piss out of a boot with the directions on the heel! I recall an incident when 1st Lt. Warren Sivertsen was a recipient of that scorn. Sivertsen, who was in charge of securing the bivouac area when the 1st Pioneer Battalion moved to a new location, made the mistake of asking the colonel what he should do with the foxholes. The old colonel just stared at him for about thirty seconds. Then, shaking his head, he said, "Good God-almighty, lieutenant. Leave them. You can't take them with you!"

Edward H. Fee Jr., a Guadalcanal campaign veteran and former Marine pioneer, recalled another amusing incident involving Col. Rowan:

> Shortly after our arrival on the Lunga perimeter, the morning quiet was fractured by rifle fire. Apparently our first uninvited Japanese sniper, or a trigger-happy Marine Pioneer, was firing at some imaginary target. Col. Rowan, returning from his daily briefing at the division command post, came roaring up in a jeep, jumped out, and began barking orders right and left. He promptly rounded-up all available Pioneers in the battalion command post area and formed a left and right pincer movement and frontal assault unit by pointing with sweeping hand and arm signals. I watched the action from my gun position some distance away. Actually, it happened so fast most of us never realized what the flurry was all about until it was over.
>
> The old colonel fearlessly shouted instructions. The assembled assault troops soon collared that venturous individual, who turned out to be a burly, pockmark-faced Marine. He was lying on his broad backside hidden in the weeds, firing vertically into the fronded top of a coconut tree. He said he was so hungry that he wanted coconuts, and he thought that nobody would hear him or care.
>
> The red-faced, sweating, angry colonel was so mad by this time he was sputtering. The only thing that saved the cornered culprit from being stomped, tarred, and feathered was that he was much larger than the colonel. As it was, he just received a fierce vocal assault from the colonel. He was effectively court-martialed, convicted, and sentenced

on the spot. The colonel took the Marine's rifle and handed it to a sergeant standing nearby, with instructions that the private would remain disarmed for the rest of his time on the island. I don't remember if these instructions were enforced. I suspect the Marine ended up as a permanent mess-man or being reassigned to another command.

I recall another humorous incident that occurred during the early stages of the Guadalcanal campaign. It involved a corporal in B Company Pioneers by the name of Warren D. "Ace" Hartwig. When Cpl. Hartwig waded ashore on August 7, he had a wad of folding money that would choke a horse. He cleaned house while aboard the troop transport *John Ericsson*. He had won 1200 bucks in a three-day crap game. During the first couple of days ashore, Hartwig carried his gambling-winnings in a money belt. Once we were in the bivouac near the Lunga River, he decided to bury his winnings in the ground. A few days later, when we returned from patrol we found that Japanese bombers had come over, erased the burial site, and relocated Hartwig's money. Ace was devastated. He passed the word that he would pay a substantial reward to anyone finding his valued money belt.

A couple days later, a fellow Marine pioneer stopped by Hartwig's foxhole and handed him his money belt. Ace zipped back the money flap and peeled off a couple hundred bucks for himself. "Here," he said to the fellow, "Take this stuff—it's found money." He took the wad of folding money, leafed through it carefully as if he had never seen that much money before. He handed it back to Ace, saying, slowly and wearily, "I ain't got no use for money on this rotten, God-forsaken island," and walked away. It would be difficult to think there might be a place for Ace Hartwig without money. The last time I saw him on Guadalcanal, he was walking around with a deck of cards in one hand and a set of dice in the other, saying, "Ace Hartwig is the name and gambling is my game!"

I have a distasteful recollection of my first encounter with Japanese sake on Guadalcanal. This occurred when several cases of sake, at least that's what we thought at the time, turned up at the pioneer bivouac area. When the cases were opened and the bottles passed around, Marines were heard to comment that it was the worst tasting stuff they ever tried to drink. When the unit interpreter was called over to read the label on the bottles, he said: "I hate to tell you guys this, but this is fly spray, not sake!" Apparently the cases of Japanese fly-spray were picked up by mistake from a captured Japanese storage shed that housed vast quantities of rice, as well as large caches of sake left behind by the Japanese who retreated into the jungle when we came ashore on August 7.

Lt. Col. Roy Walters, then a lieutenant who commanded the 3rd Platoon, B Company Pioneers, recalled his platoon taking their first bath:

After a couple of weeks on the Canal, the men in my platoon were beginning to show the strain of being in the lines. No one had taken a bath or taken their shoes off since we came ashore. Capt. Walter H. Stephens, our company commander came by one evening and after talking with some of the men digging defensive positions nearby, came up to me and said: "Walt, your men look like hell and they smell like crap. I want you to go down to the battalion motor pool and get four trucks from Gunner Barker, load your men on these trucks and take them to the Lunga River for a bath." This made me happy and needless to say the men were delirious. (The battalion motor pool was located quite some distance from our perimeter adjacent to Henderson Field.)

The river site we selected was about fifty feet wide and very shallow on one side. The water was about a foot deep, very clear and moving slowly over some stones and pebbles, so we drove the trucks right into the river. Then about fifty butt-naked men enjoyed the bath of their lives, soaking and soaping thoroughly from head to toe.

There were really no heavy enemy air attacks during the first two weeks on Guadalcanal, just repeated small raids; six or seven Japanese bombers cruising the airfield at leisure and unloading just about as they pleased. The Marines had captured the airstrip within the first few days, yet no fighter protection arrived during the first two weeks.

I returned from one of our daily patrols during this period to find that a direct hit by a Japanese bomb turned our company bivouac area into a mass of debris. There were several casualties among those left in camp, including Company 1st Sgt. Frank Cotrufo, who sustained a head wound and concussion.

On August 15, George W. Polk, ensign and radar officer, USNR, and Maj. Hayes, USMC, led 120 men of CUB-one, Naval Aviation Repair Unit, detachment onto Guadalcanal. They set up for the operation of Henderson Field to receive the first aircraft of Marine fighter and bomber squadrons to land and engage the Japanese from the island. After two weeks on the Guadalcanal without air support, two Marine squadrons of fighters and dive-bombers roared over the Henderson airstrip. At first we scattered. Then someone shouted: "They're ours, they're ours!" It was true. We could see the red, white, and blue stars painted under their wings and on their fuselage as two of the planes deliberately peeled off over our position along the Lunga River, circled Henderson Field, and dipped their wings as a salute to the Marines on the ground prior to landing. This was a moment of great excitement. I actually saw tears of joy running down the cheeks of some members of my squad. R. Adm. John S. McCain, commander of land-based air forces in the South Pacific, had delivered.

In the gentle glow of the evening of August 20, Squadron 232, consisting of twelve SBD-3 Douglas Dauntless dive-bombers commanded by Maj. Richard C. Mangrum, found the airstrip, dragged it once, and then landed. Capt. John L. Smith's Squadron 223, made up of nineteen pot-bellied Grumman F4F Wildcat fighters tailing Mangrum, bounced down on the runway and bumped awkwardly to the parking area that flanked it. The planes had flown in from the escort carrier *Long Island*, on station about 200 miles off the Lunga Point beachhead. The Marines on the island, code-named "Cactus," now felt they had at least a fighting chance. They dubbed the two new squadrons the "Cactus Air Force."

Marine air support arrived just in time. The Japanese resumed serious air operations against Guadalcanal on August 21. Almost every day, Japanese aircraft arrived around noon to bomb the perimeter. The newly arrived Marine fighter pilots found the twin-engine Mitsubishi Betty bombers, a dual purpose attack plane that could be armed with either torpedoes or bombs, easy targets. The Japanese Zero fighter was another story.

The Mitsubishi model Zero, a maneuverable navy fighter, climbed fast and turned tightly. Its armament was good, two 20-mm cannons and two machine guns. From the standpoint of maneuverability and rate of climb, the astonishing Zero had the Wildcat outclassed. The Zero's top speed, at 340 mph, was 9 mph faster than the little midwing Grumman F4F Wildcat fighter, shaped "like a barrel on roller skates with a plank stuck through its middle." But, while the F4F Marine Wildcat fighter lacked the grace and agility of the Zero, its sturdy frame could take more punishment and kept flying when badly shot up and the armor behind the seat back saved the pilot. The cockpit of the Zero was not armored and the fuel tanks were not self-sealing. The Zero could not take lead, and incendiary bullets flamed it readily.

The Zeros' superior speed and better maneuverability gave them a distinct edge in a dogfight. When warned by the coast watcher of Japanese attacks, however, the American planes had time to climb above the oncoming enemy and preferably attacked by making firing runs during high-speed dives. Their tactics made the air space over the Solomons dangerous for the Japanese. Marine fighter pilots returning to Henderson Field after a successful dogfight with the Japanese Zeros in the skies over Guadalcanal gave the thumbs-up to the ground crew, indicating that the enemy got "the whole nine yards." [3]

On August 20, 1942, the first Marine aircraft, such as this F4F-4 Wildcat, landed on Henderson Field to begin air operations against the Japanese. Courtesy of the Marine Corps Historical Center.

The SBD-3 Douglas Dauntless was a multiseat, low-wing monoplane that carried a 500-pound bomb under the fuselage and a 250-pound bomb under each wing. It was an effective dive-bomber. The Dauntless could also put up a strong defense against enemy fighters, thanks to its rear-mounted machine guns. The Dauntless was a sturdy, dependable aircraft capable of sustained operations under punishing conditions. It proved to be a workhorse for the Marines on Guadalcanal.

The fate of Henderson Field hung in the balance for more than three months. Close air-support missions for infantry operations became a luxury during this extended emergency. With the Wildcats needed to disrupt the daily raids from Rabaul, and the Dauntless dive-bombers needed to attack Japanese shipping, the Marines on the ground often had to rely on the ten P-39 Air Cobras of the Army's 67th Fighter Squadron that arrived on Guadalcanal on August 22.

The U.S. Army's P-39 Air Cobra, a medium-altitude fighter, proved to be ineffective in high-altitude dogfights. They could not climb

The first Army Air Force P-39 Air Cobras arrived on Guadalcanal on August 22, 1942, two days after the first Marine planes, and began operations immediately. Courtesy of the Marine Corps Historical Center.

high enough to mix with high-flying Japanese bombers and Zeroes and were quickly shot from the sky. Within six days only three of the original fourteen were operational. Gen. Vandegrift withdrew the P-39 fighters from aerial combat and assigned their pilots to bombing and strafing missions outside the Marine perimeter.

The P-39 fighters, with their nose cannon and six wing-mounted .30-caliber machine guns, proved to be a formidable close-support weapon against Japanese ground forces on Guadalcanal. Adorned with a snarling shark mouths, in brilliant color combinations on the silhouettes of the engine cowlings, these fighters presented a terrifying sight for the enemy soldiers on the ground as they came swooping down out of the sky in low-level strafing attacks.

After the aircraft arrived, things started to look much better. We were still taking a beating in the air and on the sea, but at least now we could strike back and the Japanese could no longer bomb us from the air with impunity. While our air Marines and Army Air Corps pilots were tooling up for their air mission, our determination to hold onto

*The pagoda at Henderson Field served as headquarters for Cactus Air Force through-
out the first months of air operations on Guadalcanal. From this building, Allied
planes were sent against Japanese troops on other islands of the Solomons. Courtesy
of the Marine Corps Historical Center.*

the ground was soon put to the test. Over the next four months,
Marines on Guadalcanal would face hell on earth, living every minute
of every hour facing death on the front lines. It was a place and time
that tested men's souls. The slop and scum of Guadalcanal featured
clouds of mosquitoes, jungle rot, dysentery, leaches, and tropical
downpours. Marines who survived combat faced the alternating fever
and chills of malaria. A Marine wasn't pulled off the line until his
temperature was above 103 degrees.

Then there were the screams of the Japanese: "Banzai!" as they
charged our lines. They were flushed with bushido, the Samurai code
of preferring death to the disgrace of surrender. On Guadalcanal it
was kill or be killed. The Japanese code of honor made it difficult not
to kill them. The Japanese had pushed the Americans off Guam,
Wake, Bataan, and Corregidor, and they figured to do the same on
Guadalcanal.

Day after day we were bombed, shelled, and shot at, but we never got any real sleep and never any real food. We ate captured rice and foul canned fish for days to survive. To this day, I can't stand the thought of Japanese food, much less the smell or taste of it. Despite all the hardships we endured on Guadalcanal, we were determined that nobody was going to drive us off the island. We were there to stay. We were not going to let the Corps down, and we were damned sure not going to let the men in our outfit down. This determination to hold was soon put to the test in the Battle of the Tenaru.

[7] The Battle of the Tenaru

The Japanese high command, incensed at reverses ashore, began assembling troops to reinforce their scattered units, which had been routed from the vicinity of the airfield. They made plans for counterattacks against the 1st Marine Division forces defending the airfield perimeter. Lt. Gen. Hyakutake was ordered to take over the ground action on Guadalcanal and salvage the situation. He decided that the attack would begin with a part of the 28th Infantry Regiment and a Special Naval Landing Force. These units were to be followed by the Japanese 35th Brigade.

The backbone of the initial effort would consist of the reinforced 28th Infantry, a 2000-man force of infantry, artillery, and engineers under the command of Col. Kiyono Ichiki. This force had been en route to the home islands after the Midway operation when the Marine landing in the Solomons brought a change of orders. The reinforcement ships landed Col. Ichiki's forward echelon at Taivu Point on Guadalcanal during the night of August 18. While this force landed at this point twenty-two air miles east of the Lunga beachhead, some 500 men of the Special Naval Landing Force arrived at Kokumbona.

Either out of supreme self-assurance or because he knew his presence had been detected, Ichiki impetuously decided to attack at once with 1000 men instead of waiting for the rest of his regiment to arrive. As night fell on August 20 he moved his small force westward, passed along the beach area where the Marines had first landed, and at about 0300 hours gave the signal to attack. Japanese mortar shells exploded on the Marine line along the west bank of the Ilu River[1] to engage the Marines. They had intended to make it a surprise attack. The attack proved to be more of a surprise for the Japanese as Lt. Col. Edwin Pollock's 2nd Battalion, 1st Marines were dug in on the west bank and waiting for them.

At 0500 on August 21, green flares rose from the opposite bank, throwing a ghostly light over the sand spit as about 200 Japanese came charging through the surf with outthrust bayonets silhouetted against the sea by the eerie swaying light of the flares. The Marines were now face to face with the enemy. Pollock' s orders were: "Line 'em up and squeeze 'em off!" (a term used on the firing range).

The ensuing battle that erupted was fierce and savage. The Japanese were shouting "Banzai!" and "Die, Marine!" Using human wave tactics, the Japanese attempted to crush Pollock's Marines who were defending the area. Most of Ichiki's soldiers were armed with the Arisaka rifle. That crude yet highly reliable weapon was a bolt-action design like the Springfield. Unlike the Marine rifle, the Arisaka was chambered for a 6.5-mm cartridge. At the tip of the Arisaka rifle barrel was what the Japanese considered the most important weapon in the night attack, the bayonet. "Don't rely on your bullets, rely on your bayonets," said one of their training manuals. The Japanese soldier placed an almost spiritual value on close combat with edged weapons.

The first of the enemy troops ran into a single strand of barbed wire placed across the sandbar at the mouth of the river. They began hacking through it. Many were killed, but many more breached this minor obstacle, and, in hand-to-hand combat using rifle butts and bayonets, they broke into the ranks of the defending Marines. Squad after squad came running low with bared bayonets flashing in the moonlight.

They met vicious rifle and machine-gun fire that halted the charge and forced them back to the sandbar. Stumbling about and undecided on which way to turn, they found themselves trapped with Marine

This photo was found in a Japanese officer's camera. He had no further use for it, thanks to the Marines. Note the fixed bayonets on the welcoming committee. Courtesy of Guadalcanal Echoes.

mortar fire behind them and deadly rifle and machine-gun fire in front. Some chose the river, where they were cut down. Others chose to try to escape by the sea. The second assault continued into broad daylight. Unable to dislodge the Marines, who were now using machine-gun fire and canisters from two 37-mm antitank weapons to decimate his troops, Ichiki sent part of his force south along the east bank to cross the Tenaru upstream in an attempt to outflank the Marines.

The stagnant waters of the Tenaru were stirring. Concealed beneath floating palm tree branches and blobs of seaweeds, Japanese swimmers were crossing the river and the lagoon behind the sandbar. Throughout the night of August 21 Ichiki continued his assault from the far side of the river. All night the Marines antitank guns, machine guns, and artillery continued to cut his men down.

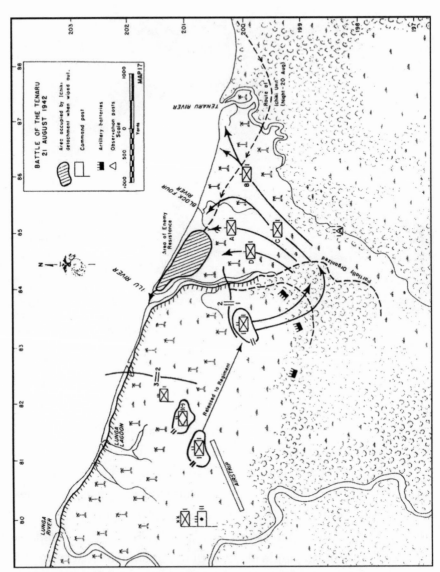

Map of the Battle of the Tenaru, August 21, 1942. Courtesy of the Marine Corps Historical Center.

Pollock's Marines had thrown back two desperate attacks. Hundreds of silent bodies sprawled on the sand testified to the serious wound inflicted on a persistent enemy. But how gravely were the Japanese hurt? The sporadic chatter of Nambu light machine guns, the slower and more methodical sound of hidden heavies, further movement in the shadows of the coconut palms across the river—all suggested to Lt. Col. Gerald C. Thomas, the division operations officer, that in spite of the battering they had absorbed, the enemy was still very much alive.

"We aren't going to let those people lie-up there all day," he said, and proposed immediate envelopment of the enemy position. Gen. Vandegrift concurred and released the division reserve, the 1st Battalion of Cates's 1st Marines, commanded by Lt. Col. Lenard B. Cresswell.

Thomas explained the scheme of maneuver: Cresswell would cross the river upstream of the Japanese as soon as possible, turn ninety degrees north, fan out, and drive toward the sea, while Pollock's battalion would keep the enemy pinned down from the west bank. Shortly after noon, Col. Cresswell's battalion completed its concealed deployment to the rear of a line of departure along the edge of the jungle that enclosed the coconut grove to the south. When the attack jumped off, it moved slowly but steadily in an attempt to envelop whatever remained of the attacking force, which now seemed to be concentrated behind the tongue of land that reached toward the sandbar.

As the Marines closed in, supported by light M3A1 Stuart tanks and the 1st Marine attack aircraft that had landed on Henderson Field the day before, the Japanese were pounded by artillery and air strikes. The remnant of Ichiki's forces were caught in a crossfire between Cresswell's advancing 1st Battalion and Pollock's 2nd Battalion dug in on the west bank of the river near its mouth. Marine sharpshooters picked off those who tried to run into the sea, their bobbing heads made easy targets. Meanwhile, Marine tanks spitting canister rounds flushed out Japanese still hiding in the coconut grove. The steel treads crushed and mangled the Japanese living, dead, and dying until, as

Gen. Vandegrift put it, "The rear of the tanks tread looked like meat grinders."

My unit, B Company Pioneers, had been moved up from our defensive position on the Lunga River to act in reserve. Initially, we didn't know how many men the Japanese had and what the situation was ashore. All we knew was that there was one hell of a battle being waged on the beach to our front. We could hear their Nambu machine guns and mortars blasting away, along with the enemy's cries of "Banzai." The Marines answered with everything they had. My God, it was butchery. The men in the 1st Marine Regiment stacked them up like cordwood on the sand bar. The Japanese tried to cross the sand bar two or three times, but each time their casualties were enormous. Throughout the morning, the Marines went to work on what was left of Ichiki's men.

Later that day, my company was ordered to move through the battle area to clear away any remaining snipers or stragglers and to assist in the recovery of the dead and wounded. As we crossed the sandbar, I knew we were at war. What a sight! In the brutally fierce sun, the Japanese soldiers killed by the Marines lay half-buried in the sand at the mouth of the river and had begun to puff and swell. The stench had started to sweep the whole area. I vividly recall the battle's aftermath— all made a scene difficult to describe, but never to be forgotten.

Reconnoitering cautiously across the spit, we found hundreds of dead Japanese heaped in rows on the sandbar. Hundreds more, dead or dying, were strewn along the beach, floating in the river or its lagoon, or blasted to bits in the palm grove on the far side of the river. A bulldozer, the only one to reach shore during the landing, began to plow a common grave in the palm grove, and the muddy brown waters of the Tenaru ran crimson with Japanese blood.

The Marines had eliminated the elite storm-trooper detachment of the Japanese Army. But in truth, we had accomplished much more. The myth of Japanese invincibility, fractured at Tulagi, Gavutu, and Tanambogo, was shattered at the Tenaru.

Japanese soldiers of the Ichiki detachment lie dead on the beach after they were shot trying to outflank the Marines. This group moved through the surf and attempted to attack from the north. Courtesy of the Marine Corps Historical Center.

By late afternoon, the battle of Tenaru was over. It was, as Gen. Vandegrift stated, "a war without quarter." Close to 800 Japanese soldiers had been killed, 15 were taken prisoner, and a small number had escaped through the jungle. Marine casualties were 34 dead and 75 wounded. It was the first significant victory for the Marines on Guadalcanal.

The 1st Marine Regiment and attached units had achieved a decisive victory against the most elite unit in the entire Japanese Army, which until Guadalcanal had won every battle they had fought. They started their initial charge with screaming waves of men charging against Marine lines—bayonets against machine guns. In the end, Col. Kiyono Ichiki, the battle-seasoned Japanese Army veteran who led this impetuous attack, tore his battle flag to threads, burned it, and committed hari-kari.

Thus, the first Japanese attempt to recapture Henderson Field had failed. Adm. Tanaka, in command of Japanese reinforcement effort during much of the campaign, later had this to say about the disaster: "I knew Col. Ichiki from the Midway operation and was well aware of his magnificent leadership and indomitable fighting spirit. But this episode made it abundantly clear that infantrymen armed with rifles and bayonets had no chance against an enemy equipped with modern, heavy arms. This tragedy should have taught us the hopelessness of 'bamboo-spear' tactics."

Col. Kiyono Ichiki, a battled-seasoned army veteran, who was the leader of the 900-man Japanese force that attacked the Marines at the Tenaru River the night of August 20–21, 1942. Courtesy of the U.S. National Archives.

At the Battle of the Tenaru, Vandegrift's Marines received a shocking introduction to the Japanese soldier. He was a tough and fanatical foe who often displayed a total disregard for his safety in battle. When defeat was certain, he invariably fought to the end, preferring death to surrender. Those few Japanese who did surrender did so because they were usually too weak or ill to resist capture or to commit suicide.

The Japanese foot soldier was well trained in jungle warfare and had never before been defeated in battle. They were also very sneaky. Soldiers would lie motionless in the sand and play dead until you passed. Then they would jump up and stab you with a bayonet or throw a grenade. Of course, they would kill themselves, but they

As a colonel, Gen. Cates (center) commanded the 1st Regiment on Guadalcanal. Standing with him are Lt. Col. Cresswell, Lt. Col. Pollock, Lt. Col. McKelvy, and Lt. Col. Stickney, also Marine officers. Courtesy of the Marine Corps University Archives.

would take some Marines with them. When asked what he would do the next time, one Marine pioneer participating in the mop-up operation said, "I'll stick 'em first."

After the Battle of Tenaru the Marines on Guadalcanal learned to throw away the rule-book. It became a war of "kill or be killed." I know that I didn't intend to take any prisoners because they were trying to kill me. In order for me to survive, I had to kill them first. I passed the word to my men: "Kill the Jap bastards. Use your bayonet!"

Patrolling continued in all sectors, and on August 27 the 1st Battalion, 5th Marines under Lt. Col. William E. Maxwell met a strong body of enemy troops near the village of Kokumbona, west of the perimeter. The battalion had made an amphibious landing without incident at about 0730, but later ran into the Japanese force dug into positions throughout a narrow coastal gorge. Maxwell was beyond artillery range of the perimeter, and although the 2nd and 5th Battalion of the 11th Marines fired diversionary missions east of him in Matanikau Village, the Japanese facing the infantry Marines seemed inclined to make a strong stand rather than to slink off into the brush, as they had frequently done in other such engagements.

Faulty communications and other difficulties bogged down the Marine attack. Lt. Col. Maxwell withdrew his forces to comply with a portion of his patrol order, which required him to return to the perimeter by nightfall. Maxwell's decision to with draw early did not set well at division headquarters. Maj. Donald W. Fuller, the battalion executive officer, assumed command of the 1st Battalion, 5th Marines two days later.

That same day, August 30, two more Marine air squadrons, VMF-224 and VMSS-231, flew into Henderson Field. The air reinforcements were more than welcome. Steady combat attrition, frequent damage in the air and on the ground, and scant repair facilities and parts kept the number of available aircraft a dwindling resource. The 6th Naval Construction Battalion (Seabees) arrived at Guadalcanal on September 1. As the Solomons aerial war grew fiercer, the Seabees began working on Henderson Field and the new nearby Fighter Strip One.

It became clear that the Japanese were focusing their effort in the Solomon Islands on regaining the vital airfield on Guadalcanal. The enemy poured fresh troops onto the island via a shuttle of ships and barges coming down the slot each night. The 1st Marines had destroyed the Ichiki detachment along the Tenaru River on August 21, but the Marine division had too few troops to secure the entire perimeter.

As much as he needed additional aircraft, Gen. Vandegrift critically needed more combat troops to bolster his defense of Henderson Field. After three weeks, Vandegrift concluded the Japanese had little interest in counterattacking Tulagi. He decided to transfer the combat-tested combined raiders and parachute battalions, both under Col. Edson's command, as well as their backup the 2nd Battalion, 5th Marines over to Guadalcanal from Tulagi. This move gave the division commander a chance to order out larger reconnaissance patrols to probe for the Japanese.

Vandegrift realized that the Tenaru battle was only a prelude to more serious attempts to retake the few precious acres of terrain his Marines had won. There were many signs of intensified actions outside the position so precariously manned. Native scouts reported Japanese landings to the west at Tassafaronga and Kamimbo Bay and to the east near the abandoned village of Tasimboko. During the first week of September, Vandegrift—a prudent man, but not a hesitant one—decided to strike somewhere in sufficient strength to knock the gathering enemy off balance. He could no longer wait to find out what was going on around him, but he dared not undertake any operation that could not be completed in daylight hours.

The general faced the sort of tactical problem for which textbooks provide no solution. With the recent arrival from Tulagi of the 2nd Battalion, 5th Marines, now both of his infantry regiments were at full strength. But the beaches he must defend against anticipated attack from the sea stretched from the Tenaru to a point west of Kukum, a distance of some 8000 yards. His six infantry battalions were not adequate to defend this frontage, provide the depth, and supply necessary reserves. To gain some operational flexibility, he had on the last day of August ordered Gen. Rupertus to ship the raider and parachute battalions to Guadalcanal.

Upon arrival on Guadalcanal, the raiders and parachutists now consolidated into a provisional battalion, moved into defensive positions on the south rim of the perimeter, inland from the airfield where they dug in. After reviewing Japanese naval activity and native scouting reports that indicated the enemy was concentrating fresh troops near the village of Tasimboko, Edson, the new consolidated unit commander, and Col. Thomas hatched a plan to raid this eastern terminus of the Tokyo Express on September 8. Intelligence initially placed about 250 Japanese at Tasimboko with their defenses located west of the village and facing Henderson Field. Edson planned to land to the east of the village and attack them from the rear.

The available shipping for this hastily arranged operation consisted of two APDs and two small, converted California tuna boats, called "yippies," so the raider commander divided his force into two waves. The raider rifle companies would embark on the evening of September 7 and land just prior to dawn, then the tiny fleet would shuttle back to the perimeter to pick up the weapons company and the parachutists. Since the APDs were needed elsewhere for other missions, the Marine force would have to complete its mission and re-embark the same day.

On the evening of September 7, native scouts brought news that the enemy force at Tasimboko had swelled to several thousand. Division planners discounted these reports at first, believing that they were greatly exaggerated or referred to remnants of previously defeated information. But when the raiders landed at 0520 hours on September 8, they immediately realized that the natives had provided accurate information. Not far from the beach, Marines discovered endless rows of neatly placed life preservers, a large number of foxholes, and several unattended 37-mm antitank guns.

Later that night, the raiders embarked at Kukum in two destroyer-transports, the *Manley* and *McKean*, and two diesel-powered yippies. Three nights earlier a group of Japanese destroyers had caught two other destroyers-transports, the *Gregory* and *Little*, off Lunga Point and sunk them. The landing was made at Taivu Point just east of Tasimboko before dawn on the morning of September 8. They met no opposition on the beach.

D Company of the 1st Raiders (little more than a platoon in strength) remained at the landing beach as rear security while the other two companies worked their way toward Tasimboko. The raiders soon ran into stubborn resistance, with the Japanese firing artillery over open sights directly at the advancing Marines. Col. Edson sent one company wide to the left to flank the defenders. But as they advanced, they were hit by mortars, and the Japs' light machine guns began their chatter.

Edson knew he was in for one hell of a firefight; the biggest thing he had was a section of 60-mm mortars that were ineffective against the heavier Japanese weapons. He immediately called for an air strike by Marine Dauntless dive-bombers and shark-nosed Army P-39 Air Cobras already on station to bomb the gun positions and to strafe the suspected strong points ahead of him. As the action developed, the APDs *Manley* and *McKean* returned to Kukum Beach at 0755 hours and the 1st Parachute Battalion (less C Company) embarked within twenty-five minutes.

Edson began an envelopment movement, through marshy land and thick growth. As the battalion advanced slowly against a heavy volume of fire, some of his raider units had lost internal contact during the stiffening battle, but these faults were corrected at about 1130, approximately the same time the 208 parachutists joined D Company ashore and went into defensive positions adjacent to them.

Edson, fearing that he might be moving into a Japanese trap, already had radioed division twice and asked for reinforcements, to include another landing to the west of Tasimboko in what was now the enemy rear. In reply, division ordered the raiders and parachutists to withdraw. Edson persisted, however, and led a coordinated attack against the firm opposition. Early in the afternoon, Edson's combined force overran Gen. Kawaguchi's rear base in the village of Tasimboko. They found the place empty of Japanese but full of booty.

The captured booty was overwhelming but there was no time to load these captured weapons, equipment, and food. They found several artillery pieces, Nambu rifles, ammunition, clothing, rice tins, rations, equipment, and a powerful radio transmitter, all of which could have been used to advantage. But having neither time or means to carry much back to Kukum, everything the raiders laid their hands on, with the exception of a half-dozen Nambu rifles with magazines and ammunition, was systematically destroyed.

Col. Edson viewed the scene with satisfaction. At 1600 hours he ordered all troops to embark. During the fast run back to the Lunga Point perimeter, Edson discovered almost every member of the raiding party was sagging under the heavy load of tinned crab, sliced beef packed in soy, and flasks of sake. The men had also helped themselves to large stocks of British cigarettes, bearing a Netherlands East Indies tax stamp.

The raid was a minor tactical victory with major operational impact on the Guadalcanal campaign. At a cost of two killed and six wounded, the Marines had killed twenty-seven Japanese. The enemy suffered more grievously in terms of lost firepower, logistics, and communications. Intelligence gathering at the scene also revealed some details about the coming Japanese offensive. The latter facts would allow the 1st Marine Division to fight off one of the most serious challenges to its tenuous hold on Henderson Field.

According to Edson's after-action report, the Japanese were prepared for an attack from the west, not from the east, and the Marines sneaked in their back door. Casualties were small on both sides (the two never really came to grips), but the raiders and parachutists found and destroyed much material and supplies, including some 75-mm artillery.

Luckily for the raiders, Gen. Kawaguchi's main body had already moved further west, and the Japanese general was under orders to keep moving. Higher headquarters at Rabaul had detected a major American convoy moving to Espiritu Santo (it was carrying the 7th Marines from Samoa). Kawaguchi was ordered to seize the airfield before those troops, assumed to be destined for Guadalcanal, could reinforce the American garrison.

On September 9, Edson met with division planners to discuss the result of the raid. Intelligence officers translating captured documents indicated that up to 3000 Japanese were cutting their way through the jungle southwest of Tasimboko. Edson was convinced that they planned to attack the unguarded southern portion of the perimeter. From an aerial photograph, he picked out a grass-covered ridge that pointed like a knife at the airfield. Col. Thomas agreed. Vandegrift, just in the process of moving his command post into that area, was reluctant to accept a conclusion that would force him to move yet again. After much discussion, he allowed Thomas to shift the bivouac of the raiders and parachutists to the ridge to get them out of the pattern of bombs falling around the airfield.

The combined force moved to the new location on September 10 and quickly discovered that it was not the rest area they had hoped to enjoy. Orders came down from Edson to dig in. The raiders and parachutists found the process of constructing defensive positions tough going. There was very little barbed wire and no sandbags or heavy tools. Men digging in on the ridge itself found coral just below the shallow surface soil. Units disposed in the flanking jungle were hampered by the thick growth. Both units were smaller than ever, as tropical illness, poor diet, and lack of sleep combined to swell the number of men in the field hospital. Those still listed as effectives often were just barely so.

Edson faced a tough situation as he contemplated how to defend the ridge area. Several hundred yards to the right of his coral hogback was the Lunga River; beyond it, elements of the 1st Pioneer and 1st Amphibious Tractor Battalions had strong points. More than a mile to his left was the tail end of the 1st Marine Regiment's positions along the Tenaru River. With the exception of the kunai grass–covered slopes of the ridge, everything else was dense jungle. His small force, now about the size of a single infantry battalion but lacking all the heavy weapons, could not possibly establish a classic linear defense.

Edson placed the parachutists on the east side of the ridge, with B Company holding a line running from the slope of Hill 80 into the jungle. The other two companies echeloned to the rear to hold the left flank. B Company of the raiders occupied the right slope of Hill 80 and anchored their right on a lagoon. C Company placed platoons strong points between the lagoon and the river. The remaining raiders were in reserve near Hill 120. Col. Thomas moved 2nd Battalion, 5th Marines into position between the ridge and the airfield and reoriented some of his artillery to fire to the south. Artillery forward observers joined Edson's command post on the front slope of Hill 120 and registered the guns.

Meanwhile, Gen. Kawaguchi's brigade faced its own troubles as it fought through the jungle and over the numerous slimy ridges. The rough terrain had forced the Japanese to leave behind their artillery and most of their supplies. Their commander also detailed one of his four battalions to make a diversionary attack along the Tenaru, which left him with just 2500 men for the main assault. To make matters worse, the Japanese had underestimated the jungle and fallen behind schedule. As the sun set on September 12, Kawaguchi, realized that only one battalion was in its assembly area and none of his units had been able to reconnoiter their route of attack. Kawaguchi tried to delay the jump-off schedule for 2200 hours, but he could not contact his battalions. Without guides and running late, the attack blundered forward in darkness and soon degenerated into confusion.

During September 10–12, while Kawaguchi and his brigade of more than 3000 men were cutting their way through the jungle to get into position to attack Henderson Field and Col. Edson's combined force of raiders and parachutists dug in on the ridge to defend it, my unit, the Marine pioneers, continued to patrol along the Lunga River, into the jungle foothills south of the airfield. Small patrols, up to platoon strength, were the mainstay of the battalion's intelligence effort and would remain so. However, with the recent report of Kawaguchi forces moving in this direction, division command found reasons to have the 1st Pioneer Battalion intelligence effort extended out beyond the perimeter.

The increased sighting of Japanese patrols out beyond our perimeter was a matter of great concern for Col. Rowan. It didn't come as a surprise to anyone when word came down from battalion that B Company would establish a strong outpost about 600 yards forward of the battalion's main line of resistance. I can't remember if I volunteered for this assignment, or if I was selected, but I suspect it was the latter since 1st Lt. Sivertsen, the battalion intelligence officer, had already informed me that he was going to request that I take the patrol out. In any event, I soon found myself lining up volunteers and making the necessary preparations to move out.

Normally, I would take out a twelve-man squad on patrol. This time, due to the nature of the mission, I decided to take a reinforced rifle squad that included a machine-gun section, communications team, and a medical corpsman. The company's proper weapon, the heavy water-cooled machine gun, was carried dismantled. One man carried the barrel assembly, another the tripod, and a whole squad the ammunition, in heavy metal boxes.

The patrol left the perimeter that afternoon, a file of more than twenty men, winding down a narrow trail. I had a few last words for the men. "Keep those canteens out of your mouth. If you don't save water, you'll regret it before this mission is over." Safe drinking water was a precious commodity in the jungle and must be conserved.

The lead squad went through the tunnel of the trail, where kanaris treetops laced together high overhead shut out the sun. There were strange birdcalls that sounded like a human cry. One sounded like someone being strangled, shouting, "I'm all right!" One squawk was like the sound of two wooden paddles being clapped together. The steamy heat increased with each step. I was near the front of the column with my Browning automatic rifle man. Behind me were the machine-gun section, corpsman, and a two-man communications team.

Our pace was extremely slow because the men taking the point had to use machetes to hack out a path through the jungle wide enough for the machine-gun section to move through. We also had to hand-carry extra ammunition boxes, cartons of grenades, and C-rations. My attached communications team had the difficult task of carrying a reel of communication wire and laying a landline as we moved forward. It took us about two hours to reach the selected outpost site.

The dense jungle floor made clearing the site very difficult. In the last hours of daylight, the machine-gun section set about the task of emplacing their guns, improving fighting holes, and fields of fire forward of their gun positions. I was not pleased with our progress—our fields of fire were not complete. In fact, our visibility was so limited the enemy would be almost on top of us before we could see them.

To offset this disadvantage, I had three of my demolition assault-squad, Cpl. Alfred Myers, Pfc. Edward Swierk, and Pfc. Frank Minerowicz, fashion booby trap hand grenades with partially loosened safety pins attached to trip wires, which could trip the unwary feet of the enemy approaching our gun positions. By this late time, dusk was settling into in the jungle. The clicking of the picks and the rasping of the shovels fell silent. I watched as my men straightened up so they could see the last flight of parakeets skimming over the jungle, the brilliance of their plumage vanishing with the fading light.

The jungle seemed to flow around our small clearing like a silent, dark sea. The men settled down for a long, chilly, damp night. A routine fifty percent watch was in effect—meaning that in each two-man fighting hole and machine-gun pit at least one man was awake, if not necessarily alert. The outpost was ready. We all knew what we had to do: detect any movement of enemy troops to our front and prevent a surprise attack. If engaged by any sizable enemy force, our orders were to withdraw to the main line of resistance.

Whatever sleep we might have gotten was interrupted shortly after midnight by a volley of rifle fire. Orange tracers cut through the darkness. One of our machine guns opened up, answered by the rapid chatter of a Japanese Nambu light machine gun. Flares bathed the area in bright light. I saw the Japanese coming toward us—silently, not a banzai attack, but slowly and deliberately, as though they expected little opposition. I held my rifle with the sling wrapped around my arm, just as I had learned to do in boot camp. I knelt on one knee in my fighting hole and waited until I saw them clearly, then yelled: "Commence firing! Give 'em hell!" I started firing and kept firing until the Japanese soldiers stopped coming. I stared into the darkness, but all I could see or hear was the cry of the wounded being dragged away. I passed the word to cease fire.

We were to learn after a survey of the area the following morning that three Japanese soldiers were killed and several wounded by booby-trap grenades and small-arms fire during this short but fierce engagement. Our only casualty was a man in the machine-gun section who sustained severe burns to both hands while attempting to remove a jammed ammunition belt from a .30-caliber water-cooled Browning machine gun. He was treated by the medical corpsman, who administered a shot of morphine, sprinkled the burns with sulfur, and applied a sterile dressing on both hands. He would eventually be evacuated to the division field hospital.

Quiet fell late that night. I managed to halt a bit of nervous firing by some of the men. I passed the word that I didn't want another man to fire one damn round unless they could see the enemy. I said, "Let them get in close before you open up. You can't stop them unless you hit them." This action was drastic, but necessary, as our ammunition supply was being depleted too rapidly.

At dawn the enemy decided to try to kill us from a distance; a big artillery piece or mortar battery opened up. I heard a rush of air as something big whizzed past me, and then a loud explosion somewhere behind me. They had not found the range yet. Despite this bit of good fortune, we knew we were outnumbered and outgunned, and the decision was made to pull back to our perimeter. After securing the outpost site, we began the burdensome task of retracing our steps over the rugged jungle terrain. Some of the men who failed to conserve water in their canteens learned that the last drink meant more to them in this hot humid environment than they ever dreamed it would.

After our first successful combat patrol, the men spent more of their time adjusting to their new role as infantrymen. Leading a patrol was often stressful, but I had decided that if I had to die, I would rather do it on patrol where I had some control rather than just huddle up in a foxhole watching the enemy bombers fly overhead.

The last patrol I took into the jungle along the Lunga perimeter was one that I'll never forget. We had been sent out to check reports that a large concentration of Japanese had been sighted in the area. It didn't take long to find out that the reports were true. We kept finding discarded Japanese equipment all along the trail. As we penetrated deeper into the jungle, we located a Japanese bivouac site that had recently been occupied. We found bags of rice and uncovered a cache of green sake. There was damn near two quarts of the stuff, which tasted something like home-brew, but much stronger.

I knew enemy probing forces were operating in this area, so I began to start my men back to our lines. We hadn't gone very far before the Japanese opened up on us. We took cover, and I set up a field of fire with my Browning automatic rifle man, and I told the rest of my patrol to withdraw to a more tenable position and dig in. It was a brief firefight, and I guess the Japanese patrol decided that the Arisaka 6.5-mm rifle was no match for the Browning and the accurate fire delivered by my '03 rifle. I positioned myself behind a large coconut tree and picked them off one by one at long range. Once the Japanese broke off the engagement and disappeared into the jungle, we rejoined the remainder of the patrol dug in nearby and returned to our unit on the perimeter. We were to learn later that this was a small probing force from Gen. Kawaguchi brigade now advancing toward the airfield.

When we got back to camp, I immediately reported to Capt. Stephens, who in turn passed the information on to 1st Lt. Sivertsen,

"Patrol Leader Returns Fire." Drawing by Capt. Donald L. Dickson. Courtesy of the Marine Corps Historical Center.

who was responsible for coordinating the 1st Pioneer Battalion's intelligence-gathering effort. He requested that I accompany him to the division command post, where we met with Col. Thomas and Col. Edson, who happened to be there at the time. I told them exactly what had happened and pointed out on the division situation map where my patrol made contact with the enemy. I showed them the exact location of the Japanese bivouac site. Col. Edson concluded that the information I gave him reinforced other intelligence reports he had received. I think he realized then that the Japanese were not going to hit our flanks, but were going to come at us from behind—at Henderson Field.

After studying intelligence reports, captured Japanese documents, and the terrain from Lunga Point back beyond the airstrip, Gen. Vandegrift noted the grassy ridge south of Henderson Field that could command the field and serve as a point of assault. Vandegrift decided this ridge must be defended and he assigned Col. Edson's combined unit of raiders and parachute troops, who were already dug in on the ridge, to the task.

In the meantime, the 3rd Battalion of the 1st Marine Regiment was moved over to defend the Tenaru River, which snaked its way inland for two miles. On the west, the perimeter was defended by another line of Marines, the 1st Pioneer Battalion, and northwest of the ridge company-sized composite outposts were to be placed at strong points west of the Lunga River. One was manned by men of the 1st Pioneer Battalion, the other by men of the 1st Amphibious Tractor Battalion.

The fact that Gen. Vandegrift had to use specialists as infantrymen showed how thin the perimeter was in spite of the number of troops ashore. He wasn't worried, however, because in the final analysis this old-breed warrior knew that the individual fighting man, operating as a member of a squad, platoon, or company, would win the battle. The men being used to fill the gaps were Marine riflemen first and specialists second.

The meeting at the division command post was breaking up on the morning of September 12, when Col. Thomas asked Col. Rowan to stay behind. Rowan was directed to proceed immediately to move a company of Marine pioneers to a previously designated strong point on a ridgeline west of the Lunga River. Col. Thomas stressed the point that it was imperative that the company being deployed be in place and fully operational prior to darkness.

After a hastily held conference at the 1st Pioneer Battalion command post, orders were issued for B Company Pioneers to proceed across the Lunga River and move west of the outpost perimeter to a position soon to be known as "Pioneer Ridge." The men would carry enough C-rations, water, and ammunition to sustain them for forty-eight hours.

At 1300 hours, Capt. Stephens called out the command, "Move out!" I kicked off the advance with the command, "Take the point! Scouts out!" My squad was assigned to the advance position. There were twelve of us, and it was our assignment to go ahead of the main body and establish contact with the enemy. On the command to move out, my two scouts took the point. My Browning automatic rifle man and I followed directly behind them. The other members of my squad followed in single file. The main body of the company followed some distance to the rear, but close enough to maintain contact.

In single-column formation, we plowed steadily along the jungle trail running parallel to the Lunga, until we reached a sandbar where the water was shallow enough for us to wade across. After we forded the Lunga, we paused long enough for the men to remove their canvas leggings, pour the water out of their boondockers, and squeeze the water out of their socks. Next to a Marine's weapon, it's imperative that he keeps his socks dry while out on patrol, for a soldier can't walk very far with wet socks inside rough laced high-top field shoes.

Once we left the riverbank, the jungle suddenly became stiflingly thick. It was enemy territory in earnest. Our column moved in absolute silence. Capt. Stephens whispered to the man in front of him and to the rear to pass the word along for the men to keep a five pace interval so as not to give snipers bunched targets. The message was passed forward and backward along the line in a whisper: "Keep five paces. . . . Keep five paces."

It is almost impossible to describe the creepy sensation of walking through the dense jungle. As we sneaked forward, the tense feeling steadily increased. The next word passed from the head of the main

One thing Guadalcanal didn't have a shortage of was water. It seems the Marines' socks were never dry. Courtesy of the Marine Corps Historical Center.

body came slowly, in whispers, "Keep a sharp look out to the right and left. . . . Keep a sharp look out to the right and left. . . . Keep a sharp look out to the right and left." As if we had to be told! After this, another kind of message came back along the line—the click of bullets being slipped into the chamber of the weapons.

Moving single file through the thick jungle was slow going. Capt. Stephen, bothered that the company was stuck in a slow-as-molasses mode, passed the word forward for me to take the point and to pick up the snail's pace. It seemed rather strange to be walking erect. Our jungle training in peacetime had stressed the need for slithering along on our bellies, or at least creeping on all fours like animals. But we didn't even stoop because it was imperative that we keep moving at a rapid pace in order that we arrive at our designated objective and be in position prior to darkness.

Suddenly, three or four rifle shots rang out up ahead of us. They were the high-pitched Japanese kind. Almost at once, I sent a message back along the line: "Hold it up. . . . Hold it up. . . . Hold it up." "Corpsman!" somebody shouted. "Pass the word back for a corpsman. We've got a wounded man here!" We stopped for a short interval to silence the Japanese sniper and to get the company medical corpsman forward to treat a wounded Marine. The wound was not life threatening, and after medical treatment he was able to remain with the column as we started to move again.

I recall the sniper incident as if it happened yesterday. I moved forward to the location where the Japanese sniper held us up. I saw the dead sniper laying face down on the jungle floor, where he had fallen from the top of a nearby kanaris tree after being shot. The lead scout's comment was, "This is the Jap son of a bitch that shot my buddy." While saying, "You know, it doesn't pay to be shooting at a Marine with a rifle," he took his foot and rolled the body over on its back so I could see that he had been shot right between the eyes.

Moving through jungle-choked ravines, across boggy streams and over steep hills was an exhausting process under the best of circumstances, and more so while carrying rifles, machine guns, grenades, ammunition, and rations. The struggle to continue our forward progress under these conditions caused us to sweat profusely. The wet skivvies would cling to your body like a second skin.

After a couple hours trudging under heavy combat packs and lugging extra machine-gun belts and bandoleers of rifle ammunition, we halted on the crest of a broad and fairly high ridge that looked down over the whole area of battle. Exhausted due to the strenuous climb and scorching heat, B Company Pioneers established a hasty perimeter on a hillcrest west of the Lunga River. After the exhausting and strenuous climb to the top of the ridge, one of my scouts, an old farm boy from the Deep South, said, "You know something, Sarge? If we worked a horse this hard in this kind of heat, we'd all go to jail."

The ridge rose to command a panoramic view of the bay as far west as Point Cruz, where the Japanese reinforcements were being off-loaded. If there was any doubt that the Navy had really left us stranded without air or naval protection, it was completely dispelled at this point. We knew it was only a matter of time before these Japanese reinforcements coming ashore would move around our perimeter.

Our immediate concern was to prepare our positions for the night, but first we took time out to eat. We had eaten a good lunch before we left camp, but that had been more than six hours ago, and we had done quite a bit of work in that time. We flopped down wherever we happened to be and wolfed down our C-rations. We had a choice of menu: meat and vegetable stew, corned beef hash, or meat and beans, straight from the can—cold but delicious. I also had a few cans of captured Japanese crab meat in my pack that I shared with my squad; it tasted real good. For dessert, we had a chocolate C-ration bar.

After eating, the exhausted men dug in as best they could. It was very difficult to prepare fighting positions on the ridge. The ground was hard as steel, and the men had trouble chipping out a slight indentation deep enough to provide some degree of protection from small arms fire and shrapnel. All we had to dig with was our bayonets and entrenching tools. Hacking a foxhole out of coral was palm-blistering, back-breaking work, and it took me some time to chop out a dugout deep enough and wide enough to cram myself into it so that my ass was a few inches below the surface.

Gradually, our bivouac settled down for the night. The men snuggled into whatever comfortable spots they could find. They couldn't find many, because the composition of ridges on Guadalcanal was mostly crumbled coral—not the stuff of beauty rest. I took off my pack, cartridge belt, and canteen, folded my poncho double, and settled down. There was nothing to serve as a pillow except my pack, which was full of ration cans, or my steel helmet. I finally found that the most comfortable arrangement was to put my helmet on and let it contend with the coral. All we could do then was wait.

War is nine-tenths waiting in line for chow, waiting for mail, for an air raid, for dawn, for reinforcements, for orders, for the men in front to move, for relief. All that night, we waited and we waited for the enemy to attack. The plan was for the pioneers to dig in and hold. We held the high ground, and thus had the advantage of position, so essential to the scheme of battle.

Meanwhile there was a beehive of activities occurring at the division command post, which was set up on the southern, landward side of the airstrip. After a month of nerve-wracking indignities caused by Japanese naval bombardment and air attacks, Col. Twining, the assistant chief of staff operations, dubbed the site "Impact Center South." Gen. Vandegrift decided that it should be moved.

About a mile south of the runway, the ground sloped up to a grass-covered ridge. It ran south for more than half a mile, roughly parallel to the Lunga River, which flowed west of it. On either side, in the ravines and flatlands, the rainforest encroached. Imagine a saurian creature waddling south, body somewhat bent, tail to the airfield, snout toward the mountains, with three stumpy legs on either side— irregular spurs that reach out into the jungle. On it back were three distinct knobs or rises. Japanese officers gave it the apt name "Lizard Hill," and the Marines referred to it as "Lizard Ridge."

For its new command post, the Marine command chose the lizard's left rear leg, an L-shaped spur that hooked back toward the airfield. On the southern slope of the spur, away from the airfield, D-1 officers put up tents that served as sleeping quarters. Being on the landward side of he spur, they were somewhat sheltered from naval gunfire. This location had little else to commend it, as the officers soon learned.

Close to where the spur joined the main body of the ridge, a jeep park was established, from which a short trail led into the forested brush-covered headquarters area, where tents for the enlisted personnel were located. Also located in this area was a tarp-covered field mess tent. Toward the airfield to the north the 11th Marines, the artillery regiment, set up its own command post on the southern slope of the spur, away from the airfield.

More than division headquarters was moving toward the ridge. Gen. Kawaguchi's four battalions, among others, were approaching. After leaving Tasimboko, they had hacked their way inland, at first close to the coast, then up river valleys across terrain that grew progressively rougher as they worked into the network of coral ridges. Kawaguchi was planning a three-pronged attack, aiming at weak points in the southern part of the perimeter.

One battalion would peel off and strike across the Tenaru some two and a half miles above its mouth. Three battalions would continue through the rugged ridge country until they were in position to attack Lizard Ridge. Col. Oka's battered troops in the west would hit at the point where the 5th Marines' organized defenses ended and a more lightly held series of outposts began, southwest of Kukum. Kawaguchi planned, of course, that all three pushes were to be made at the same time.

Worried about the weak defenses at the other end of the ridge, where the new command post was being set up, Gen. Vandegrift had moved Col. Edson's raiders and parachutists to the lizard's snout. There they were to set up defensive points and patrol to their front for a few days before being relieved by the division's reserve battalion, the 2nd Battalion, 5th Marines, which moved over from Talagi. The pioneer and engineer battalions continued doing what they had done for five weeks, manning a sector of the vulnerable southern, landward side of the perimeter.

The 1st Pioneer Battalion (minus its B Company on a ridge west of the Lunga) held an outpost position just south of Henderson Field between the Lunga and the north spur of the ridge occupied by Edson's force. Farther to the east and across the right spur from the pioneers was the area of the engineer battalion. Between the two positions was the division forward command post that recently had been moved from its former, bomb-pocked position near the airfield.

A battalion of 105-mm howitzers moved into position just south of the airfield to back up the tenuous defenses. Marine and native patrols reported Kawaguchi was getting closer, but no one knew just when or where, or in what numbers, he would try to break through to the airfield. As an effort to get the command post out of the regular Japanese bombing pattern, the move to the ridge was a failure. When the command post shifted locations, so did the pattern of bombing. Enemy pilots began aiming at Lizard Ridge, not the airfield, to soften defenses against the impending attacks.

[8] The Battle of Bloody Ridge

At the ridge overlooking the airfield, Col. Edson prepared his men for the impending payoff battle. Bald, but for its kunai grass, nameless, and bumpy, the ridge rose like a long, thin island from the dark green sea of the jungle. It lay a short mile south of the airfield, sloping toward the Lunga River to the west and the Tenaru to the east. Deep, heavily wooded ravines surrounded the ridge on all sides. It was an ideal approach to the airstrip. Whoever held the ridge commanded Henderson Field. Whoever held the airfield, held Guadalcanal.

Edson's disposition placed his two parachute companies on the exposed left flank and tied them in with Raider B Company, which held the ridge knoll in the center of the Marine line. C Company Raiders extended down the west slope of the ridge in contact with the pioneers, who would guard this jungle flank. Raider A Company, on a high knoll to the north and to the rear of B Company, was Edson's reserve. An increment of the 1st Pioneer Battalion was holding a hill overlooking the west bank of the Lunga well to the right of C Company Raiders, and elements of the 1st Engineer Battalion were on another hill, to the left of the 1st Parachute Battalion. Edson faced a tough decision as to how best to deploy his small force of raiders and para-Marines to defend the ridgeline. He decided on the strategy of individual units of about platoon strength disposed at intervals along the main line of resistance. There were open fields of fire only in the center of the positions where the main line of resistance crossed the

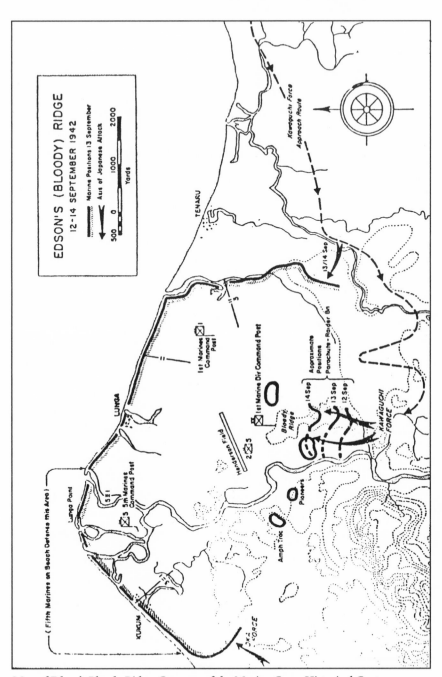

Map of Edson's Bloody Ridge. Courtesy of the Marine Corps Historical Center.

grassy ridge, but even there the abrupt slopes and broken ground made coordination of fires difficult. In the last hours of daylight, the troops improved their foxholes and their fields of fire, but the resulting positions were neither continuous nor complete.

As darkness fell on the ridge above Henderson Field, Col. Edson's men were dead tired, and their strength was 300 men in foxholes along the ridge. Behind them was Gen. Vandegrift's forward command post, and behind that was the division reserve of a battalion of the 5th Marines and the artillerymen from the 5th Battalion, 11th Marines, with their guns sighted in on the crest of the ridge and the Japanese positions to the south. Beyond all the Marines lay Henderson Field, the prize the Japanese had vowed to capture and the Marines to defend.

As the exhausted Marines on Guadalcanal were sweating it out, a Japanese naval task from Adm. Yamamoto's combined fleet was moving into position to launch a major attack. Shortly after 2200 hours on September 12, Guadalcanal night was lit up with ghoulish green flares as the Japanese warship began their bombardment. But on this night the airfield was not the prime target. Gen. Kawaguchi had radioed to Rabaul a description of the Marines disposition, and the bombardment unit opened up on the ridge where the Marines were.

Anyone who was on the hill overlooking the west bank of the Lunga (soon to be called Pioneer Ridge) that night will never forget the pounding we took from the Japanese warships. Shortly after 2200, the night's pitch darkness was transformed into the brightness of day. The Japanese warships had turned their searchlights on the ridge, sweeping the area with bluish-white lights that seemed considerably brighter than they were.

The searchlights were actually the eyes of a mighty enemy naval armada that swept into Sealark Channel to deliver the promised final knockout punch. Soon the men hunkered down on the ridge heard the sound of naval gunfire, saw the gun flashes offshore, and heard the sigh of the shells, a *swoosh-swoosh-swoosh* sound, rather like a steam

Capt. Donald L. Dickson said of this watercolor, "I wanted to catch on paper the feeling one has as a big shell comes whistling over. There is a sense of being alone, naked, and unprotected and time seems Endless until it strikes somewhere." Painting by Donald L. Dickson. Courtesy of the Marine Corps Historical Center.

locomotive straining to climb a steep hill. The shells came whizzing by, bursting near us. Some Marines on the ridge nearly panicked. The huge shells detonated with ear-splitting metallic cracking sounds. The concussion lifted us from the ground. We found ourselves face down on the ground wishing we were dug in twenty feet deeper.

We lay within a hundred yards of where the shells were landing on the forward slope of the ridge, so close you could almost taste the pungent gunpowder. We could hear the cutting sound only experienced on the receiving end of naval gunfire. Heavy, gray smoke drifted our way, bringing with it the unmistakable odor emitted when high explosives are detonated. The explosions were sharp and loud, followed by a swishing sound of hot flying shrapnel, as the metal cut through the trees on the forward slopes of the ridge. If the objective of the Japanese warships was to terrorize us, they were successful. If it was to soften us up for a frontal attack or to force us off the ridge, they had failed.

There is nothing more demoralizing than naval gunfire. You can hear each round leave the ship and come in like a freight train.

A member of my squad recalled "trying to dig a hole with his nose" as the large shells exploded and "trying to get down into the ground just a little bit further." I shook and trembled all through the attack, more afraid for my life than I had ever been before. Somehow I gathered up the inner strength to control my fear. For the sake of members of my squad who were shaken up, I had to appear fearless. Most of them were shell shocked and walking around in a daze.

I recall one member of my squad was still in his hastily dug foxhole, shaking like a leaf. I prodded him in the ass with the butt of my rifle, and said "Get up." He said, "What in the hell do you want me to do?" I said, "I'll tell you what I want you to do. Get your ass out of that foxhole, pick up your rifle, and help me kill every one of them Japanese sons of bitches coming up the ridge before they kill us."

When the naval barrage subsided, the expected attack on the ridge did not happen. We could hear the Japanese thrashing about in the hollow below the ridge. They appeared to be shaken and disorganized by the effect of their own naval bombardment, leaving some of us to believe there had been some miscalculations by the Japanese high command—that they had intended an all-out attack that night, but were hampered by failure of some of their contingents to arrive on schedule. Hence, they put on only half a show.

They did succeed in penetrating our forward lines on the right flank, where our company was holding the slopes of the ridge. Several Japanese soldiers wriggled forward through the underbrush on the lower slopes, probing our positions. They made no major contact with the Marine pioneers dug in along the top slopes of the ridge. We moved with caution all through the night as Japanese fired off several flares and snipers took pot shots in our direction.

Dawn on September 13 brought the usual retirement into the jungle by the attacking forces. The previous night had been a rehearsal for the main show. The enemy apparently decided to withdraw to fight at another time and another place. We were to learn later that the enemy probing force we encountered on Pioneer Ridge on the night of September 12 was from Col. Oka's battalion moving in from the west to join Gen. Kawaguchi main attack on Henderson Field.

The worst night at Guadalcanal was September 12–13, when Kawaguchi's brigade nearly broke through Edson's thin line of raiders and parachutists holding a grassy knoll overlooking Henderson Field. The battle began with a barrage of incoming shells from Japanese war-ships offshore, followed by an outbreak of rifle and mortar fire. Japanese soldiers crawled forward through the underbrush on the lower slopes, probing the Marines' positions. It was a harrowing night. For those on the firing line, a few hundred yards away, it was a hellish one.

From about 2200 hours until daybreak on the 12th, two of Kawaguchi's battalions made a series of charges against the Marines' lines. The Japanese surged out of the jungle behind a cloud of smoke shouting "Totsugeki."[1] The attackers bent the defenders in a semicircle around the ridge's knob, where they were making their stand. In the melee, Edson and his officers somehow managed to keep their men well enough organized to hold in the face of mortar barrages, followed by determined charges. Col. Edson pulled back to higher ground, leaving an open grassy no-man's-land between his line and the Japanese. Edson said, "There is only us between the airfield and the Japanese. If we don't hold, we will lose Guadalcanal."

The main thrust of the night came against Edson's left flank. Boiling out of the jungle, the enemy soldiers attacked fearlessly into the face of rifle and machine-gun fire, closing to bayonet range. They were thrown back. They came again, this time against the right flank, penetrating the Marines' positions. Again they were thrown back. A third attack closed out the night's action. Again it was a close affair. Edson told his men to hold, and they stood their ground.

We had a weapon the Japanese did not have, one that was probably decisive in this otherwise unequal battle: the battalion of 105-mm howitzers. Col. Pedro del Valle's artillery began pounding the attackers as soon as they had withdrawn to regroup after their first unsuccessful attempt to break through Edson's lines. The barrage continued through the night, often churning up the ground only 100 or 200 yards ahead of our own troops. Once, when Edson called urgently for a concentration, he reported back to the artillery commander: "Perfect. Now march it back and forth." And they did.

Together the mixed units under Edson's command and the artillery saved the day, rather the night. By about 0230 hours the assaults were petering out. Edson informed division, "We can hold." Col. Gerald Thomas, the division operations officer, told Lt. Col. "Wild Bill" Whaling, who had just taken command of the 2nd Battalion, 5th Marines, the division reserve, to reinforce Edson immediately.

Col. Whaling was a veteran fighter, but this was no night for a battalion-level Pickett's Charge up the backside of Edson's desperate defense. He ordered his three rifle company commanders to advance independently by guiding on the path they had reconnoitered the previous afternoon. Here they were fed into the lines to strengthen the left flank. On that side a small enemy group had broken through just east of the division command post and got into an unsuccessful fight with a company of engineers. Before dawn two more efforts, more feeble than the earlier ones, were made to break through on what became known as "Bloody Ridge." They were thrown back. As soon as the sun was up, five P-39 Air Cobras added to the Japanese misery, swooping low to strafe as the remnants of Kawaguchi's force gathered beneath the island canopy.

On the morning of September 13, Edson called his company commanders together and told them: "They were just testing, just testing. They'll be back." He ordered all positions improved and defenses consolidated and pulled his lines toward the airfield along the ridge's center spine. The 2nd Battalion, 5th Marines, his backup on Tulagi, moved into position to reinforce again.

The next night's attacks were as fierce as any man had seen. The Japanese were everywhere, fighting hand-to-hand in the Marines'

"The Raging Battle for Bloody Ridge." Painting by Capt. Donald L. Dickson. Courtesy of the Marine Corps Historical Center.

foxholes and gun pits, and filtering past forward positions to attack from the rear. Sheffield Banta, a feisty bantam cock of the old Marines, had been division sergeant major until recently promoted to the warrant-officer rank of Marine gunner. Banta shot one Japanese who infiltrated the new division forward command post. Col. Edson appeared wherever the fighting was toughest, encouraging his men to their utmost effort.

The man-to-man battles lapped over into the jungle on either flank of the ridge, and the pioneer and engineer positions were attacked. The 2nd Battalion, 5th Marines were fed into the fight. Artillerymen from the 5th Battalion, 11th Marines, as they had on the previous night, fired their 105-mm howitzers at any called target. The range grew as short as 1600 yards from tube to impact. The Japanese finally could take no more, and they pulled back as dawn approached.

The Japanese left more than 600 bodies on the slopes of the ridge and in the surrounding jungle; another 600 were wounded. The remnants of the Kawaguchi force staggered back toward their lines to the west, a grueling, hellish eight-day march that saw many more of the enemy perish. The cost to Edson's force for its defense was also heavy. Fifty-nine men were dead, 10 were missing in action, and 194 were wounded. These losses were coupled with the casualties of 89 men of the parachutist's original strength.

Both Col. Edson and Maj. Kenneth Bailey were awarded the Medal of Honor for "their heroic and inspirational actions." Edson's citation took note of his "cool leadership and personal courage." Bailey's described his "great personal valor while exposed to constant an merciless enemy fire and his indomitable fighting spirit."

It was daybreak of September 14 on the ridge. A rosy sun was rising almost directly to the left of the Marine front, lighting the battle that was now over. There was only an occasional shot and *boom* sound of a booby trap body as elements of the 1st Pioneer Battalion moved through the battle area to clear away any remaining snipers and stragglers and to assist in the recovery of the dead and the wounded.

War correspondent Richard Tregaskis wrote in his diary:

I went out on the ridge later in the day, to have a look at the Bloody Ridge battle ground. I climbed the steep knoll where our troops had made their stand and turned back the Japanese drive. The hill was silent now. The small fires smoldered in the grass. There were black, burned patches where grenades burst. Everywhere on the hill were strewn hand-grenade cartons, empty rifle shells and ammunition boxes with ragged rips in their metal tops. The Marines along the slopes of the hill sat and watched quietly as I passed. They looked dirty and worn. Along the flank of the hill where a path led, I passed strewn bodies of Marines and Japanese, sometimes tangled as they had fallen in a death struggle. At the top of the knoll, the dead Marines lay close together. Here they had been exposed to rifle and machine-gun fire and grenades.[2]

Dead Japanese soldiers on Bloody Ridge, Guadalcanal. Courtesy of the Marine Corps Historical Center.

At first light on the morning of the 14th, the men in B Company Pioneers secured their gun positions, gathered up their personal gear, made horseshoe rolls, and buckled up their field packs. It took us two hours to withdraw from Pioneer Ridge, although we'd spent an entire afternoon getting up to it. We knew the way back, we hadn't known the way in. After recrossing the Lunga River, we rejoined the rest of the battalion in time to take part in the three-day mop-up operation still in progress, as the Japanese survivors tried to retreat to the coast through the dense jungle.

The Japanese lost half of their men during the battle of Bloody Ridge, and many more in mopping-up operations. Almost all of the Japanese alive on the morning of September 14 either died of wounds or fell desperately ill as they tried to retreat to the coast through the dense jungle, out around our perimeter. And yet, Bloody Ridge marked only the beginning of the end—a fact made plain to the Marines by a Japanese prisoner who stood among his slaughtered countrymen and

A view of the scene after the Battle of Bloody Ridge was over. Courtesy of the Marine Corps University Archives.

said, "Make no matter about us dead. More will come. We never stop coming. Soon you will all be Japanese."

Kawaguchi had started his ill-omened venture with more than 6000 members of the emperor's finest five infantry battalions and supporting troops. Of these, some 400 had been lost off the islands of Santa Isabel and Savo as they were being barged to Guadalcanal. In addition, 800 were killed, wounded, or missing in the Battle of Bloody Ridge. In Japanese doctrine, any unit taking more than one-third casualties was considered *zenmetsu* (annihilated), and the two battalions attacking the ridge had suffered far worse than that. But so had the 1st Raiders and 1st Parachutists since their first landing in the Tulagi area. Both were ready for relief and evacuation.

Although our casualties were not heavy compared to those of the Japanese, the defenders of Henderson Field were too shorthanded to pursue the enemy. In three actions at the ridge, the grassy field by the Tenaru, and the other ridge beyond Kukum, we lost 59 dead and 204 wounded. But the division reserve had already been committed to the southern defense sector, relieving raiders and parachutists. Edson, for one, thought there were still some 2000 Japanese lurking in the rainforest to the south. In this, he was wrong. Kawaguchi's shattered brigade was withdrawing. It faced other enemies as deadly as Marines—exhaustion, heat, hunger, starvation, and malaria.

One Japanese battalion made its way back to Koli Point. The main body headed west. Abandoning weapons and many of their wounded, scrabbling for nourishments from forest plants as rice supplies ran out, they straggled in little groups over steep hills and through tangled ravines. Painfully they made their way south of Mount Austen and across the upper reaches of the Matanikau. The leading elements gained the beach at Point Cruz three days after the defeat at Bloody Ridge.

It should be noted that all enemy action on September 12–14 did not occur on the ridge itself. The Japanese made several attempts to support Kawaguchi's attacks on it with thrusts against the flanks of the Marine perimeter. On the east, enemy troops attempting to penetrate the lines of the 3rd Battalion, 1st Marines were caught out in the open on a grassy open plain and smothered by artillery fire; at least 200 died. On the west, the 3rd Battalion, 5th Marines, holding ridge positions covering the coastal roads, fought off a determined attacking force that reached its front lines, and B Company Pioneers withstood a probing attack on a ridge later dubbed "Pioneer Ridge" by Oka's battalion. Casualties were reported by the 3rd Battalion, 1st Marines and B Company Pioneers in both of these engagements, but they were light compared to the number sustained by the attacking force.

The victory at Bloody Ridge gave a great boost to the home front morale, and reinforced the opinion of the men ashore on Guadalcanal that they could take on anything the enemy could send against them. At upper command echelons, the leaders were not so sure the ground Marines and their motley air force could hold. Intercepted Japanese messages revealed that the myth of the 2000-man defending force had been completely dispelled. Sizable naval forces and two divisions of Japanese troops were now committed to conquer the Americans on

Guadalcanal. Cactus Air Force, augmented frequently by Navy carrier squadrons, made the planned reinforcement effort a high-risk venture. But it was a risk the Japanese were prepared to take.

It had been a close call at Bloody Ridge. Some 2000 Japanese, backed by another 1000 who never got into battle, had almost broken through Edson's 400 men. We can only speculate about what would have happened if several hundred Japanese soldiers had overrun the airfield. Their primary targets were the planes and artillery. They would have overrun the division command post, putting the Marine nerve center out of action at a crucial time.

In later years, Vandegrift recorded in his memoirs: "The Battle of the Ridge was the most critical desperate battle in the entire Guadalcanal campaign. Our own American officers and men proved themselves to be the best fighting troops that any service could hope to have. Had the Japanese assault been successful, we would have been in a pretty bad condition." Indeed, we would have been.

[9]   **After the Ridge**

After the Japanese were stopped at Bloody Ridge, Gen. Vandegrift decided to reorganize the defensive perimeter into new sectors for better control, giving the pioneers, engineers, and amphibious tractor battalions sectors along the beach. He had infantry battalions man the other sectors, including the inland perimeter previously held by the 1st Pioneers, engineers, and amphibious tractor battalions, and extend his western perimeter to the eastern bank of the Matanikau.

On September 22, the recently promoted Lt. Col. Samuel B. Griffith assumed command of the 1st Raider Battalion. He was told to chase the Japanese the hell out of the area from Kukum Beach to the Matanikau River, which meant that he would have to kill a great many of them. Griffith was given the 1st Raider command because recently promoted Col. Merritt "Red Mike" Edson had assumed command of the 5th Marine Regiment.

There was ironic justice in this reassignment. When Edson had been appointed to lead the 1st Raiders, early in 1942, he had skimmed off the cream of officers and NCOs in the 5th Marines to fill his own ranks. If the regiment had not measured up thus far on Guadalcanal, it was due in part to the 1st Raiders' raid on its best men. Now he would have the job of bringing up to the mark units he had earlier depleted.

The 1st Pioneer Battalion, under the command of Col. George Rowan, was moved over to the Kukum Beach area to provide support for the 1st Raider Battalion and the 5th Marines. We carried out our role as pioneers, and defended a strip of coconut plantation and strands of beach about one mile long. This same area was previously manned by the 5th Marines, and more recently by the 1st Raider Battalion.

Our new defensive position off Kukum Beach seemed like a nightmare landscape to me. Deep zigzagging fighting holes split the ground, and on the edge of the coconut grove and along the shoreline where charred remains of Japanese Zeroes, planes that had crashed and burned with their pilots. Manning this violent scene were bearded, gaunt, hungry, and lonely-looking Marine pioneers. They went about their assigned task with no outward signs of emotion.

After more than thirty consecutive days on the front line, we were a sorry-looking lot, with bloodshot eyes, unshaven faces, and dirty-tattered dungarees. Our socks were gone and our skivvies were rotting away. We needed this lull from battle and time in bivouac to recoup. The password was given out, and those men not manning the machine-gun positions on the perimeter fell asleep shortly after dusk. I was kept awake by grotesque shapes looming about me, and the unfamiliar Southern Cross glowing in the sky. A few men stirred after midnight to relieve themselves.

Planes were droning over the sea, but their motors suddenly cut off. A flare, drifting on a parachute, lit the camp with a weird green glow. We looked for planes, but the firing came at us from the sea, where the Japanese ships stood close in, unchallenged. The ships battered the pioneer battalion bivouac area in the coconut grove. Much of the grove was combed by flying fragments from exploding shells, and men screamed in agony. Trees were torn and broken, and many tumbled to the ground.

Daylight revealed a scene of smoldering fire and smoke throughout the bivouac area. Dazed and shell-shocked pioneers wandered aimlessly about the scattered debris. "Some G-damn rest area," a pioneer yelled. Another pioneer yelled, "Yeah, it's safer in the lines than this

The interior of the former Japanese barracks converted by the Marines into a hospital on Guadalcanal. Courtesy of the Marine Corps University Archives.

damned place. At least we could shoot back there. Here all you can do is get in a hole and pray." I thought the faces of the men in the grove this day were already much older than when we first landed.

At dawn, the dazed and sleepless men went about the grim task of treating the wounded and burying the dead. Unconfirmed reports were that three pioneers had been killed during the night. L. Cdr. Albert J. Bertram, the battalion surgeon, and his medical staff treated twelve wounded. Jeep ambulances moved the more seriously wounded to the division field hospital for further treatment.

This would be a day for digging in. Men who had not dug holes attacked the earth with any digging instrument they could get their hands on. Those who had already dug their holes would dig deeper. One thing we became experts at was digging foxholes and underground bunkers. I think mine was at least six feet deep. I recall some of my men making a comment that I would need a stepladder to get in or out. I didn't worry about getting in, but I did solve the problem of getting out by digging a step-up exit on one end. Usually, these hastily dug fighting holes were four feet deep and six feet wide, with an earthen sandbagged barricade to the front. They were essential in providing some degree of protection from enemy mortar or artillery fire and in fending off an enemy ground attack. Getting in and out of deep foxholes and underground bunkers proved to be one hell of a battle when the Japanese Sons of Heaven started lighting up the place with a searchlight and then lobbing in 5- and 6-inch shells during the middle of the night.

Throughout the daylight hours, the coconut grove rang to the strokes of the axes. Big coconut trees damaged by the shelling came crashing down. They were chopped into logs and dragged over wide sandbagged holes to make bunkers. Corrugated metal, old tarps, more sandbags—everything we could lay our hands on—were put on top of those bunkers. Japanese officers often wrote in their war journal that "Marines were actually not genuine jungle fighters because they always cut the jungle down." They were not wrong. Not only did we chop timbers to reinforce bunkers and gun positions, we cleared the jungle for fields of fire in front of our gun positions.

Another priority that day was to erect a company field mess hall where Sgt. Woodrow M. "Rip" Collins, our company mess sergeant, and field cook John C. Studdard, prepared our first hot meal in many days. As I recall, we had beef stew. I'm not sure if the beef came from a can or one of the scrawny cows I saw wondering through the coconut grove earlier. I didn't ask any questions, but I think one could safely assume that the horse they called "Reckless" tied to a nearby coconut tree was used in the roundup of the fresh beef.

When aging survivors of the Guadalcanal campaign get together, the story about Reckless is a topic of conversation. No one seems to know for sure where the horse came from. Most likely he was one of the horses used by Capt. Charles Widdy, the Australian who managed the Lever Brother's Plantation on the island prior to the Japanese occupation. Two members of the 1st Pioneer Battalion who claimed ownership of Reckless at different times provide this account.

Cpl. Phil Bessor, Headquarters Company Pioneers, obtained possession of the horse, complete with bridle, saddle, and rope, shortly after the pioneers moved into their new bivouac area off Kukum Beach. Within a week, Col. Rowan started to raise hell about the horse. He objected to the piles of horse manure around the command post. Battalion sergeant Maj. Paul Adams told Bessor that the horse had to go, so he sold it to Sam Russo in B Company Pioneers for fifteen bucks. Sam Russo admits that he purchased the horse from Bessor, but swears he only paid five dollars for the mighty' steed.

It is not known how the horse got the name "Reckless," but he was the only living creature on the island that didn't seek cover in a foxhole or bunker during enemy air raids, naval bombardments, and artillery and mortar attacks. The title seemed appropriate. Old Reckless did get nicked a few times by flying shrapnel, but after a little first aid administered by the company medic, he was raring to go again.

One of the things the horse was used for was to round up a few head of skinny cattle that roamed among the palm groves. The British abandoned the cattle when they left the island. Marine pioneers had high hopes that a do-it-yourself round-up and slaughter operation would add fresh meat to their meager food supply. A call went out for former cowboys to round up the beef and for our company mess sergeant and for his butchers to do their thing. The system for obtaining fresh meat was just swinging into high gear when it was abruptly stopped. After a number of reported food poisoning incidents attributed to the slaughter and preparation of fresh beef under less-than sanitary-conditions, Operation Slaughterhouse was ordered out of business.

Another pioneer who recalled Reckless is Roy Walters, who was a lieutenant at the time. He said: "I don't remember who owned the

When the Japanese took to the hills in the Solomons on August 7, 1942, they left herds of fine horses. During the calm between battles the Marines held roundups in true Western style, putting the horses back to work. Courtesy of the Marine Corps University Archives.

horse, but I do recall that I had shared riding privileges that I exercised quite frequently. I rode him bareback at a gallop around the coconut grove whenever we had a little free time between combat support operations, air raids, and shelling attacks."

At our new bivouac site at Kukum Beach, we were able to enjoy a hot meal each day. That was a special treat considering what we had to eat while deployed in the front lines along the Lunga. There the only food we had after the C-rations ran out was from the bags of rice we captured from the Japanese. I recall that for several days, we were fed a steady diet of captured rice for breakfast, captured rice for lunch, and captured rice for supper. Some of this rice was ridden with boll weevils. But when you're starving, you begin to look at those insects not as weevils, but as a source of protein.

On the afternoon of September 23, we were to enjoy another long-awaited treat. A truck from division came by to drop off a pile of gray canvas sacks at our company command post. It was the first mail to reach the troops since we landed on Guadalcanal. Each man seemed happy at the mere thought of getting mail. It was as if you had given him a hundred dollar bill. That evening was an orgy of reading. Most of the men had three or four letters each. They set about in circles; besides reading them several times to themselves, they read pieces of letters to one another. Their letters from home seemed to give the men a sense of hope and strength to survive.

Later that evening in a short V-mail letter to my mother, I wrote, "I did not forget to get down on my knees and say a silent prayer, thanking God for helping me to live through the first day ashore and ask for his help in the long and bitter days of combat that were to follow." I made a promise to myself: "If I live through this war, I'm going to find an isolated farm somewhere and spend the remainder of my life in peace and quiet." (In reality, this would have to wait until after two more wars, Korea and Vietnam, and until my retirement from the Corps in 1971, some thirty years later.)

That night the war stood still for a moment as my thoughts returned to home and my family. Prayer and old-time gospel music was woven into the fabric of my life. By closing my eyes and listening, I was immediately transported back in time to an old wooden front porch attached to a farmhouse with a rusty tin roof. In my mind I could hear my father playing his harmonica and see my mother wearing her faded gingham

This V-Mail letter form was used most exclusively because it was the only writing material readily available at the time on Guadalcanal.

apron. Her weathered hands stripping and breaking beans as she tapped her foot in tune to the ancient hymn, "Shall We Gather at the River." My father could really play that mouth harp.

It was thought that our new bivouac site at Kukum was a quiet sector and we would not see much action, that it would provide the men a chance to relax and release the tension of battle. That proved to be a false assumption on our part. After being subjected to a daily dose of bombing and shelling attacks, the Marine pioneers were quick to dub that area "Impact Center West."

The pioneers were on the far end of Henderson Field's runway, located on the northwest side in the direction of the Japanese air base at Rabaul. Consequently, the Japanese bombers' approach to the target

"Big One Coming." Drawing by Capt. Donald L. Dickson. Courtesy of the Marine Corps Historical Center.

runway was directly overhead. In fact, they had already released their bomb load three miles out as they normally came over at an altitude of 20,000 feet and a speed of 265 mph. The bombs came whistling downward in about forty-five seconds and arched directly over the pioneers' bivouac area. Even though the main target was Henderson Field, we got our share of them, at least the ones that fell short.

The worst time in a bombing attack is the moment when you can hear the bombs coming down. You feel helpless. You unconsciously pull your helmet down over your ears, and you think very intensely of the fact that it's purely a matter of chance whether or not you will be hit. You also think about those who have been critically wounded or killed during previous bombings, and in your imagination you suffer the shock of similar wounds. While your mind is racing through these thoughts, your ears are unconsciously straining to gauge the closeness of the bombs from the swishing sound they make.

At the time of our arrival at Kukum, the Japanese had virtually uncontested day and night control of the waters around Guadalcanal. Enemy submarines surfaced and plied back and forth about 8000 yards offshore. We watched with a feeling of indignation as these menaces from the sea, with their Japanese battle flag flying atop the conning tower, boldly patrolled the waters off Kukum Beach. Out of complete frustration, the Marine pioneers manning gun positions and operating in the beach area would fire at the enemy submarines. Results were disheartening, hardly justifying the expenditure of ammunition, which was already in short supply. A battery of 5-inch coastal guns of the 3rd Defense Battalion kept the submarines at a respectful distance, far beyond the range of rifle and machine-gun fire.

It didn't take the Japanese long to realize that they had very little opposition, and they then began a daily harassment routine. In midafternoon, Japanese planes would fly overhead in tight V-formation and drop a string of bombs. As darkness set in, just one plane would appear, dropping flares and a bomb, then disappear. It was followed by another and another throughout the night. Those bombings did little damage except to the nerves of exhausted Marines, who yearned to sleep. These nightly menaces from the air were given nicknames. A single-engine nocturnal visitor, usually a floatplane, was "Louie the Louse," and a two-engine night bomber was "Washing-Machine Charlie."[1]

Almost every night, Washing-Machine Charlie harassed us. He would fly over our bivouac area and drop one or two bombs. He never hit anything of value, except the one time he hit the mess storage tent, scattering over the area what little food we had. Almost every night, too, destroyers and submarines shelled us from the sea. We learned to sleep through most of it.

One night, no sooner had we fallen asleep, than a floatplane, "Louie the Louse," flew over. He circled back and dropped flares on us. They were weird colors: orange, blue, and pink. Nobody moved. The flares lit the area up so brightly that you could read a newspaper. I felt sure the pilot did it so the Japanese forward of our defensive perimeter could see well enough to attack us. There were plenty of Japanese in the area. But all they did that night was fire a burst of machine-gun fire at us about every thirty minutes.

The sights and sounds of war became a part of our daily routine. We'd hear these explosions most any time of the day or night, and the concussion would shake the ground. I'd hear an explosion and some-body would say, "There goes another one!" Sleep? Forget it. The constant shelling from the sea and bombing from the air kept us awake at night. We never knew when they were going to come. It's a terrible feeling, just sitting there in a foxhole, watching the bombs dropping all around you. It left us feeling helpless, and the Japanese were really giving us hell then.

Despite the daily pounding by Japanese planes and naval gunfire, the pioneers made an effort to maintain their senses of humor. A widely told story related how Col. George R. Rowan, our battalion commander, was riding in a jeep at night on Guadalcanal along the coastal road during the period of nightly shelling. The jeep's head-lights had been covered with flat paint, with narrow slits to let slivers of light show. Every few minutes a voice would come out of the dark-ness: "Turn off them G--damn lights." After a while, Cpl. Fletcher W. "Shorty" Sanders, the young driver, at the end of his patience, bel-lowed back: "I can't! I'm driving the G--damn colonel!"

Although our bivouac area was infested with mice and rats, the most loathsome creatures we had to content with were the damned stinking land crabs. They were everywhere. Their size ranged from a few inches to more than a foot across. Those ugly, ravaging plunderers hid by day and roamed at night. Before putting our boondockers on each morning, we shook them to make sure those creatures hadn't crawled into them overnight. If we didn't, we'd be apt to get one hell of a nasty bite.

Anything stored or left standing without surveillance was not safe from those scavengers. U.S. mailbags and anything else that had already been opened became their special domain. Packages from home were ripped open, shredded, and devoured by the land crabs. What they didn't finish, the ants carried away. We were only able to get rid of the land crabs by stepping on them or pounding them with our bayonets and entrenching tools. After they were squashed, we had to shovel them up and bury them in a hurry. Dead land crabs in Guadalcanal's hot humid environment emitted a nauseating stench.

The stinking crabs were not the only loathsome creatures we had to deal with on Guadalcanal. One morning I woke up covered with damned red ants. While some of my men got a good laugh out of my reaction to them, I didn't see anything humorous about the ordeal. Not only did their bite hurt like hell, I ended up having to shave off my month-old, well-cultivated, and self-admired beard to get rid of those miserable creatures. I shaved my face, but left my mustache on. One of my men made the remark shortly after I shaved, "Hey, Sarge, you don't look rough and ready without your beard. Your face looks more like a 'shave-tailed' second lieutenant." My responses to that clown was, "Yeah, have you every seen a 'shave-tailed' second lieutenant with a mustache?" The only consolation about that whole ordeal was that I still had my mustache to enhance my image as a seasoned jungle fighter.

This breather in bivouac provided us with the time to clean and repair our weapons, as well as an opportunity to evaluate their capabilities and limitations, following the time-honored tradition of all armies to discard surplus equipment. Most Marines were proud of their marksmanship with the bolt-action Springfield '03, the Browning automatic rifle, and the Colt automatic .45 pistol. The venerable Springfield kicked like a mule but its well-aimed rounds would have impact on an enemy 500 yards down range. The reliable Browning would become a faithful friend on many jungle patrols or night defensive fire engagements with the enemy.

The Reising a .45 submachine gun was made in two different models, the 50 and the 55. The Model 50 had a full wooden stock and a

During a lull in the fight, a Marine machine-gunner takes a break for coffee, with his submachine gun on his knee and his .30-caliber light machine gun in position. Courtesy of the Marine Historical Center.

compensator attached to the muzzle, a device that reduced the upward muzzle climb from recoil. The Model 55 had a shorter barrel and no compensator. Its use was primarily by parachutists, tank crews, and others needing a compact weapon. Both versions of the Reising fired .45-caliber ammunition, the same as the Colt automatic pistol and the Thompson submachine gun.

The Reising submachine gun didn't have too many friends in the 1st Marine Division, especially in the 1st Raider and 1st Parachute Battalions, considering that's where a majority of the machine guns went. As we evaluated our equipment, raiders and para-Marines figured it was a good time for them to toss the ridiculous Reising submachine gun. What a lemon, a real piece of junk. The Reising's major shortcoming was its propensity for jamming. This was due to both a design problem in the magazine lips and the fact that magazines were made of soft sheet steel. The steel used allowed excessive rust to form in the tropical humidity of the Solomon Islands. The weapon's safety mechanism didn't always work, and if the butt was slammed down on the deck, the hammer would set back against the mainspring and then fly forward, firing a chambered cartridge. The design allowed the entry of dirt into the mechanism, and close tolerances caused it to jam. It doesn't matter how many bullets a weapon can fire per minute, if it cannot fire when you want it to. Then it isn't much good.

The Reising design flaws made it unreliable under combat conditions. The machine guns failed to function with alarming regularity, and a number of them were discarded on Tulagi, Gavutu, and Guadalcanal. The Reising was withdrawn from use before the end of the war when other submachine became available. In its place came the Tommy gun, firing twenty- or thirty-round clips. I got hold of a Thompson, a real submachine gun, while the pioneers were taking part in the mop-up operation during the Battle of Bloody Ridge. The Tommy gun, with its full-automatic capability, made it well suited for firefights in jungle warfare. It became my choice of weapon for the remainder of the campaign.

While the Reising submachine gun proved to be a dud, we were quick to appreciate the value of the Browning automatic rifle, the good old workhorse of World War I vintage. It proved to be an excellent weapon to develop and sustain the desired base of fire. Regardless of the size of the fire team, the Browning always occupied the key spot. The .30-caliber light and heavy machine guns both proved to be effective in defensive positions, but had certain draws-backs in operations, such as combat jungle patrols.

The overall weight of the Browning .30 caliber, 1917 water-cooled heavy machine gun with its tripod was 85 pounds. This made it cumbersome and difficult to carry through the jungle. The light machine gun had a tendency to overheat during sustained automatic fire and required frequent barrel changes. Each weapon had a cyclic rate of fire of 400 to 500 rounds per minute. Proficiency with the Browning air-cooled light machine gun, however, required the discipline that could only come from long practice.

The enemy on Guadalcanal would soon learn that a Marine marksman armed with a Springfield '03 rifle is a dangerous man at a great distance. Many tend to forget the range of such a rifle and the tremendous power of its bullet. The Springfield was easy to clean in a battle zone and would seldom clog due to dirt. The bolt could be removed and cleaned quickly, in just a matter of seconds, which is more than can be said for the more complex weapons.

After each patrol or combat engagement, I field-stripped my rifle and cleaned everything thoroughly to remove dirt or moisture. The metal parts received a light coating of rifle oil, while the wooden stock was hand-rubbed with boiled linseed oil. That rifle never failed me and was in better condition when I turned it in—after obtaining a Thompson submachine gun—than when it was issued to me at Parris Island in January 1940.

Initially, I didn't carry a sidearm on Guadalcanal. My only weapon was the '03 rifle. This situation soon changed. During our first company combat patrol along the Lunga River, Lt. Harrell P. "Dusty" Rodes, my platoon commander, was seriously wounded and had to be evacuated off the island. I was allowed to keep the .45-caliber pistol he carried, and it became my sidearm for the remainder of the Guadalcanal campaign. It was my constant companion. I lived with that pistol. I ate with that pistol. I slept with that pistol. It was never out of my sight. If it were not in its holster, it was close enough that I could reach it. I carried that pistol with confidence—and in fear.

By the time we encountered Japanese soldiers on Guadalcanal, we were well aware that we were up against the best jungle fighters in the world. Action reports coming in from the Tulagi and Gavutu operations confirmed the fact that the Japanese soldier was a ruthless and

"Marines' Best Friend." Drawing by Capt. Donald L. Dickson. Courtesy of the Marine Corps Historical Center.

dangerous foe who would never stop trying until killed or crushed. That is one reason why Japanese corpses were piled high along the Tenaru River, atop Bloody Ridge, and in front of gun positions in the Guadalcanal jungle.

By the middle of September, we knew a lot about Japanese soldiers that wasn't contained in any training manual. They were very sly, using camouflage to conceal themselves as they moved around in the jungle.

A Marine dressed in the garb of a Japanese sniper demonstrates how a sniper would ascend a palm tree on Guadalcanal. To assist his climb, he uses climbing spikes, which tie onto his field shoes and ease the climb. He is also wearing clothing designed to blend into the fronded treetop. Courtesy of the Marine Corps Historical Center.

They were also good snipers. Many of the Japanese were equipped with tree spurs made of strong steel wire, which they used to shinny up the smooth boles of the palm trees to the fronded tops to get in position for sniping. Enemy snipers were especially effective at promoting terror. Anyone who served in the jungles of Guadalcanal will attest to this fact. Hidden in the fronded tops of palm coconut trees or other camouflaged surroundings, the Japanese snipers were feared as much or more so than the deadly booby traps placed to impede our advance on the ground.

Japanese soldiers were equipped and outfitted to meet the clawing jungle growth with two pair of trousers—not one—with heavy shirts, gloves, and cloth-covered helmets that made no sound when they brushed against tangled trees and vines. They wore soft clover, hoof-type, two-toed, rubber-soled shoes called *tabis*. The big toe fit into one compartment, and in his progress through the jungle, the Japanese soldier could feel any object beneath his feet that might roll or twigs that might snap and thus reveal his presence.

Japanese equipment in use on Guadalcanal was well adapted to jungle fighting. The Japanese had no artillery or tanks on the island during the early phase of the campaign, but they had mortars, automatic arms, rifles, hand grenades, and knives. The short, mildly recoiling, and easy-handling Arisaka Scout Type 38 Carbine, with chambered-in 6.5-mm rounds, had open sights and scope and was a favorite weapon for the Japanese sniper. The trigger on the Arisaka rifle was two-stage with plenty of over-travel.

Another distinctive Japanese weapon was the Model 89 50-mm mortar. Popularly known as the "knee mortar" to the Marines, it was light and easy to employ. The mortar's nickname was derived from its distinctive concave base plate that enabled it to be mounted in the ground, on a log, or on a fallen tree, as a Marine on Guadalcanal painfully discovered after having his leg shattered. Effort were swiftly undertaken in the field to educate all combat troops in the safe and proper handling of these very useful weapons.

The Japanese hand grenades were designed to injure and stun the enemy, but lacked the force that would make them dangerous to the Japanese soldier, who followed them closely to come to grips with the stunned opponent. They could be used at short range. Our own pineapple-shaped, serrated fragmentation grenades, by contrast, were more effective, and the man who threw one must be far enough away or it would blast him and his antagonist at the same time. We took them out of their cases by the hundreds, pulled the pins, and threw them downhill into the noise below. They wrought havoc and a shrill chorus of shrieking arose.

The Japanese proved themselves to be ruthless, treacherous, fanatically brave, and thoroughly skillful. As Gen. Vandegrift said, "In order to meet them successfully in jungle fighting, we shall have to throw away the rule book of war and go back to the tactics used during the French and Indian Wars."

If the exhausted pioneers hoped to rest and refresh themselves in a peaceful coconut grove east of the Matanikau for long, then they were mistaken, for there was still work to be done and battles to be fought. We performed pioneer support task during the day and when darkness finally fell, we manned fighting positions on the perimeter. Most of the Japanese attacks came in the hours of darkness, where they had a distinct advantage in training, equipment, and experience.

By the time we arrived at Kukum Beach, the application of military explosives had become the preoccupation of my demolition assault squad. My work with explosives continued until I was generally accepted as the battalion demolition expert. Neither antitank nor antipersonnel mines were available, and while there was no substitute for these, the ingenuity of the pioneer demolition specialist to fabricate these items from existing materials met an urgent need. The method used would not pass muster with any ordnance safety inspector, and I always warn others when I talk about this technique not to attempt it themselves.

The first step was to send out my best scroungers to moonlight requisition empty 5-inch shell cases, cement mix, nails, nuts, and bolts. The next step was to assign two smashers to pulverize cast TNT blocks with wooden mallets. Then our packers would pack the loose explosives into the empty shell cases primed with prima-cord and cap off the open end with mortar and fuse that was detonated remotely. Antipersonnel mines and booby traps were fabricated the same way, except that shrapnel-producing metals, such as nails, nuts, and bolts, would be inserted with great care inside the empty shell casing along with the explosives.

This endeavor to construct homemade mines in a combat environment was a dangerous undertaking that was performed only in a defilade site some distance from the company bivouac area. Needless to say, only volunteers worked on the assembly line in this operation. Once the mines were fabricated, they were stored temporarily in a nearby explosive magazine.

My assault demolition squad was called on to lay what I believe were the first antitank and personnel mines used in the South Pacific theater in World War II. We laid approximately 500 improvised mines, which enabled us to partially cover a strand of beach that Gen. Vandegrift didn't have men to cover.

We also spent a number of days attached to the 5th Marines, where we deployed improvised antipersonnel mines forward of their defensive positions. While there, we assisted and instructed units on the lines in the use of hand grenades as booby traps. One of our problems with grenades on Guadalcanal was that they were painted yellow—the color used in stateside training. We repainted them olive green and hung them on wires strung between trees to dry.

While attached to the 5th Marines, Col. Edson expressed his concern about enemy tanks crossing the sand spit at the mouth of the Matanikau River. I advised him that I could come up with some improvised bangalore torpedoes (a piece of metal tubing filled with high explosives) and install them like land mines fused to be control detonated from our position on the east bank of the river. As I recall, his comment was, "Lets get it done!"

The operation, dubbed "Bangalore Torpedo," got under way early the following morning. Our mission, simply stated, was to advance to the Matanikau and mine the sand spit at the mouth of the river. The sand spit, which had already soaked up a considerable amount of Marine blood, provided the only east-to-west route for tanks, artillery, and wheeled vehicles. First Lt. Warren S. Sivertsen, who was leading the patrol, was one of the most admired and respected officers in the 1st Pioneer Battalion. His expertise was primarily intelligence and planning. He served on the battalion staff and seemed to have a knack for coming up with "missions impossible."

My twelve-man demolition assault squad from B Company Pioneers formed the nucleus of the force. A radioman and two wiremen from battalion communication, two men from the battalion intelligence section, and a medical corpsman augmented it. Each man was armed to his own taste and heart's content. Most carried rugged bolt-action Springfield rifles. A few had Thompson submachine guns, an automatic or semiautomatic firearm with a short barrel and a stock, fired from the shoulder or hip. Two men in the demolition assault squad carried Browning automatic rifles. Almost all carried knives and bayonets, slung from their belts, fastened to their packs, or strapped to their legs. Some carried pistols, and their pockets bulged with grenades. Others who were not satisfied with one bayonet carried two. Communication and demolition specialists carried the tools of their trade in special leather carrying cases attached to their belts.

We moved out from the pioneer bivouac area at Kukum into the tall coconut grove and then down the worn road winding like a puzzle toward the beach. We swung left and marched west along the coast in the direction of the Matanikau. The palms thinned out as we reached the wire at the outmost area of our perimeter. The guard at the A Company Pioneer outpost warned us that there were Japanese snipers ahead. From here we proceeded with caution, keeping our eyes to the ground constantly, nervously scanning the undergrowth on our left. Knowing that there might be snipers in your midst makes you nervous, but it was beneath our dignity to fall on the ground and crawl. We ended up walking along, feeling like clay pigeons on a skeet range.

Although the distance of one and three-quarter miles between Kukum and the mouth of the Matanikau River was not great, our column was slowed by the sluggish pace of the men in my demolition squad who were hand-carrying twelve improvised bangalore torpedoes with '03 rifles slung across their shoulders. It was midday by the time we reached the 1st Raiders' encampment near the mouth of the

Matanikau River. We needed a break. We chowed down on C- rations and a canteen cup of hot coffee, courtesy of the raiders' field mess.

While the men were on break, I accompanied 1st Lt. Sivertsen to a meeting at the 1st Raider Battalion command post. We discussed our mission with Maj. Kenneth Bailey, the battalion executive officer. He agreed to provide machine-gun fire support from positions already in place on the east bank. He also advised that a half-track would be available on call. (The half-track was officially known as LVT, landing vehicle tractor. The front part of the vehicle has regular trucks wheels, the rear runs on tractor treads. Mounted with a 75-mm gun, the half-track and its seven-member crew were very effective against tanks, and its .50-caliber air-cooled machine gun was likewise effective against enemy aircraft and personnel.)

Our rested patrol was reformed and we pushed ahead. We moved cautiously between bursts of firing until we could see the river and the curving spit of gray sand that closed it's outlet into the sea and the shadowy coconut grove across the river where the Japanese were positioned. The word was passed to hold it up.

I was crouching behind a large mangrove tree when Sivertsen, looking quite calm and walking erect, came over. He apparently wasn't at all afraid of the sniper fire. He looked at me and said, "Hondo, now it's all up to you. You know what we have to do. Let's get 'er done." I said. "Aye, aye, Sir." He was the only officer in the 1st Pioneer Battalion who ever called me by my nickname, "Hondo." We had established a strong bond, and we both respected and trusted each other.

At this point, the patrol split up into two groups. I was to lead a group that included the demolition assault squad and two wiremen out to the sand spit at the mouth of the Matanikau. While the improvised bangalore torpedoes were being buried as antitank mines in a zigzag pattern, the wiremen laid a trunk line back to a control bunker on the east bank of the river so the improvised mines could be detonated remotely. The other group, which included the radioman, two men from the intelligence section, and the medical corpsman, remained with 1st Lt. Sivertsen at the control point on the east bank near the mouth of the river. At this position, Sivertsen maintained radio contact with the raider's command post and coordinated operation bangalore torpedo.

My group moved across the river's mouth, where a gray sand spit thrust through the shallows toward the enemy. To our right was the sea. To our left was a tangle of growth on the west riverbank that extended to a thick coconut grove. We had barely begun our mine-laying operation when enemy machine-gun fire exploded from the grove. The Japanese were positioned along the riverbank, totally camouflaged in the underbrush, not more than fifty yards away.

To this day, I don't know how all of us got out of there alive. I quickly sized up the situation and yelled, "Let's get the hell out of here!" "Take cover behind the coconut logs to your right." The bullets were literally coming through our legs and hitting our heels as we darted for cover. If those Japanese machine-gunners had been able to shoot a little higher, they would have had us all.

Once we reached some cover behind the coconut logs, I realized that I had been hit. I felt my heel sting and looked down to find that half of my shoe heel had been shot off and that blood was oozing through the heel of my sock. While the coconut logs that had washed up on the sand spit provided some cover, we were in an untenable position. I never felt so helpless in my life. We were being heavily fired upon and could see little gushers of water and puffs of sand where the bullets from the automatic weapons hit all around us. Yet we couldn't return fire because we couldn't see a damn thing from our defilade position.

Tom Shields, one of the wiremen sat on the ground, repeating over and over again; "Oh my God, I've been hit! I'm hit! I'm hit! It's my leg. They got me in the leg." However, it was only a flesh wound and he calmed down once the team member who hunkered down next to him removed the belt from his trousers and used it as a tourniquet to stop the bleeding.

I was concerned that the Japanese would start lobbing a few mortar rounds our way because we presented a prime target bunched up there like a flock of sheep. The covering force on the east bank finally suppressed the enemy machine-gun fire. Once the Marine half-track moved into position to lay down a base of protective fire, my group, bringing our walking wounded with us, joined 1st Lt. Sivertsen and the remainder of the patrol on the east bank of the Matanikau River.

When we arrived on the east bank, Sivertsen observed that I was bleeding from a foot wound. He said to me, "Hondo, you'd better get that taken care of." He yelled for the corpsman, and John "Doc" Moore came running. He cleaned the heel area and applied a sterile gauze compress and a tight bandage where I got nicked. That stopped the bleeding and allowed me to continue my role in the operation. Doc Moore also treated Tom Shields, but because his wound was more serious, he recommended that Tom be evacuated to the field hospital for further treatment.

It really pissed me off to learn that that the mission was being considered as too risky and might be aborted. I could not believe that after what we had gone through and done, and after sustaining casualties, they would even consider aborting the mission. Just because we failed once didn't mean that we shouldn't try again. We still needed what we had sought—the antitank mine field at the mouth of the Matanikau River.

Lt. Sivertsen became somewhat impatient with my persistent attitude. He finally said, "Enough!" With that, I made no further effort to convince him that we should go back to the sand spit and get the job done. But my persistence must have had some influence, for a short time later he informed me that the mission was still a go. He slapped me on the back and said, "Go get 'em, Tiger," and we did. That time, two Marine half-tracks were deployed to provide mobile fire support, which the enemy decided not to challenge.

There have been several recorded versions of how Japanese tanks were destroyed while trying to cross the sand spit during the ensuing Matanikau battles. That would certainly indicate that antitank mines destroyed or disabled some of them. Guadalcanal veteran CPHM John F. Moore recalls that while on patrol along the Matanikau River during an offensive operation, he saw the lead tank in a Japanese column blown apart by the improvised antitank mines we placed on the sand spit at the mouth of the river. One large section of the tank's left track was blown at least fifty feet into the ocean when the mine exploded. The use of improvised bangalore torpedoes as land mines during the Guadalcanal campaign was not the first such use in modern warfare. Confederate 8- and 10-inch Columbia artillery shells, called "torpedoes," were used in a similar manner in the Peninsula Campaign at Yorktown during the Civil War.[2]

Doc Moore, who was a pharmacist's mate first class at the time, was one of the most admired and respected medical corpsman in the pioneer battalion. He constantly volunteered to go out on patrol and was willing to expose himself to enemy fire in order to treat wounded Marines and pull them to a safe area. Navy medical corpsmen like John Moore were among the most courageous men on Guadalcanal. They ran many times into enemy fire to save a life, with nothing in their hands but a first aid kit. To do that takes plenty of guts. All the naval hospital corpsmen that I knew in the war were a credit to the Marine Corps. John Moore, now deceased, was among the best.

Another preoccupation of my demolition section was dealing with a variety of unexploded Japanese ordnance. This ordnance included bombs that failed to detonate on impact, torpedoes that ran aground on the beach, artillery projectiles, mortars, and grenades. Placing a counter-charge and detonating it from a safe distance destroyed most

"The Unspoken Bond." This memorial at the National Naval Medical
Center, Bethesda, Maryland, is dedicated to the hospital corpsmen
who served with the Marines in the Pacific during World War II. "Doc"
was the special comrade who pulled them to safety, patched their
wounds, and shared their foxholes. Established in war and ennobled
in peace, this bond will always endure. Photograph by Sam Y. Kim.
Courtesy of the National Naval Medical Center.

of the dud-fired ordnance encountered. In some cases, the fusing
mechanism had to be removed by hand. This proved to be extremely
hazardous because, at that time, we had not been trained in the
deadly art of defusing Japanese ordnance. All we could do was say a

prayer and hope for the best. There was no way of telling whether this unexploded ordnance contained a time-delay or antidisturbance fusing device, which, when activated, could blow you into a million unrecognizable pieces.

I recall one incident on Guadalcanal when the only option was to disarm a Japanese torpedo that missed its target and beached. When asked by the battalion operation officer if I could do the job, my immediate inclination was not only to tell him no, but "*Hell* no!" Discretion being the better part of valor, I simply told him that I didn't know a damned thing about Japanese torpedoes and suggested that we ask the Navy for assistance.

The Navy unit at Tulagi agreed to send over a rated torpedoman and the minelayer *Southmore*. While I can't speak for the Navy torpedoman who assisted me during the rendering-safe procedure, I recall my heart was beating like a tom-tom drum. Fear drained the strength from my body until I was near complete exhaustion. Marines do not openly express fear, but this time I was frightened and needed God's help. I prayed that he would guide our hands, as we were operating more on courage than skill. Our prayers were answered.

Once that eighteen-foot-long monster from the sea (with its 500-pound high-explosive warhead) was disarmed, it was hoisted aboard a small barge and towed across the channel to the naval base at Tulagi, where later it would undergo an analysis by a technical evaluation team from Pearl Harbor. The Navy and Marine commanders signaled a "well done" message.

I had a number of close calls while working with explosives and unexploded ordnance on Guadalcanal. One incident that stands out in my memory was when I was nearly buried alive. My demolition team was engaged in blasting a crater on a coral ridge where the 5th Marines new command center was to be located. After a series of blasts, we paused briefly to evaluate the results. I decided to let the other members of my team take a coffee break with a nearby 5th

Marines security unit, while I climbed down into the crater to measure its depth and width. As I began my exit, I heard the dull, throbbing roar of approaching enemy aircraft. By the time I reached the lip of the crater, the all too familiar sight of Japanese two-engine Mitsubishi Betty bombers appeared west of Savo Island. They were flying in a wide V-formation flight pattern that would take them directly over our position and onto their primary target, Henderson Field. At least that's what I thought at the time, but for some unknown reason one or more of the bombers jettisoned their bombs early. I recall looking up and seeing a string of bombs coming down directly overhead. From there on out everything is somewhat murky, I don't recall if I jumped back into the crater or if I was blown in by the blast of an exploding bomb. I do know that I literally had to be dug out after the attack and that I was a mess. I escaped with ruptured eardrums, temporary loss of sight, and initially experienced difficulty in walking. My equilibrium was shot all to hell.

As I recall, there were several reports of Marines being killed or wounded during this enemy air attack. By some miracle of God, I survived. I recall 1st Lt. Sivertsen, who was in the area shortly after the bombs exploded and supervised my recovery from the crater, asking: "Are you alright?" I said, "I can't see, Sir. I can't see." He said, "You'll be okay, Hondo." He clapped me gently on the back and said, "Doc Moore will take good care of you. You're going to be alright."

For several days my eyes were covered with some type of sulfur ointment bandage and I had to be led around the bivouac area by a seeing-eye volunteer. Later, while in Melbourne, Australia, I underwent eye surgery at the 4th Army General Hospital to remove scar tissue caused by flash burns. After the bomb explosion my eardrums felt like they had been lanced a hundred times. It is a wonder my hearing had not been impaired more. One Navy physician who examined me some years later told me that my eardrums were so scarred they resembled a "battlefield." Today, some sixty years later, I still have a constant ringing in my ears, which I characterize as a thousand crickets in my head. I wake up in the middle of the night with my mind silently screaming, "Mitsubishi! Mitsubishi! Mitsubishi bombers!"

By the end of August it was clear that the struggle for Guadalcanal was going to be long and bitter and that additional reinforcements would be required. Gen. Vandegrift continued to press for operational control of the 7th Marines left on the island of Samoa. The top Navy commanders, Adm. Ghormley and Adm. Turner, still favored developing a base at Ndeni in the Santa Cruz Islands as a backup for Guadalcanal or a fall-back position if Guadalcanal was lost. Vandegrift strongly opposed sending the 7th Marines to another island in the rear when they were so badly needed on the Canal. Even after Adm. Turner had agreed that the regiment was needed on Guadalcanal, he wanted to land it, not within the Lunga perimeter, but at Koli Point.

In the original plans for the Solomons operations, the 2nd Marine Regiment was slated to occupy Ndeni in the Santa Cruz Islands. But at Vandegrift's request, Adm. Turner released two battalions to help seize the Tulagi group. In consequence, most of the regiment was ashore when Turner had to pull out on August 9. Ndena had to be scratched as a target—temporarily. Col. John M. Archer, commander of the regiment, and about 1400 of his officers and men were still aboard the ships. They landed in Espiritu Santo, where they were ordered for the time being to reinforce the local garrison. Most of them would remain there until mid-September.

During his visit to Guadalcanal on September 12–13, during the Battle of Bloody Ridge, R. Adm. Turner personally saw what the Marines ashore were up against. Gen. Vandegrift later said he thought Adm. Turner's visit with the Marines ashore "had given him religion." Turner had gotten a dose of the normal ration of incoming shells during his stay at the division command post, dubbed "Impact Center South." Before he left Guadalcanal, the admiral promised to send reinforcements and to land them wherever Vandegrift said they were needed.

Gen. Kawaguchi had been ordered to seize the airfield before its defenders' reinforcement arrived. He failed. The 2nd Marines, the original floating reserve landed on September 14, followed four days later by the 7th Marines from Samoa. The arrival of the 1st Marine Division's third organic infantry regiment would turn a toehold into solid footing. The Japanese on the island were temporarily in disarray. More than 3000 fresh and well-trained troops would make it possible for the Marine command not only to strengthen the cordon around the airfield but to expand it and to pursue more vigorously the battle-scarred enemy to the west.

Shortly after Battle of Bloody Ridge, Gen. Vandegrift and his staff decided to move the command post back to its original site in the northwest corner of Henderson Field. The shift meant that his hard-worked communication personnel that had just finished laying reels of telephone wire to the spur of the ridge now must relay the network. For a week or two after the mid-September battle, there was a beehive of activity along the Lunga perimeter as units were shifted, supplies brought in by the 7th Marines were moved to the dumps, and the division nerve center was reestablished at Impact Center South.

The latest promotion list had resulted in a fistful of new colonels—more than the table of organization called for. Gen. Vandegrift had the unpleasant duty of deciding which ones to send home for reassignment to other units where they were needed. The departure of the chief of staff, Col. William C. James, was no surprise. It was obvious from the outset that Col. Thomas was the guiding mind and driving force of the 1st Marine Division. Clearly, he was the staff officer on whom the general leaned most heavily. He was given a field promotion to full colonel and made chief of staff. Twining succeeded him as assistant chief of staff. Another new full colonel, whom Gen. Vandegrift decided to keep on Guadalcanal, was William J. "Wild Bill" Whaling, executive officer of the 5th Marines.

On September 18, the long awaited 7th Marines, reinforced by the 1st Battalion, 11th Marines, and other division troops arrived at

Guadalcanal. The Navy had accomplished its mission—the 7th Marines had landed—but at a terrible cost. Japanese submarines hit the Navy covering force for the American reinforcement and resupply convoys hard. The carrier *Wasp* was torpedoed and sunk. The mighty battleship *North Carolina* shuddered as a Japanese torpedo tore a big hole in her side.[3] She turned and went streaking south. The mighty ship took a hard blow but didn't come close to sinking. The *North Carolina* returned to Pearl Harbor, where the crew was greeted by bands and a surprise reception. After repairs, the ship rejoined the fleet. The destroyer *O'Brien* was hit so badly it broke up and sank on its way to dry dock. About the only good after the devastating Japanese torpedo attacks was that the *Wasp*'s surviving aircraft joined Cactus Air Force on Guadalcanal.

When the 7th Marines landed on Guadalcanal in September 1942, the campaign on that island already had been raging for several weeks. The hungry, haggard, hard-pressed men of the 1st Marine Division welcomed the new arrivals because the 7th Marine Regiment was a fresh, well-supplied, well-trained force that constituted a huge shot in the arm for the beleaguered defenders. The only thing the regiment lacked was combat experience.

During the movement to the Solomon Islands, word was passed among the Marines about the threat of enemy air attacks and the need for rapid unloading to get the vulnerable shipping away from the deadly waters around Guadalcanal. By the time the ships arrived off Lunga Point, the Marines aboard were keyed up and expecting the worst. The remainder of the day the Marines moved at a feverish pace to unload everything they could before the convoy departed that evening.

The arrival of reinforcements was a welcome sight for the Marines stranded on Guadalcanal. I went to the beach and saw a convoy of troop transports and cargo ships steaming into sight. Several warships provided a screen that could be seen on the horizon. All along the beach our weary veterans stood and watched the process pass. We had been talking about reinforcements and waiting for a long time, and there were boatloads after boatloads of them. They wore clean combat uniforms, new helmets, and talked tough and loud as they came ashore.

We knew that it would take some time for these men, as it had with us, to get rid of that loud surface bravado and develop the cool, quiet fortitude that comes with battle experience. But, at least the new arrivals were fresh and strong. We had less than a full division of men on Guadalcanal. It was said no troops would be taken out of this place, except by doing it feet first. We needed all the fighting men we could muster.

With the 7th Marines came tanks, an artillery battalion, engineers, medical and motor transport companies, aviation ground crews, and communication personnel. With more than 4000 officers and men, Col. Webb brought rations, gasoline, and post-exchange supplies. The latter included 20,000 small round aluminum boxes. In breakfast lines several days later, each Marine was issued Trojans gratis. With no women for miles, these condoms could not be used as a contraceptive, but they proved to be most effective for preserving such perishable items as matches, cigarettes, candy, and letters from sweethearts in the States. The men would also put them over the end of their rifle barrels to keep them dry and clean. We also received our first atabrine tablets. The bright yellow quinine pills were supposed to prevent malaria. We would take one a day.

Navy coxswain manning the Higgins boats bringing the Marines ashore were amazingly efficient souvenir hunters. With one, I swapped a box of Hershey's chocolate bars in exchange for a Japanese battle flag I removed from the body of a dead Japanese sniper during a patrol along the Lunga River. What a wonderful thing that was. I had to stretch them over a mighty big company headquarters group. They ate those candy bars like frogs eating flies, but I did manage to save a few bars for the skipper and myself. Marines on Guadalcanal didn't miss an opportunity to remove souvenirs from their dead or captured enemy.[4]

Shortly before dusk, the ships pulled out, carrying with them the remnants of the 1st Parachute Battalion. The departing para-Marines had been in the thick of it from the beginning. Although they were never afforded the opportunity of a combat jump, they had borne the brunt of the fierce fighting on Gavutu and fought courageously alongside the 1st Raider Battalion during the epic Battle of Bloody Ridge. The reason for the para-Marines' early departure was bluntly stated in Gen. Vandegrift's battle diary: "They desperately needed rest. . . . Their thinned ranks speaks more eloquently than words, they have suffered and endured."

Also departing aboard these ships were 162 wounded Marines, eight Japanese prisoners, and many of the older, senior officers picked, for the most part, in the order they had joined the division. They were now being sent back to the States. There they would provide a new level of combat expertise in the training and organization of the many Marine units that were forming. Col. George R. Rowan, our battalion commander, was one of the departing officers. I noted at the time that no one in the battalion came down to see him off. I guess it was because he was such a son of a bitch, they were glad to see him go. Maj. Robert G. Ballance, the battalion executive officer, assumed command of the 1st Pioneers Battalion.

A separate supply convoy reached the island at the same time as the 7th's arrival, bringing with it badly needed aviation gas, bombs and our first resupply of ammunition since D-Day. We witnessed a heartbreaking incident on the beach where the 7th was unloading. A Douglas dive-bomber was circling low overhead, presumably in a holding or landing pattern. Suddenly anti-aircraft guns on one of the ships opened fire. At least one other ship joined in, and the bomber began trailing smoke. The pilot headed toward the beach to crash-land, but ran into more fire. The stars on the plane's wings were plainly visible, but the newcomers refused to believe the plane was ours. When the poor devil crashed in the water, a great cheer went up from the new arrivals on the beach, who moments before had stampeded into the palms. Those of us who knew our own planes couldn't believe our eyes. We shouted, "Don't shoot, God damn it, it's *our* plane, it's *our* plane." But there was no stopping the firing until the plane splashed into the sea. A Higgins boat standing offshore brought in one badly shot-up member from the downed plane. The other, I suppose, was dead and went down with the plane.

As dusk approached, the 7th Marines settled into a temporary bivouac site in a coconut grove just behind the beach. There was no doubt they were now in the war. Many of the trees were shattered from bombardment; wrecked planes and vehicles lay scattered among the broken trunks; and hollow-eyed, scraggly Marine pioneers and men of the 3rd Defense Battalion stood watch on guns trained up to the sky or outward over a shoreline sprinkled with flotsam of sea battles. The word was passed for everyone to dig in, but most of the men were too exhausted and many unit leaders failed to supervise, probably due to a combination of fatigue and the onset of darkness.

Just after midnight the men of the 7th Marines were roused by enemy aircraft dropping flares to illuminate the target area, the airstrip next to their bivouac site. The ships opened fire. Marines without fighting holes hugged the ground or frantically scraped at the earth with helmets, bayonets, and bare hands trying to dig holes deep enough to get into. The shelling lasted for half an hour. In this baptism of fire, the 7th Regiment lost several men, both dead and wounded. Additional casualties were the result of friendly fire—the men were firing at an imaginary enemy in the darkness.

The trigger-happy 7th was the subject of much scorn and merriment among the rest of the division, though most of those who were laughing had acted the same way just a few short weeks ago. Word went out that Vandegrift expected the newly arrived unit commanders to be more aggressive in controlling friendly fire at night. Indiscriminate firing wastes ammunition, which was already in short supply.

Col. Lewis B. "Chesty" Puller, commander of the 1st Battalion, 7th Marines lost patience with the uncontrolled shooting. He passed the word that there would be no more firing at night without explicit orders from him. Marines were otherwise to rely solely on their bayonets. His angry reprimands helped instill calm. The problem gradually disappeared as the green troops of the regiment had the chance to taste actual combat, to get the feel of their weapons, to kill, to be fired at, to hear the noise of battle, and to get over their first fight. Before long, they would be amused by new arrivals, going through the same process of adjusting to war.

The value of the 7th Marines lay not only in the numbers of battalions it added to the division, but also in their size. All were close to full strength, while Vandegrift's other units were badly deflated by casualties and sickness. In addition, two of the battalion commanders, Puller and Lt. Col. Hanneken, provided the type of leadership Vandegrift desired. They were a welcome addition to the senior stalwarts on hand such as Col. Edson and Col. Whaling.

The division wasted no time in putting the 7th Marines to work. On September 19, the first day after landing, the 2nd and 3rd Battalions moved into the two southern sectors. They covered the area from the bank of the Lunga River running east to the flank of the 1st Marines, in position along Alligator Creek. It was flat ground blanketed by jungle, except in the center, where there was a low, north-south rise covered with kunai grass.

With most of his divisions assembled for the first time, Vandegrift was able to apply pressure on the Japanese still stubbornly hanging on the west bank of the Matanikau. But of those units landed originally, none could muster any where near full strength. Although battle casualties had not yet reached 1000 men, twice that number became noncombat casualties. Despite this fact, Gen. Vandegrift did not contemplate a purely passive attitude. He planned an active defense. With forces now available, he could both hold what he had and jab at the Japanese with limited but effective operations designed to keep the enemy off guard, off balance, and under constant strain.

Vandegrift now had ten infantry battalions, one understrength raider battalion, and five artillery battalions ashore; the 3rd Battalion, 2nd Marines, had come over from Tulagi also. He reorganized the defensive perimeter into ten sectors for better control, giving the pioneers, engineers, and amphibious tractor battalions sectors along the beach perimeter. Infantry battalions manned the other sectors, including the inland perimeter in the jungle. Each infantry regiment had two battalions on line and one in reserve.

Vandegrift also had the use of a select group of infantrymen who were training to be scouts and snipers under the leadership of Col. Whaling, an experienced jungle hand, marksman, and hunter, whom he had appointed to run a school to sharpen the division's fighting skills. As men finished their training under Whaling and went back to their outfits, others took their place and the Whaling group was available to scout and spearhead operations.

Now with the 19,200 Marines ashore on Guadalcanal, Vandegrift had enough men to expand his defensive scheme. He decided to seize a forward position along the east bank of the Matanikau River, in effect strongly outposting his west-flank defenses against the probability of strong enemy attacks from the area where most Japanese troops were landing. First, however, he was going to test the Japanese reaction with a strong probing force. Vandegrift had two reasons for striking the Japanese west of the Matanikau River. He wanted to break them up before they could cross to the east bank, from which they could punish Henderson Field with their artillery and prepare an assault on his line at Kukum, and Vandegrift wanted to occupy the east bank of the river himself.

[10] September Matanikau Action

The Second Matanikau was the first of such probing operations. This move was designed to break up an increasingly threatening concentration between Point Cruz and the Matanikau. On September 23, Vandegrift chose the fresh 1st Battalion, 7th Marines, commanded by the famous jungle fighter Lt. Col. Lewis B. "Chesty" Puller, to make a reconnaissance-in-force into the hills south and west of the perimeter. The scouting expedition was to end by September 26, on which date the 1st Raider Battalion, now under Lt. Col. Samuel B. Griffith, was to cross the Matanikau River at its mouth and march about ten miles farther west to the village of Kokumbona. The idea was that the raiders could set up a patrolling base there. All this was to be preliminary to Vandegrift's attack.

Puller's 1st Battalion, 7th Marines set out from the perimeter on September 23. Nothing was heard from him until the night of September 24. He reported meeting the enemy near grassy knoll (Mount Austen) about four miles south of the western half of the perimeter and losing seven men killed and twenty-five wounded in a sharp firefight that followed. Because of the rugged terrain, it required four men to carry back each of the stretchers on which eighteen of the wounded lay. This was one of the occasions when Puller was glad to be in touch with the division command post. He called for reinforcements.

Vandegrift sent the 2nd Battalion, 5th Marines forward to reinforce Puller and help provide the men needed to carry the casualties out of

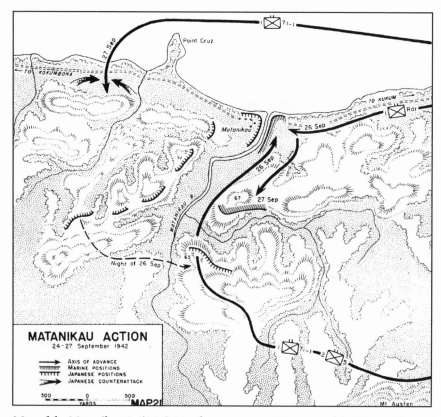

Map of the Matanikau Action, September 24–27, 1942. Courtesy of the Marine Corps Historical Center.

the jungle. Vandegrift told Puller he was on his own as far as continuing his mission or withdrawing. The wounded were placed in the care of two companies from Puller's own battalion under Maj. Otho Rogers, his executive officer, who would rejoin Puller's command three days later on the east bank at the mouth of the Matanikau River.

Now reinforced, Puller continued his patrol westward toward the Matanikau, where they found their crossing barred by heavy machine gun and mortar fire. Puller called for air and artillery support,

Evacuating wounded from the front with help of four litter bearers. Courtesy of the Marine Corps Historical Center.

but the Japanese were dug in. They were as tenacious and ready for a fight as he was. Hoping to force a crossing further downstream, Puller probed northward along the river gorge, drawing fire from the opposite bank all the way. He headed for the river's mouth. Again the two battalions ran into heavy fire and, as the four days allotted for the patrol ended, they gave up hope of gaining the other side. Although Puller had trained his troops well, the green unit did not get off to an auspicious start in its first combat engagement on Guadalcanal.

If the results were disappointing, the Puller probing operation had at least demonstrated that the Japanese were in considerable strength all along the Matanikau and were determined to hold the west bank. Vandegrift decided on a larger and more complicated effort to dislodge the defenders. By early evening hours of September 26, division operations had reached the hopeful conclusion that by committing a little more power, the enemy could be levered out of the positions he had so successfully defended during the morning. This concept was similar to the design of the August effort in the same area. As might have been anticipated, the action was to be attended by several of the difficulties that had beset the earlier operation. They were planned and conducted in total ignorance of the terrain and of the enemy situation.

By this time, the Japanese had more than 4000 fighting men on the line of the Matanikau and in reserve behind it. Some of them were hungry and ill, but reinforcements had just arrived and fresh troops were on the way. It was under these circumstances that division directed Col. Edson, now commanding the 5th Marines, to establish a command post near the mouth of the Matanikau and coordinate the propose operation.

Meanwhile, the 1st Raider Battalion, on its way to establish the patrol base at Kokumbona, had reached the vicinity of the firefight, and division directed Griffith to join with 1st Battalion, 7th Marines and 2nd Battalion, 5th Marines and to prepare for a renewal of the attack the next day. With this large provisional group now formed, Vandegrift sent Col. Edson up to take command of the expanded force.

On September 27, Griffith's understrength 1st Raiders were to do what Puller had been unable to do a few days earlier—force a crossing upriver. The raiders were to make their attempt near Jap Bridge.[1] At the same time the 2nd Battalion, 5th Marines were to cross the river near its mouth. Puller was named Edson's second in command for this operation. If the battle developed favorably, his own battalion, temporarily commanded by Maj. Otho Rogers, was to land with Higgins boats west of Point Cruz and hit the Japanese from the rear.

Nothing worked out as planned. The battalion of 5th Marines could not force a crossing at the river's mouth. Lt. Col. Griffith's raiders ran into a hornets' nest of Japanese that had crossed the Matanikau during the night to set up strong positions on the high ground overlooking the east bank of the river in the vicinity of Jap Bridge. The Japanese in these well-concealed defensive positions had put a stopper in the jungle bottleneck, which measured about twenty yards from the ridge. In a short but fierce fight, Lt. Col. Griffith was seriously wounded and the gallant Maj. Kenneth D. Bailey, who led them so brilliantly on another ridge, was killed. The Japanese kept the 1st Raiders pinned down and cut them up with mortars.

At that moment there occurred a communications muddle of major proportions. A series of garbled messages compelled both division and Lt. Col. Edson to conclude that the 1st Raiders were, indeed, across the river and ready to jump off toward the sea. Edson therefore ordered the 2nd Battalion to land as planned. Puller remained at the forward command post to assist in the overall operation. The plan was for the companies under Maj. Rogers to make an amphibious thrust at the Japanese left. They were to go west to the Kokumbona vicinity by boat, land there, and cut off the "defeated" enemy's retreat.

The Marines under Maj. Rogers shoved off just as the first of three waves of Zeroes and bombers swept overhead. The destroyer *Ballard* that was to deliver supporting fire was forced to flee. Still the Marines went west, but when they came ashore they were far short of Kokumbona. They were at Point Cruz, a small peninsula just west of the Matanikau and just north—behind—the Japanese left flank.

The Marines went in without radio communications, without naval gunfire. Before they had advanced 400 yards, the Japanese fell upon them from three sides. Fighting was vicious, and in less than five minutes Maj. Rogers and a half-dozen others were killed. The toll mounted alarmingly as the enemy swung to cut the battalion off from the beach. The situation of these Marines was critical. Lt. Col. Edson issued orders for them to pull out and asked for immediate air support. Now Vandegrift had three battalions in trouble and the last one was out of contact, the 2nd Battalion was trapped for a time behind enemy lines. The embattled Marines had spelled out "HELP" in the sand. A scout SBD dive-bomber spotted the plea.

On September 27, before a rescue effort could be put in motion, more than two dozen Japanese bombers launched an air raid over Henderson Field and along the Matanikau River, which formed the western edge of the perimeter, disrupting all division communications. Fortunately, Puller had not dallied. During the raid, he commandeered a boat and boarded Navy destroyer *Ballard*. With landing craft riding in wake, she moved at once to Point Cruz, established visual communication with the Marines surrounded on a kunai-covered knoll several hundred yards inland, and conducted a close-in boxing shoot, aiding the battalion in a fighting withdrawal down the corridor outlined by *Ballard*'s exploding shells. With them, Marines brought the bodies of twenty-four dead, and twenty-three wounded officers and men had to be carried as well.

The rescue force of landing craft moved with difficulty through Japanese fire, urged on by Puller, who accompanied the boats on the destroyer *Ballard*. The Marines were evacuated after fighting their way to the beach covered by the destroyer's fire and the machine-gun fire of a Marine dive-bomber overhead. Once the survivors of the embattled companies of the 2nd Battalion, 7th Marines got back to the perimeter, landing near Kukum, the 1st Raiders and 5th Marines battalions pulled back from the Matanikau. The confirmation that the Japanese would strongly contest any westward advance cost the Marines sixty men killed and more than a hundred wounded.

One Marine survivor of this ill-fated landing recalled:

> looking out on the Bay and seeing an old four stacker tin can, belching smoke headed toward the beach. Then I saw fire from the 5-inch guns, so I hit the ground. The destroyer fired salvo after salvo, hitting the coconut grove below us. We all let out a cheer. Trees were falling, Japanese were screaming, and we were yelling. Between the salvos, many of us stood up so we could get a better view.

Higgins boats engaged in the evacuation of a battalion of Marines trapped by enemy Japanese forces at Point Cruz, Guadalcanal, September 27, 1942. Painting by Bernard D'Andrea. Courtesy of the U.S. Coast Guard Historical Office.

After about thirty minutes, the firing stopped and I was ordered to bring down the rear guard of my Platoon. I remember laying down a base of fire to secure an area for the men to move through to the beach. The Higgins boats were already heading ashore to pick us up. I wondered if all of us would make it, or if the Japanese would cut us off. Col. Puller was aboard the destroyer and ordered the shelling which provided the survivors cover during the evacuation.[2]

Sgt. Robert Raysbrook, standing erect under heavy Japanese fire, repeatedly signaled *Ballard*'s officers that the Japanese stood between the Marine ridge and the beach. He later received the Medal of Honor, an award also posthumously conferred on Coast Guardsman Signal-man Douglas Munro, who led the landing craft to the beach. Munro was killed by enemy fire while firing a boat machine gun to protect embarking Marines. At this juncture, strafing planes appeared to cover a second wave of five evacuation boats, and just before dusk Puller's battalion arrived at Kukum Beach.

Meanwhile, Edson had ordered the raiders to withdraw. By midnight on September 27, all Marines were within the perimeter. The Second Matanikau, the name given to these series of blundering actions, exacted a toll of 267 killed and 125 wounded. Seventy-nine of these casualties were from Puller's battalion.

At the Second Matanikau, the Japanese thwarted Gen. Vandegrift's effort to gain control of the Matanikau River. In the process, a good portion of the 1st Battalion, 7th Marines (under the command of Puller's executive officer) was trapped for a time behind enemy lines. Only a daring amphibious withdrawal effort under fire saved the force from annihilation. Having suffered more than ten percent casualties (including the battalion executive officer an all three company commanders) at the end of ten days on the island, the morale of the 1st Battalion, 7th Marines was at a low ebb.

On September 30, unexpectedly, a B-17 carrying Adm. Nimitz made a landing at Henderson Field. The admiral made the most of the opportunity; he saw Edson's Ridge and talked to a number of Marines. He reaffirmed to Vandegrift that his overriding mission was to hold the airfield. Nimitz promised all the support he could give and, after awarding Navy Crosses to a sergeant and several of Marine officers, including Vandegrift, left the next day visibly encouraged by what he had seen. Nimitz characterized the Marines as "fatigued, but in high spirit." The second month on Guadalcanal ended with Marines on the ground bruised but still capable of more battles and with those in the sky steadily whittling away enemy air power.

[11] October Matanikau Battle

October was the month of the dreadful rains, the month of decisions, change, unending battle between men, ships, and airplanes, the month of the "Night of the Battleships," "Dugout Sunday," "Pistol Pete," and the month when the Marines on Guadalcanal still held on by the skin of their teeth.

By day, the Marines strengthened their line. They sent out patrols, rushed in supplies and troops, or flew from the airfield to break up those aerial attacks, which the enemy launched by day to clear the way for their nighttime movements. At night, we lay still in our holes, peering into the rain-swept darkness, knowing that destroyers were landing troops to the west or that the great, dark shapes were gliding into the bay and, at any moment, the silence might be shattered by the thundering of guns and the yelling of a new attack.

By the second week of October, it seemed things were not going too well for Vandegrift's Marines at the front. Edson's 5th Marines, or at least a part of them, had not yet reached the Matanikau. Japanese machine gun were still raising hell this side of the river. Edson told his company commanders that if they didn't clean them out before dark, they would be in trouble. They didn't, and they were. A deadly stalemate quickly developed. The Japanese hit them that night with knives and bayonets, and I Company was badly cut up. This hard-hit unit was relived by elements of the 1st Raider Battalion at 0500 on October 9.

One of the raiders called into battle said, "I suppose Edson thinks we are the only troops he can trust." A half-track also moved forward, blasting the Japanese machine-gun positions at short range with its 75-mm gun. It rained steadily and hard all day and well into the night. By daybreak, the awkward bridgehead had been established. Marines occupied the right bank, and this time division meant to hold it.

Two Marines who fought in this hellish battle—but would not fight again—were the Lenoir brothers. William W. and St. Clair Lenoir both served with me in I Company, 3rd Battalion, 5th Marines before I was reassigned to the 1st Pioneer Battalion. We were very good friends, and we often went on liberty together. Bill was killed, and St. Clair was seriously wounded when he went to his brother's aid during the battle of the Matanikau River.

Historian Henry I. Shaw Jr., in his commemorative series on Guadalcanal, gave a graphic account of the Marines' "Third Battle of the Matanikau," which occurred on October 7–9:

> The next Marine move involved a punishing return to the Matanikau, this time with five infantry battalions and the Whaling group. Whaling commanded his men and the 3rd Battalion, 2nd Marines, in a thrust inland to clear the way for two battalions of the 7th Marines, the 1st and 2nd, to drive through and hook toward the coast, hitting the Japanese holding along the Matanikau. Edson's 2nd and 3rd Battalion would attack across the river mouth. All the division's artillery was positioned to fire in support.
>
> On the 7th, Whaling's force moved into the jungle, about 2000 yards upstream on the Matanikau, encountering Japanese troops that harassed his forward elements, but not in enough strength to stop the advance. He bypassed the enemy positions and dug in for the night. Behind him, the 7th Marines followed suit, prepared to move through his lines, cross the river, and attack north toward the Japanese on

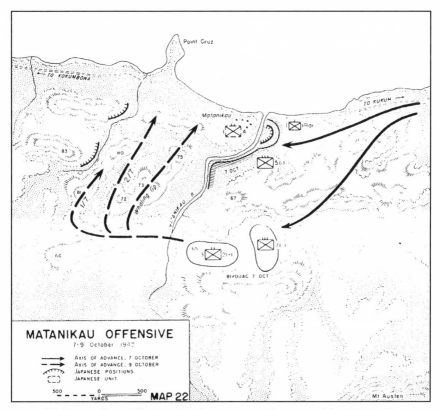

Map of the Matanikau Offensive, October 7–9, 1942. Courtesy of the Marine Corps Historical Center.

the 8th. The 5th Marines' assault battalions moving toward the Matanikau on the 7th ran into Japanese in strength about 400 yards from the river. Unwittingly, the Marines had run into strong advance elements of the Japanese 4th Regiment, which had crossed the Matanikau in order to establish a base from which artillery could fire into the Marine's perimeter. The fighting was intense and the 3rd Battalion, 5th, could make little progress, although the 2nd Battalion encountered slight opposition and won ground through to the riverbank. It then turned north to hit the inland flank of the enemy troops.

Vandegrift sent forward a company of raiders to reinforce the 5th, and it took a holding position on the right, toward the beach.

Rain poured down on the 8th. The weather virtually stopped forward progress, but did not halt the close in all day fighting around the Japanese pocket. The enemy troops finally retreated, as they attempted to escape the gradually encircling Marines. They smashed into the raiders position nearest to their escape route. A wild, hand-to-hand battle ensued, and a few Japanese broke through to reach and cross the river.

On the 9th, Whaling's men, flanked by the 2nd and then the 1st Battalion, 7th Marines, crossed the Matanikau and then turned and followed ridge lines to the sea. Puller's battalion discovered a number of Japanese in a ravine to his front, fired his mortars, and called in artillery while his men used rifles and machine guns to pick off enemy troops trying to escape what had proved to be a death trap. When his mortar ammunition began to run short, Puller moved on toward the beach, joining the rest of Whaling's force, which had encountered no opposition. The Marines then recrossed the Matanikau, joined Edson's troops, and marched back to the perimeter, leaving a strong combat outpost at the Matanikau, cleared of Japanese. Gen. Vandegrift, appraised by intelligence sources that a major Japanese attack was coming from the west, decided to consolidate his positions, leaving no sizable Marine force more than a day's march from the perimeter. The Marine advance on October 9 had thwarted Japanese plans for an early attack and cost the enemy more than 700 men. The Marines paid a price too: sixty-five dead and 125 wounded.[1]

There was another price that Guadalcanal was exacting from both sides. Illness was beginning to fall men in numbers that were equal to the battle casualties. In addition to gastroenteritis, which greatly weakened those who suffered its crippling stomach cramps, there were all kinds of tropical fungus infections, collectively known as "jungle rot," which produced uncomfortable rashes on men's feet, armpits, elbows, and crotches. It was a result of seldom being dry. If it didn't rain, sweat provided the moisture. On top of this came hundreds of cases of malaria. Atabrine tablets provided some relief, besides turning the skin yellow, but they were not effective enough to stop the spread of the mosquito-borne infection. Malaria attacks were so pervasive that nothing short of complete prostration—becoming a litter case—could earn a respite in the hospital. Naturally enough, all these diseases affected most strongly the men who had been on the island the longest, particularly those who experienced the early days of short rations.

By mid-October the Japanese had put ashore, west of the Matanikau River, about 14,000 fresh troops, a heavy field artillery regiment, and a company of eighteen-ton tanks. For the first time the enemy had emplaced artillery of longer range than our own, and the capability to shell our airfield at will. Also for the first time, the enemy had heavy armor available to counter our own and to spearhead an all-out drive to recapture Henderson Field. The Japanese had landed 150-mm howitzers. We had nothing bigger than 105-mm howitzers, too short-ranged to fire effective counter-battery. The decision by our senior military commanders to leave in Wellington, New Zealand, our own 155-mm long guns and essential sound and flash-ranging equipment necessary for effective counter-battery fire appeared to have been a serious miscalculation.

Responding to the rapid build-up of Japanese forces on Guadalcanal, a convoy with the 164th Infantry Regiment of the Americal Division aboard arrived off Kukum Beach in the early morning hours of October 13 and began off-loading.[2] The soldiers, members of a National Guard outfit, were equipped with Garand M-1 rifles, a weapon that most Marines on the island had only heard of. In rate of fire, the semi-automatic Garand could easily outperform the single-shot, bolt-action Springfields the Marines carried, but most 1st Division Marines of necessity touted the Springfield as inherently more accurate and a better weapon. This did not prevent some light-fingered Marines from acquiring Garands when the occasion presented itself. As the soldiers were landing and their supplies were being moved to inland dumps, several Marine pioneer manning gun positions on the beach or participating in the off-loading operation liberated several interesting cartons and crates, just happening to contain the new Garand rifles.

When the 164th Infantry came across the beach on October 13, they got a warm reception from thankful Marines and a hot one from the Japanese. In their first twenty-four hours ashore, their staging area in a coconut grove just off Kukum Beach was pounded as it had never been pounded before. The unmerciful shelling started shortly before noon, when several flights of Japanese bombers arrived over the staging area, relatively unscathed by the defending fighters, and began dropping their bombs. The soldiers headed for cover. Many of them found themselves sharing bunkers and foxholes with Marines at gun positions along the beach and in the nearby coconut grove bivouac area. All we could say was, "Welcome to Impact Center West, soldier," and quickly add, "Look, it's not always this bad."

Throughout the day, the men of the 164th Infantry took a pounding from the newly emplaced 150-mm howitzers. Like each new menace, the Japanese long-range guns quickly got a nickname. They were collectively called "Pistol Pete." This terrifying experience with the Japanese howitzers was only a prelude to what was yet to come. Determined to knock out Henderson Field and to protect their soldiers landing in strength west of Koli Point, the Japanese naval commanders sent a task force built around two huge battleships, *Kongo* and *Haruna*, into the dark waters of the slot to bombard Marine positions on Guadalcanal. Each one displaced more than 36,000 tons and was nearly 750 feet long. They could cruise at thirty knots and carried 1360 men.

The *Kongo* and *Haruna* stood about ten miles out, near Savo Island. Both ships were armed with 500 specially designed 14-inch naval artillery shells, a type never before used against land targets. The basic component of the shell was more than 600 inner steel cylinders, each filled with a highly incendiary mixture of magnesium alloy and barium nitrate. When detonated, each cylinder emitted a jet of flame that burned at more than 3000 degrees Celsius for about five seconds. Their bursting radius was between 200 and 400 feet. These lethal incendiary shells were extremely effective in destroying aircraft in the parking area near the runway, and much of our aviation ordnance and fuel supply. Explosions in these nearby storage dumps sent white-hot searing flames roaring high into the black sky and illuminated the airfield.

The most serious damage, as the Japanese intended, was to Henderson Field and the recently opened auxiliary fighter strip with nearly a thousand 14-inch shells. Japanese planes harassed the perimeter for the balance of the night. The deluge of steel put much of the Cactus Air Force out of commission, destroyed nearly the entire stockpile of aviation fuel, and killed forty-one Marines. Fortunately, there was less damage to the fighter planes and pilots, dispersed on the grassy field that served as Fighter One. Prior to the attack thirty-nine dive-bombers had been conditioned to fly. After the night only three were operable. In the bombardment that night a Marine group commander, his executive officer, flight officer, and two pilots were killed.

Satisfied that they had dealt a knockout blow to Henderson Field, the mighty Japanese battleships *Kongo* and *Haruna*, now firing 14-inch high-explosive shells, and their three destroyer escorts, *Uranami*, *Ayanami*, and *Shikanami*, unleashed a terrible shelling attack on the Marine perimeter where the newly arrived 164th Infantry Regiment was bivouacked.

This baptism of fire on Guadalcanal by Japanese warships in the early morning hours of October 14 was one none of us who were there would ever forget. There must have been a spiritual angle to the baptism as well, for undoubtedly a lot of Marines and soldiers emerged from the affair more thoughtful Christians than they had been since childhood. I recall several soldiers from the newly arrived

164th Infantry shared our command bunker during the eighty minutes of sheer hell delivered by the Japanese battleships. They were terrified and kept asking, "What can we do? What can we do?" I told them, "We can ask God to look over us and to protect us." I also told them: "Not to worry, you never see the one that will kill you."

In the morning, Marines and soldiers, awed and wide-eyed, picked up 14-inch base plates and huge chunks of shell casing. I recall that one of the recovered base plates was stamped "Made in the United States of America." Quite often during the late 1930s, I would see a truck pass our farm on its way to Norfolk, Virginia, with a load of scrap iron. I became interested in where so much scrap iron was going, and I soon learned that it was going to Japan and Germany. It started coming back at us in the early forties in the form of bullets, shells, and bombs.

October 15 was a sad day. Six Japanese transports were brazenly off-loading within sight of Kukum Beach, and there wasn't a damn thing we could do about it. Our aviation gas was exhausted. Some of our planes miraculously survived the pounding they got the preceding two nights, but they were helpless without fuel. The Japanese had the run of the waters around Guadalcanal, and they had landed unknown thousands of troops in the previous two nights. They had made determined attempts to knock out the airfield, and had come close to succeeding, what with bombing, artillery shelling, and naval gunfire.

It was disheartening watching ships bearing thousands of fresh enemy troops unload a few miles to the west. As some of the Marines said, "They're landin' 'em faster than we can kill 'em." After two days and nights of bombing and shelling, only three of our dive-bombers were able to take off. Two of the three fell in bomb or shell craters before they could get off the ground.

Again ground crews feverishly patched up damaged planes that were not beyond repair. Within an hour of sunrise, four dive-bombers attacked the transports through heavy anti-aircraft fire and a screen of Zeroes. Later, small groups were able to continue the pounding. By the end of the day three transports were beached and burning. Three were able to pull away. All six had unloaded their troops and cargoes. Three of the gallant Douglas Dauntless dive-bombers were shot down that day.

There was a chilling message from Gen. Geiger's air command the morning of October 15, when Japanese transports were unloading to the west: "We have no more avgas." When the few planes then flyable were fueled, they said, the supply would be exhausted. Marines started a desperate search for caches of aviation gas that might have been forgotten. As a precaution against air raids and naval shelling, dumps of gas had been widely scattered. Drums were partly buried and covered with earth. Marine aviation personnel found about 100 drums. Marine pioneer found 200 or more in their area. Another 100 turned up near Kukum, where a new fighter strip was being built.

The arrival of the 164th Infantry brought Vandegrift's strength on Guadalcanal to slightly over 23,000 men. But this regiment brought something more to thousands of filthy and tired Marines. The arrival of the soldiers was a signal that somewhere, someone was interested in trying to hold Guadalcanal, and some day in the distant and unpredictable future we would get off this cursed island, if we lived that long.

As the thousands of fresh enemy troops off-loaded to our west on the night of October 15 began to advance toward our position, a message from Maj. Robert G. Ballance, our commanding officer, was read to all hands:

> The time has come for all good men to show their guts. While the situation is tense, it is not hopeless. We, too, have a Navy and they may be nearer than we know. Remember Midway!
>
> Now what the hell, you joined this outfit to fight, and fight. I've every confidence in you that you will. Forget about this dying business; you can't live forever. Think instead about killing, concentrate on squeezing off those shots; make every round land in one of those

"Pistol Pete," a Japanese long-range artillery piece captured during the drive on Kokumbona. Courtesy of the Marine Corps University Archives.

little yellow bastards. They kill easy. Sure we'll get bombed, sure we'll get shelled, sure its tough to take it, but I want every damned son-of-a-bitch in this outfit to stay in his position and keep thinking, "Let 'em come, brother, let 'em come," and when they do, acquit yourself like the Marine you are. If die we must, we'll do it with our boots on and our face to the Japs. KEEP COOL, and good luck.

The night Maj. Ballance put out this masterpiece, one of our company commanders told his cooks to put out the best possible chow, because it could very well be the last meal our boys would ever eat. It was a rugged night.

After a night of unmerciful pounding by the Japanese Pistol Pete long gun, I walked through the B Company bivouac area early on the morning of October 16 to check on the men and to assess our damages. The company runner appeared and told me that the skipper wanted to see me.

As soon as I walked into the command bunker, I knew Capt. Stephens was highly pissed off. He was pacing back and forth like a caged animal, cursing and venting his anger at the Japanese shelling. As he saw me, he stopped pacing and turned in my direction, but didn't say a word. His eyes were cold as steel as he stared at me, and his chin quivered as he stroked his black goatee. I waited for a few moments, and becoming impatient, I said, "Skipper, did you send for me?" He said, "Yes, I did. That Japanese Pistol Pete is a damn nuisance. I want you to get yourself a satchel of explosives, go up there, find that miserable SOB, and blow it all to hell!"

"Sir," I said real respectful like, "We've had ground and air surveillance in that area for the past week and they couldn't locate the gun. How do you expect me to find it?"

I knew what was coming when he didn't respond. His left eye started to blink and his face began to twitch. This was a peculiar trait he always exhibited when he was impatient and was in no mood to discuss the matter further. At this point, I knew the subject was closed, so I told him that I would take the patrol out, but suggested that we coordinate our efforts with division intelligence. He finally said, "I'll have Capt. Sivertsen take care of that. You just get your men together and get ready to move out."

I rounded up four Marines and a Navy corpsman and headed down to the command bunker for a quick briefing by newly promoted Capt. Warren Sivertsen, the battalion's intelligence officer. He had just returned from a briefing at Division G-2 and provided us with the latest reports and information concerning friendly and enemy activity west of the Matanikau River. He handed me a map with a red circle on it showing where division intelligence figured Pistol Pete was located. That point was generally between Point Cruz and Tanambogo, three miles beyond the Marine line. "You'll spot it in a clearing. We think it's camouflaged. Blow it up." I thought to myself at the time that might be easier said than done. The map also showed the location of our most forward observation post west of the Matanikau River, where we were to depart and reenter our lines. Capt. Sivertsen ended the briefing by saying, "Okay. Good luck, guys." I said, "Thanks, Sir, we just might need it."

As we were leaving the command bunker, I overheard one of the scouts assigned to my patrol from the battalion intelligence section mutter: "That's one hell of a big area they've marked on that map. Looking for Pistol Pete there will be like looking for a needle in a haystack!" I didn't make any comment at the time, but I did address his concern at my final briefing before we left camp. Before the briefing, we enjoyed a hot meal that Mess Sgt. Ward had prepared for us at the battalion field mess tent.

At the final briefing, my remarks were short and to the point. I reminded them that we were going on a dangerous mission, but because they were all volunteers, I didn't intend to dwell on that point. What I did emphasize was that this was a reconnaissance patrol and that no fighting would take place unless absolutely necessary, "We're not gonna be lookin' for a fight. Recon ain't about playing hero—its about gatherin' intelligence and blowing Pistol Pete all to hell if we can locate it." I stressed the need for stealth and speed, stating that to be successful, we must reach our objective undetected. Then we would have to get in and out quickly. This would require that we travel light. The word was: "If you can't shoot it, eat it, or drink it, don't take it."

I ended my briefing by asking if there were any questions. When there was no response, I decided to briefly address the map issue. I said, "I am aware that some of you may be concerned about the difficulty of locating Pistol Pete in such a large area, especially at night. I don't see this as a problem since it's not my intention to go thrashing about the jungle at night looking for a damn Japanese gun. We'll take up a position and wait for Pistol Pete to start firing, then we will move forward as close as possible, lay low until it stops firing and the gun crew is on stand down. Then, and only then, we'll attempt to sneak in and place explosive charges in the gun's breach or tube, then get the hell out of there."

Once the final briefing was over, I focused my attention on last-minute details, namely checking weapons, explosive charges, and the equipment the men would be carrying. Since each member of the patrol was armed with the weapon of choice, my concern was primarily about the amount of ammunition they carried. I wanted to make sure they didn't weigh themselves down. As for me, I only carried one extra thirty-round clip for my Thompson submachine gun.

Safety precautions were always a matter of great concern when we carried explosives in a combat environment. That's why I had one of my two demolition men carry the prepared explosive charges in a back pack, while the other one carried the detonators crimped to short safety fuse in a special carrying case. The detonators were to be inserted in the explosive charges at the appropriate time, once we arrived at our objective.

Before moving out, we checked each other to make sure nothing we wore or carried would make noise when we moved or shined during daylight or at night. I was really impressed by the individual effort the men had made to meet the requirement for stealth and speed. I commented: "You men look like Indian scouts from the Montana Blackfoot tribe." Steel helmets were discarded in favor of a plain cloth headband knotted in back of the neck. We wrapped strips of cloth (puttees) around our legs, and shoes were covered with canvas designed to muffle the noise as we moved through the jungle. The two scouts and I carried the special Marine raider stiletto stabbing knife, which had a double-edged, seven and a half–inch tapered blade with a sharp point.

After some additional effort to blacken our faces, tape and make some final adjustments to our equipment, I gave the signal for the patrol to move out. We moved down the winding trail from our bivouac area toward Kukum Beach, where we swung left and moved west along the coast in the direction of the Matanikau River. We were able to maintain a quick pace because we were traveling light. After a couple of hours on the trail, we crossed the Matanikau at the sand spit. The patrol then moved inland up a ridgeline until we reached the forward listing post indicated on the map we were carrying.

Here we took a coffee break. During that time, I made a point to coordinate our plan of re-entry into our lines with the listing post gun crew. We also confirmed the passwords "lollipop" and the counter sign "lollygag," which we would be using. We chose these particular words because of the difficulty the Japanese had with the "el" sound.

We waited for darkness to come. Then I said, "Alright you men, listen up! When we move from here, we travel in single file with two scouts in the lead. There will be no more smoking or talking. All communications will be in a low whisper or by hand and arm signal." My last words to the members of the patrol were, "You must move like one man and think like one man. If you don't, you'll be dead." I decided we would travel initially along the beach, either along the sand washed ashore by the waves or just off the beach, where the tall kunai grass and brush would provide some cover.

We moved along the shoreline for about two hours until we came to a wide-open area with no cover to conceal us. We moved inland a short distance into a cluster of bushes and tall kunai grass. We were just above a trail running parallel to the shoreline and waited there until we could get oriented. As we waited, two Japanese soldiers walked directly below on the trail. They went about thirty yards after passing us, turned left off the trail and down to the beach in the general area we had just left. This had us concerned. Did they know of our existence? Were they looking for us? Or were they just on a routine patrol?

As we waited to make sure the Japanese soldiers didn't return, I sent the scouts out to find a safe way to cross the open area. They came upon a ditch formed by erosion, and there was very little water in it. There was a three-quarter moon that night, and a few clouds over the area, so visibility was fair. I whispered to a member of the patrol to stay close as we crept to the ditch that would provide us cover. We crawled like alligators, on our stomachs, hands, and knees. We went like that across the open area until we reached a wooded area of mostly coconut trees.

I decided that we would travel through the wooded area some distance from the shoreline. We did this for a couple of hours, but with great difficulty. Branches hit us in the face and shrubs scraped our clothing. We constantly tripped over limbs and splinters from shattered coconut trees. We were making a lot of noise. We finally decided to work our way toward the coastline, where we could move faster, more quietly, and get a better look at what was in front of us. We swung right and traveled north through a wooded and highly vegetated area for some distance before we reached a much-traveled path leading toward the beach.

With the scouts in the lead, we headed up the path in the general direction of Point Cruz. We had no sooner begun to move out when we ran smack into a six-man Japanese patrol coming down the same path. Those soldiers were eating and chattering away. There was nothing between us but fifty or sixty feet of open air. We quickly reversed our direction and moved ahead of them down the same path, but I am sure we walked much faster. As soon as the path took an abrupt turn to the right and put some vegetation between us, we jumped to the right and slid under some downed coconut trees. They went right by us, still talking and eating out of bowls with chopsticks.

When we could no longer see, hear, or smell the Japanese patrol—and believe me we could smell them, for there was a heavy odor of fish and garlic in the air when they passed us—we headed back up the path parallel to the shoreline. The shoreline was sparsely wooded with scrubby trees, affording very little protection. From this point we quit walking and began to creep and crawl, standing up only when we were in the tall jungle growth. After traveling a short distance,

I gave the signal for the patrol to move closer to the beach so we could get a better view of the coastline.

In the distance, Savo Island appeared like a dusky hump on the horizon. I looked up the coastline as far as I could see. It was empty, so we settled down behind a sand dune. We sat in the sand and listened to noises of the jungle at night, the winds rustling among the palms along the shoreline, and watched the sea, the endless rolling sea. I heard a pounding sound, and at first I couldn't identify it. It sounded familiar, but I could make no sense of it. It was the surf—the waves were pounding rhythmically onto the black sand. The stars were plentiful, but it was the darkness of the sand on the beach that seemed so strange. It was as if there was nothing beneath my feet. I felt as if I were floating on a raft at sea.

Somewhere behind us, most likely along the Matanikau River, we could hear the sounds of a firefight. The *rat-tac-tac* of a Japanese Nambu machine gun sputtered and paused. A Marine weapon was quick to respond. Members of the patrol sat in silence, each comforted by the other's presence. We were tired, but attentive to every detail.

I looked at my watch. It was midnight. Almost as if on signal, we heard a flare pop, lighting the sky until it looked almost like daylight. Everyone froze, no one moved until the flare had burned out. We decided to get the hell off the beach just in case we had been spotted. We pulled back far enough to find some cover behind a large boulder and a patch of kunai grass, but remained close enough to where we could see up the coastline ahead without the palm trees blocking our view.

When there was no enemy response to our presence, I thought I'd get up and take a look. Boy, did I get an eye full! What I saw, took my breath away. Up ahead at a distance, I could see the gray shapes of Japanese troop ships west of Point Cruz, and I could hear the noise of landing craft bringing Japanese reinforcements and supplies ashore. All along the beach were these small boats coming ashore, hundreds of them, each carrying twenty or thirty Japanese soldiers.

We could hear the big guns already ashore banging away, and the familiar rumbling *swish, swish* sound of the large shells sucking up the air as they passed overhead on their way toward their target, Henderson Field. If there was any doubt that the Japanese had more than one Pistol Pete, it was completely dispelled at this point. From our position, we observed orange flashes from several locations when the big guns were fired, which indicated a well-dispersed artillery battery of long guns in the area.

It became apparent that the Japanese artillery barrage we were observing was a diversion tactic to cover the reinforcements coming ashore and to cause a disruption of air operation at Henderson Field. It also was apparent that our chances of getting close enough to slip in and blow-up any of these big guns were zero to none. Not this night, for the Japanese were swarming all over the place.

At this point, I decided we should withdraw. There was nothing else to be accomplished on this mission. On the return trip to our lines, we decided to travel along the inland trail running parallel to the shoreline as much as possible. En route we were challenged several times and shot at twice. After about two hours on the trail, I could tell that the men were getting tired and needed to rest, so we went off to the right and flopped down in a grassy spot under a tree.

Our break was soon interrupted by the chatter of Japanese soldiers walking through the jungle in our direction. There were six or seven of them. They came within thirty feet of us. If they had come any closer they would have walked right on top us. I had the safety off my Thompson submachine gun in anticipation of just that. Luckily a nearby path that ran parallel to us saved the day. They hit the path, turned right on it, and went inland up a ridge. Every one kept their cool.

After this encounter, we continued in a southeasterly direction down a narrow dirt road running parallel to the beach. We followed this road quite a distance and then stopped for a rest. After about ten minutes we heard what sounded like a vehicle coming up the road from the south. We scrambled like mad to get off the road and take cover in some tall kunai grass.

The truck went by with its headlight beams passing right over us. It stopped about fifty yards beyond us. We heard them talking, then the truck drove on. All this time our hearts were in our throats and the adrenaline was flowing like mad. They had stopped for about five minutes, but it seemed like an eternity. We were afraid to get in a firefight with them because we felt if that happened it would only be a matter of time before we would be caught. I decided to stay off the road when we continued on.

I passed the word to move out. Almost immediately, the lead scout hit the ground, and the rest of us followed suit. Unbeknown to us, the Japanese truck had dropped off a two-man patrol that was bearing down on us. I tapped each scout on the leg to get their attention and gave them the signal to take them out by using their Marine stiletto knives. The scouts wriggled forward on their bellies like salamanders to get in position for the attack. I stayed right on their heels. The lead scout, with the advantage of surprise, was successful in bringing his man down. The second scout was not so fortunate, as the Japanese soldier he engaged had time to react and put up a desperate fight for survival. When I saw my scouts' knife drop to the ground, I realized he was in trouble, so I lunged forward to administer the *coupe de grace*, the finishing stroke.

Knife fighting does not come natural to most men, but my scout was struggling for his life. I knew the Jap was my enemy, and he knew I was his. We grappled. He was smaller, but stocky and strong. He was brave—they all were brave. My stiletto prevailed, but the memory still haunts me. He is one of my nightmares. He comes without a face.

During the melee with the Japanese patrol, one scout sustained a rather nasty gash on his arm that required some medical attention. Our medical corpsman, rushed forward and dressed his wound. While the scout was being treated, other members of the patrol were busy moving the Japanese bodies and cleaning up the site in general. At this point we could hear the sound of a vehicle heading in our direction. I assumed it was the same truck that dropped off the two-man patrol and was returning to pick them up. Realizing the urgency of the situation, I decided to make tracks going east, as fast as we could. Doc assured me that despite the loss of blood the scout would be able to keep up, and he was right. That scout was one tough gung-ho kid.

After several close encounters, we somehow made it back to our perimeter unscathed. When morning came, we approached the forward listing post we had left the day before. We were challenged as we approached our lines, but after giving the password we were allowed to move forward to be recognized. Once safely behind our own lines, I passed the word that the smoking light was on. While most members of the patrol smoked a cigarette, I sat down to enjoy my pipe. I kept the pipe and tobacco pouch in my map case, and only smoked occasionally to relieve the tension after a combat action.

Although we were unable to destroy Pistol Pete, for all intents and purposes, the patrol was deemed a successful mission. We obtained valuable information regarding the increased enemy activity in the Point Cruz area. We also were able to confirm the fact that we were being harassed not by one, but by a well-dispersed battery of Pistol Pete long guns in that general area. Shortly after returning from the Pistol Pete patrol, I assumed the position of acting company first sergeant, replacing 1st Sgt. Frank Cotrufo, who was promoted to the rank of warrant officer (Marine gunner) and reassigned. Initially, I had some doubt about becoming the company's first sergeant. I knew there would be a certain amount of animosity among some more senior NCOs, especially those who had developed a "bunker mentality."

It was no secret that that I had little to no patience with officers or NCOs in a leadership position who were more concerned about staying alive than fighting the enemy. You can't win a war huddled up in a foxhole or bunker. I suspect one of the reasons my commanding officer leaned on me so much was that I was young and unattached. The psychology of warfare, what goes on in peoples' minds, figures into the events on the battlefield. If you're lovesick or if you've got a wife and kids back home, you're not likely to be volunteering to lead a patrol into enemy territory or to take on other high-risk combat missions.

Different people have different perceptions of what makes a good leader. For my part, I'll stick with the maxim that history is about people, leaders, and the led. When you get right down to a small unit level, there are elements of leadership that are tried and true. Never tell your men to do something you won't do yourself. "Follow me" are the operative words, not "Go take that hill." Always see to their needs first—food, shelter, clothing, and equipment. Push them near the breaking point, but never beyond it.

I never had any trouble with my outfit. We had a job to do, and we did it. For the next two months, I met my new challenge head-on. There was no time to worry about bruised egos. We had a mission to accomplish, and it was my job to see that the commanding officer's orders were carried out. I learned that in order to be a good leader you must stand firm for what you believe in, no matter what kind of adversity you face.

My ability to handle that new position of leadership was soon put to a test. Once again the pioneers were sent into the line as infantrymen. The word was passed, "Stand by to move out in the morning. We're moving up to the frontlines. Get all your foul-weather gear ready, and be sure your machine guns are oiled and your ammunition belts are dry. Try and get as much sleep as possible. There will be an early reveille."

At 0500 hours on October 20, the word was passed to move out. We made a forced march from our bivouac area at Kukum Beach, where we crossed a narrow valley filled with waist-high kunai grass just west of where the new Fighter Two landing strip was to be located. From there we swung right until we reached a ridge line where we could take up battle positions in support of the 3rd Battalion 1st Marines, holding the east bank of the Matanikau River.

It was quiet for most of the day, except for the artillery fire from the west. Then late in the evening, a mortar round struck the lines of the 3rd Battalion. The bombardment soon intensified, with most of the shells directed at our forward positions along the main perimeter for several hundred yards where we were dug in. Gen. Sumiyoshi was clearly trying to pin the Marines on the line while preventing reinforcements from using the main trail running parallel to the Matanikau River.

All through the night, snipers took pot shots at us and probed our lines. A torrential downpour developed before dawn and continued unabated throughout the following day. It was too overcast for air activity, and the artillery fire the troops heard seemed too far away. There was little to do for most of the evening, except to hunker down and wait for the miserable weather conditions to improve.

The ponchos helped, but rain infiltrated them. Soon a spot here, a spot there, got wet. I still have vivid memories of the miserable condition we endured that night and the next day. I was in a muddy foxhole, and my poncho was leaking like a sieve. The bottom of my foxhole had two inches of water, and the water kept rising. My feet were propped up to keep my last pair of socks dry. Next to a Marine's weapon, it's imperative that he keep his shoes and socks dry. With the damp came chills, and before long there were a lot of miserable Marines. The only consolation was that across the Matanikau there were undoubtedly a lot of miserable Japanese.

The Japanese artillery fire that began at 1800 hours on October 20 was a clear signal that Gen. Sumiyoshi was sending his diversionary forces into battle. As soon as it became obvious that the Japanese artillery fire of the early evening would soften the way for a major assault, recently promoted B. Gen. Pedro "Pete" del Valle, the 11th Marine artillery commander, committed his twelve 75-mm guns and 10 of his 105 batteries to the endangered zone. Division headquarters was gambling its main support on the premise that the assault on the Matanikau front would be the only Japanese activity of the night.

On October 20, the same day my company was ordered into the lines, an enemy patrol accompanied by two tanks tried to find a way through the line held by Lt. Col. William N. McKelvy Jr., 3rd Battalion, 1st Marines. A sharp-shooting 37-mm gun crew knocked out one tank and the enemy fell back; meanwhile the Japanese continued shelling the Marine position with artillery. Near sunset the next day, the Japanese tried again, this time with more tanks than before, but again a 37-mm gun knocked out a lead tank and discouraged the attack.

On October 22, the enemy paused, waiting for Gen. Maruyama's force to get into position inland. On the 23rd, the date planned as the day of the Sendai Division's main attack, the Japanese dropped a heavy rain of artillery fire on McKelvy's force to get into position near the Matanikau River mouth. Near dusk, nine eighteen-ton medium tanks clanked out of the trees onto the river's sandbar, eight of them were quickly riddled by 37-mm antitank guns. The one tank that got across the river had one of its tracks blasted off by one of our previously buried improvised bangalore torpedo buried as a land mine. A 75-mm half-track finished it off in the ocean surf.

On the night of October 23, Gen. Sumiyoshi began his attack across the Matanikau. During the day there were the usual air raids, but the bombers unloaded on the shorelines far from the airfield. Pistol Pete fired intermittently through the day, hitting the new naval base at Lunga Lagoon. (The base had been driven out of Kukum.) As night fell, the big howitzers' firing grew steadier and more purposeful. Joined by lighter artillery and mortars, Pistol Pete shelled deep into Marine positions then drew their fire back to concentrate on the east bank of the Matanikau. It was the closet thing to an artillery preparation the Japanese ever managed to achieve on Guadalcanal.

The following day the enemy was pounded by massive artillery fire, as all battalions of the augmented 11th Marines rained shells on

Marine officers observe the battle scene. In the background five enemy tanks lie smashed and harmless on the sand spit across the mouth of the Matanikau River, Guadalcanal. Courtesy of the Marine Corps Historical Center.

the massed attackers. The Japanese suffered hundreds of casualties and three more tanks were destroyed. Later, an inland thrust by the enemy further upstream was easily beaten back. The abortive coastal attack did nothing to aid Maruyama's inland offensive, but did cause Vandegrift to shift one battalion, the 2nd Battalion, 7th Marines, out of the lines to the east and into the 4000-yard gap between the Matanikau position and the perimeter. This move proved to be providential, since one of Maruyama's planned attacks was headed right for this area.

Japanese infantry and tanks were blown apart by the 11th Marine artillery, mortars, and improvised antitank mines placed on the sand spit. Several hundred Japanese were caught at the edge of the trees by the Marine artillery batteries south of Kukum, and hundreds were killed in the devastating fire by 2200 hours, when the gunners were ordered to stand down. The 1st Marine Division had twenty-five Marines killed and forty wounded that night. Many of the wounded were hit by enemy mortar and artillery fire.

This is the way a Japanese counterattack ended in the disaster for the enemy. Late at night the Japanese forces attempted to break through lines in force. The following morning the beach area was a gruesome sight, as Marines had foiled the attempted break-through. Courtesy of the Marine Corps University Archives.

Then-Colonel Clifton B. Cates, who commanded the 1st Marines through months of heavy combat in terrible jungle conditions, later wrote: "McKelvy's battalion finally received credit that was due it. The 1st and 2nd Battalions had previously been given official commendations for their work at the Tenaru River. Now, the 3rd Battalion received a citation. Naturally, I was very proud. I was fortunate in having three good battalion commanders in Lt. Col. Leonard B. Cresswell of the 1st Battalion, Lt. Col. Edwin A. Pollock of the 2nd Battalion, and Lt. Col. McKelvy of the 3rd Battalion. All were later decorated with the Navy Cross." (Lt. Col. William W, Stickney assumed command of the 2nd Battalion, 1st Marines on September 24, when Lt. Col. Edwin A. Pollock was named Executive Officer of the 1st Marines.)

In the meantime, my unit, B Company Pioneers, was moved from the east bank of the Matanikau to a new location, where we would be in position to reinforce Puller's battalion. It was dug in along a ridge-line east of Henderson Field. We came clanking down from our defensive position on the east bank of the Matanikau in a chilling drizzle. We would spend a couple of days in our bivouac area at Kukum Beach while awaiting the 911 call. I marveled at the hot meal our Mess Sgt. Rip Collins and his cooks had prepared for us. They must have raided the food-supply of a newly arrived Army unit.

[12] Second Assault on Bloody Ridge

Like all Marines, the pioneers were first and foremost riflemen. They were rushed up to the line during skirmishes when every man and every rifle was needed. They responded to trouble calls. The second assault on Bloody Ridge was one of those times.

In late October, our company was rushed into the lines with the 1st Battalion, 7th Marines. Once again the B Company Pioneers moved up to fill a gap that had been breached in a few places on the ridge. It was a debacle, but I think we held our own. The infantry was delighted to have the pioneers go into the lines with them because we had such firepower. We had machine guns galore. We also had the semiautomatic weapon of choice, the M-1 Garand rifle, recently obtained through moonlight requisition from the Army's 3rd Battalion, 164th Infantry Regiment.

On October 25, the men of B Company Pioneers awoke to the sounds of a fierce battle being waged south of Henderson Field. Little did we know at the time that our company would be joining the fray before the end of the day. A desperate battle was once again underway on Bloody Ridge. The Marine unit defending the ridge perimeter overlooking the airfield was Lt. Col. "Chesty" Puller's 1st Battalion. Puller had to cover the whole sector of 2500 yards with his understrength battalion, which required spreading his men thin and putting in the line all except those in the mortar section.

When the Sendai Division set out toward Edson's Ridge, Lt. Gen. Masao Maruyama appraised his officers and men of the stakes: "This is the decisive battle between Japan and the United States in which the rise and fall of the Japanese Empire will be decided. If we do not succeed in the occupation of these islands, no one should expect to return alive to Japan. We must overcome the hardships caused by the lack of material and push on unendingly by displaying invincible teamwork. Hit the proud enemy with an iron fist so he will not be able to rise again."[1]

On the night of October 24, in a blinding rainstorm, Lt. Gen. Maruyama's forces had launched their attack against Col. Puller's 1st Battalion. The attack began about 2130 hours, when a Marine listing post opened fire on the advance elements of the Japanese 29th Infantry Regiment, and pulled back to our lines. The Japanese had finally hacked their way through the jungle to the south of the Marines and were launching their attack. They had crossed the upper reaches of the Lunga River and were now just south of Bloody Ridge.

To support their attacks, they had nothing more than machine guns. All of their artillery and mortars had been abandoned along the Maruyama Trail. Gen. Maruyama had hoped for bright moonlight to orientate his troops, but the clouds and rain made the night black. The clash with the outpost was unavoidable and tipped off the Marines. The front lines were quiet for about two hours, until suddenly they attacked Puller's battalion east of Bloody Ridge.

Six battalions of the Sendai Division charged out of the jungle, attacking in Puller's area near the ridge and the flat ground to the east. The Marines replied with everything they had, calling in artillery, firing mortars, and relying heavily on crossing fields of machine-gun fire to cut down the enemy infantrymen. A wedge was driven into the Marine lines, but that was eventually straightened out with repeated counterattacks. Puller soon realized a strong Japanese force capable of repeated attacks was hitting his battalion. He called for reinforcements, and the Army's 3rd Battalion, 164th Infantry, commanded by Lt. Col. Robert K. Hall, was ordered forward. Also ordered forward was B Company Pioneers.

By 0330 on the morning of October 25, the Army battalion was completely integrated into the 1st Battalion, 7th Marines lines and the enemy attacks were getting weaker and weaker. The return fire laid down by Puller's reinforced battalion, including a smothering artillery barrage, was just too much to take. Gen. Maruyama pulled his men back to regroup and prepare to attack again.

Meanwhile, in our bivouac area, B Company made final preparations to go forward. The men busily cleaned and checked their weapons to insure that they were operating properly. Ammunition was distributed for the extra bandoleers and machine-gun belts they carried. Canisters of grenades and packages of C-rations were also passed out. Those items were carried in their combat packs.

Late in the afternoon, word was passed: "Stand by to move out." B Company Pioneers formed up in a column of platoons formation. A forward hand signal by Capt. Stephens started us on a force march that would take us from Kukum Beach to the ridge, where we would fill in a gap between two front-line units in Puller's extended line.

Light was fading fast as we crossed the mouth of the Lunga River. The skipper had us pick up the pace almost to a dogtrot. Night drops on you quickly in the jungle, and he didn't want us caught out in the dark before we reached the ridge. It was imperative that we occupy our unfamiliar defensive positions during daylight hours.

Once we reached the communication trail that led to the Puller zone, there was a guide from one of those units waiting to lead us in. When we reached the crest of the ridge, additional guides were waiting to drop off squad-sized units in fighting positions already prepared along the ridgeline. It was evident by the odor and the marks of battle that these fighting positions had been manned the previous night. The Marine pioneers were quite surprised to find machine guns, ammunition cans, and boxes of grenades in many of the fighting holes they were to occupy.

After we established radio communications with Col. Puller's battalion command post, my attention was focused primarily on making sure security was adequate in and around the company command bunker. After being briefed by a member of Puller's staff on the field telephone, Capt. Stephens requested that I accompany him on a quick tour of our lines. We really had to move out fast because darkness was setting in. We stopped briefly at some of the fighting positions along the ridgeline we were to defend. The men appeared to be in good spirits and eager to take on the enemy. Capt. Stephens had a brief conversation with his platoon commanders before we returned to the command bunker.

By the time we arrived back at the command center, the top of the ridgeline was already blanketed in a damp, heavy fog. Marines from the headquarters platoon assigned to man fighting positions in the sector around the center had already donned their ponchos to ward off the dampness of the night. Inside the command bunker, the radio was crackling with fast and furious reports of enemy activity in the area. There was no light in the bunker except for a flashlight occasionally used by the radioman. One of the men attached from the battalion communications section was manning an open field phone to Col. Puller's command post. Field phones were also opened down the line so that all platoon commanders could hear every message.

One message heard over the open phone resonated with every Marine on the ridge: "Colonel," Capt. Regan Fuller said to Puller, "I'm just about out of ammo. I've used up almost three and a half units of fire." Col. Puller said, "You've got bayonets, haven't you?" Fuller replied, "Sure. Yes, Sir." Puller said, "Alright, then. Hang on." B Company, 1st Pioneers was ready for its night of trial. Rain began to fall. It would be a long night.

After dark on the night of the 25th, the Japanese repeated the pattern of attack used the previous night. With only machine guns to augment their hand-carried weapons, groups of 20 to 200 Japanese soldiers charged out of the darkness to assault the entire length of the Puller-Hall line. The machine-gun companies with supporting riflemen against the junction of the Marine and Army battalions, where a trail led north to the airfield. The heavy concentration of artillery, mortars, small arms, and the four canister-firing 37s cut down the repeated Japanese assaults. A Company from the 1st Marine Division reserve (B Company Pioneers) came forward to reinforce, and the line held.

The Japanese took staggering losses, but continued hammering against the Marine lines throughout the night. But both of the assaults on the night of October 25–26 were thrown back. At dawn on the 26th it looked as though some enemy men might break through in the south. Col. Twining, the D-3, sent a precautionary message to the air command: "Jap's are driving hard toward Fighter Strip One. We'll probably stop them but take security measures around planes." He sent the engineers to act as security guards at the strip.

The Sendai Division hit Puller again about 1915 hours that night— the third successive night of trying to work along the east slope of Bloody Ridge. But the Marines were no longer the tenuous, hastily improvised group it had been before the arrival of the reinforcements. A lack of reserves had plagued the Marine command throughout the campaign. During the first battle at Bloody Ridge, it consisted of one understrength battalion. But Army and Marines lines south of the airfield, breached in a few places, were restored and held. The Sendai Division's back had been broken. It was clear that with the aid of the 11th Artillery and the final support of Army and Marine reinforcements, Puller's forces had been able to fend off the enemy. At daybreak the Marine positions were secure and the enemy had retreated. They would not come back. The grand Japanese offensive of the Sendai Division was over.

One of the mainstays of the Marine defense of Henderson Field was artillery in well-placed positions. Both the 37-mm antitank gun, in a sandbagged bunker, and the 75-mm howitzer were used with devastating effect against enemy formations. Often, Marine artillery fire would fall upon the Japanese before they had an opportunity to adequately prepare for an attack.

By the time the night was over, the 29th Japanese Infantry had lost 553 killed or missing and 479 wounded. The 16th Japanese Regiment's losses are uncounted, but the 164th burial parties handled 975 bodies. The Americans estimated that about 3500 enemy troops had died during the attacks. Once again, the "automatic artillery," so labeled by the Japanese in the Edson's Ridge and the Matanikau battles, helped to turn the tide. What was left of Gen. Maruyama force now straggled back over the Maruyama Trail, losing most of its seriously wounded men, as had the Kawaguchi force in the same situation during the first battle of Bloody Ridge.

That fighting in late October was probably as important as any combat on Guadalcanal. Once again, the Marines showed the Japanese that even with their bushido beliefs, they couldn't break the Marines. In the long run, that battle was the key to our victory on Guadalcanal.

Amid all the heroics of the three nights of fighting, many men were singled out for recognition, and there was an equally large number who performed great deeds that were never recognized. One Marine who distinguished himself throughout this action was Sgt. "Manila John" Basilone, who, operating in imminent danger and constantly exposing himself to hostile fire, kept the machine guns in his section of the front lines operating under almost impossible conditions. For his constant feats of heroism in this action he was awarded the Congressional Medal of Honor.

A platoon sergeant by the name of Mitchell Paige won the Congressional Medal of Honor for holding the Japanese at bay as they overran the eastern portion of the ridge. By holding his position against seemingly insurmountable odds, Paige was able to disrupt the

Japanese and prevent them from outflanking the Marine positions. In a further heroic action, Paige led a group of Marines in an attack that broke the back of the final Japanese assault. In that attack, Paige cradled a .30-caliber water-cooled machine gun in his arms as he ran forward firing into the Japanese.

For his courageous leadership and successful defense against heavy odds, Lt. Col. Puller was awarded his third Navy Cross. The action that brought him the medal occurred on the night of October 24–25. For a desperate three hours his battalion stretched over a mile-long front. It was the only defense between vital Henderson Field and a regiment of seasoned Japanese troops. In pouring jungle rain the Japanese smashed repeatedly at his thin line, as Chesty moved up and down its length encouraging his men and direct the defense. After reinforcements arrived, he commanded the augmented unit until late the next afternoon. The defending Marines suffered fewer than 70 casualties in the engagement, while 1400 of the enemy were killed. The Marines recovered several truckloads of abandoned Japanese equipment.

A few days after his men had fought off an assault on the ridge, Puller led his battalion in a new engagement to block off any Japanese attempt to escape inland. He was one of the casualties of the eight-day engagement. Chesty's wounds were significant, but not immediately life threatening. He was wounded by mortar fire, collecting, as he put it, "a fanny full of shrapnel." When the battalion medical officer pinned a casualty tag on him and ordered him evacuated, the colonel shouted: "Evacuate me hell! Take that tag and stick it you know where. I will remain in command." But the next day he was ordered to leave and yield command to Maj. John E. Weber, his battalion executive officer.

[13] The Final Phase of the Campaign

Although the Marines had won their battle on land, it would be meaningless unless the U.S. Navy could figure out a way to stop losing night battles in the slot to the northwest of the island, through which the Japanese kept sending replacement troops ashore. On November 4, 1942, after a ten-day voyage from Samoa, the 8th Marines reached the embattled island and went ashore near Lunga Point. Almost immediately, the unit was involved in heavy fighting with the Japanese, which continued through November and into December.

I recall seeing the 8th Marines come ashore. Although the worst was past, we pitied them. They looked miserable plodding along the beach under the weight of heavy combat packs and extra ammunition as they headed inland toward the Matanikau and the Japanese, but we couldn't resist needling the "Hollywood Marines" from sunny California. That name came about because the 2nd Marine Division occasionally furnished men for movie productions.

Another group of Marines we often referred to as "Hollywood Marines" was the 2nd Raider Battalion. They sailed aboard converted World War I four-piper destroyers and landed on the island from Higgins boats. Col. Evans Fordyce Carlson's unit scrambled ashore on Guadalcanal and went into bivouac at Aola Bay, about forty miles east of Henderson Field, while the mop-up on Guadalcanal continued. Carlson's assigned mission was to clear out a Japanese force

A Marine Corps landing operation takes place on the far end of the island of Guadalcanal. These Marines are part of the 2nd Raider Battalion. Courtesy of the Marine Corps University Archives.

along the Gavaga River, where the U.S. Army's 164th Infantry was fighting.

Early on November 8, the 2nd Raiders left their base camp at Bino and advanced inland along a mountain trail. Warily, they moved through the tall kunai grass and humid jungle. Coming upon a Japanese outpost, some of the raiders opened fire. But the Japanese machine guns were in good dugout positions and replied, pinning the 2nd Raiders down, but not for long. A signal was given to spread out and take cover, and the word was passed for the mortar section to lay down a couple of rounds. The Japanese scattered in all directions. The 2nd Raiders pushed on, moving as stealthily as their enemy and hitting them whenever they could. Sometimes it was almost too easy for the raiders to find and kill the Japanese. Sometimes, said Col. Carlson, "It was like shooting ducks from a blind."

Carlson's force had intended to spend a week patrolling and harassing the enemy, but it stayed more than a month. The 2nd Raiders destroyed remnants of the enemy on the Upper Lunga River and collected valuable information about enemy operations and the terrain.

A raider battalion, a specially trained group of Marines, hikes over rugged terrain during operations on Guadalcanal. Note the native guides. Courtesy of the Marine Corps University Archives.

It was a difficult time for the 2nd Raiders, but they moved fast and hit the enemy hard. They existed mainly on rice and C-rations. Sometimes they joined their native guides in a repast of air-dropped Australian corned beef (called "corned willy" by the Americans). The weather was unpleasant. Sometimes it would suddenly start raining with monsoon force. Then the rain would just as abruptly stop. The rain provided no relief from the heat, and the temperature would again be 120 degrees.

After more than thirty days, the 2nd Raiders followed a native guide twenty-five miles along back trails to the Bino base camp. Their mission was completed. The raiders had high praise for the heroic natives who assisted them and the other U.S. troops on Guadalcanal. Carlson's 2nd Raiders had marched 150 miles and killed 488 Japanese troops, with a loss of 16 Marines dead and 18 wounded. Some of the Marine Corps observers called the 2nd Raiders' operation on Guadalcanal the greatest single patrol of World War II.

Col. Carlson was a professional soldier of legendary courage in the U.S. Marine Corps tradition. He was a strong believer in comradeship between officer and men, and he maintained that the paternalistic caste system had no place in the armed forces of a democracy. He was an intrepid field commander who led his raiders to everlasting fame. Nevertheless, Carlson's raiders were looked upon with disapproval by certain officials. After Guadalcanal, the 2nd Raiders were consolidated with three other battalions into a Marine raider regiment. Carlson was placed second in command, but his gung-ho system was discarded. He was awarded a second Gold Star in lieu off a third Navy Cross for his leadership and heroism. Stricken with malaria, he was sent home in the spring of 1943.

On November 8, while Gen. Vandegrift's forces were still maneuvering to pull the string on the Japanese along the Matanikau, V. Adm. William Halsey, who had been given command of the Navy's South Pacific Area on October 26, 1942, came to Guadalcanal. Halsey came in without fanfare, put on Marine dungarees and boondockers, and rode in an open jeep around the perimeter. His staff officers begged him to stand up, to wave, to do anything that would let the Marines know that "Bull" Halsey was there. He refused. It would be "too dam theatrical," he said, it would be an affront to the weary men who had held this island for the past three months. Halsey went to Vandegrift's headquarters for lunch and a briefing by the general and his staff. The next day Halsey flew back to Noumea, heartened that Gen. Vandegrift still thought that he could hold, convinced that men with such courage could never be defeated.

Under the aggressive leadership of V. Adm. Halsey, the Navy won their battles—including a three-day air and naval engagement in mid-November 1942 that wiped out a Japanese cruiser, damaged two others cruisers and a destroyer, and tore up eleven enemy transports with 10,000 troops aboard. This engagement may have been the turning point in the fight for Guadalcanal. Halsey later speculated that if that battle had been lost, the troops on Guadalcanal would have been cut off, as they were at Bataan, and supply lines to New Zealand and Australia would have been cut.

Sometime after midnight on November 13, we were awakened by naval gunfire. The island trembled to the mighty sound of naval warships engaged in battle just off our shore. A star shell rose, and it was terribly bright as it arched downward. Giant tracers flashed across the night in orange arches. Sometimes we would duck, thinking they were coming at us, only to find that they were miles away.

A pinpoint of light appeared in the middle of the darkness and it kept growing until it illuminated the entire skyline. We were suddenly bathed in pale yellow light, and there was a momentary, clutching fear as we felt Guadalcanal shift beneath us. Some great ship had just exploded. We lay on the ground, almost breathless and watched as the battle raged on throughout the night.

We had no way of knowing it at the time, but we had witnessed one of the most furious sea battles in naval history. At least 800 U.S. naval officers and enlisted men who had gone into battle that night did not live to see the sun rise. The five cruisers and eight destroyers in the opposing force led by R. Adm. Callaghan suffered heavy loses. Only three destroyers escaped damage. The cruiser *Juneau* plus four of our destroyers were sunk. The cruisers *Atlanta, Portland*, and *San Francisco*, and three other destroyers were heavily damaged. The *Atlanta*, R. Adm. Norman Scott's flagship, was the first ship to catch the shells and torpedoes. At least one torpedo had pierced the *Atlanta*'s hull. The force of the explosion had lifted her completely out of the water and set her down, shuddering and crippled. The Japanese lost the battleship *Hiei* and two destroyers, with four others damaged heavily.

At the break of dawn all available airplanes rose in pursuit of the enemy fleet. These included a flight of P-38s from the 39th Fighter Squadron that left Milne Bay on November 13 and flew directly to Henderson Field. From the shore, we could see a Navy cruiser dead in

U.S. Army troops land on the beach at Guadalcanal. They relieved leatherneck fighters who, to a large extent, captured the island. The Army now had to hold it. Courtesy of the Marine Corps University Archives.

the water, with fires still burning forward. Every landing boat at Kukum Beach was being dispatched to pick up survivors and bodies floating in the water. Marines ashore, almost to the man, volunteered to assist in this effort.

I led a detachment of Marines aboard one of the dozens of small boats sent from Kukum. We cruised slowly, picking up men in the oily water. Practically all of the Japanese preferred to die, and most were allowed to do so. After struggling to avoid our rescue efforts, however, some were forcibly pulled into the boats for purposes of interrogation.

The scene of this rescue operation will forever be etched in my memory. I vividly recall that the water was filled with floating bodies as far as the eye could see. Surviving sailors yelled and waved frantically, while trying to keep their wounded and dying shipmates afloat. One rescue

USS Alchiba *(AK-23), aground and afire off Lunga Point, Guadalcanal, in late November 1942, after being torpedoed by Japanese submarine 1–16. Note the men in foreground, who are probably handling cargo unloaded from* Alchiba *while she was fighting her fires. Courtesy of the Naval Historical Foundation.*

craft carried Marines with rifles. They circled around the area firing at sharks attracted to the blood in the water. Some of the wounded we rescued had been attacked by sharks but managed to survive. Others did not. Our rescue efforts continued throughout the day. Floating bodies were pulled from the oily water and taken ashore to a temporary morgue for processing. I participated in the gruesome effort until noon, when I was diverted to another high-priority assignment.[1]

November 28 turned out to be a sad day for the pioneers on Guadalcanal. The troop combat cargo ship *Alchiba* that brought us to the island on August 7 was torpedoed. She was lying offshore, with smoke pouring from her forward hold. Off toward Tulagi, destroyers could be seen crisscrossing, dropping depth charges. Patrol planes were circling in the sky looking for the submarine. After-action reports indicated that the torpedo was fired from a Japanese submarine that penetrated the screen. The *Alchiba* burned for several days, but was later salvaged. The USS *Alchiba* and its gallant crew will long be remembered as one of the first ships that brought supplies of rations and ammunition to Marines stranded on Guadalcanal. This was a perilous mission that required slipping by Japanese submarines that stood steady guard over the waters surrounding the island.

Through December and into January, elements of the 2nd Marine Division, with other Marine Corps and Army units, made a final drive toward the west, with the support of air and naval gunfire. On three dark nights in early February 1943, while combined force of Marine and Army units approached Gen. Hyakutake's force from two sides, the last Tokyo Express raced down the slot. They evacuated Hyakutake's 13,000 sick, wounded, and starving survivors—all that were left of the 40,000 that they put ashore. Guadalcanal was finally declared secure on February 8, 1943.

[14] Guadalcanal in Perspective

Four things are mentioned in all accounts of Marine troops on Guadalcanal: heat, mud, mosquitoes, and bombs. Each day around noon an air-raid warning was sounded and everyone ran for foxholes and dugout air-raid shelters. So regular were these attacks that the enemy planes' arrival became known as "Tojo Time," in ironic homage to the Japanese prime minister. But nearly two-thirds of the men on Guadalcanal were knocked out of duty by health problems, far more than suffered from bombs or bullets. The two thin meals a day never satisfied and soon the hardy young men who'd been so eager to see combat turned into gaunt, sunburned zombies, their uniforms in tatters, their socks gone, and their underwear rotted away.

By late November 1942, the Guadalcanal campaign was all but over for the 1st Marine Division. The reason, bluntly stated in Gen. Vandegrift's battle diary, was that it was no longer capable of offensive operations. "The Division's tragic condition wasn't the result of battles lost or of men killed or wounded. Malnutrition, malaria and other crippling jungle diseases had done what the enemy had failed to do. . . . Day by day, I watched my Marines deteriorate in the flesh. Although lean Marines are better than fat Marines, these troops were becoming too lean."

The sick list of the 1st Marine Division in November included more than 3000 men with malaria. The men of the division still manning the front-line foxholes and the rear areas, if any place within Guadalcanal's perimeter could properly be called a rear area, were plain worn out. They had done their part and they knew it.

We had great leaders on Guadalcanal. One standout was Maj. Gen. Alexander A. Vandegrift, commanding general of the 1st Marine Division, Reinforced. He was a professional, a soft-spoken, tough-minded commander in the mold of Stonewall Jackson. Vandegrift, like Jackson, was particular in explaining to those around him that the victory at Guadalcanal belonged to his men and not to him. Vandegrift never doubted the capabilities of his Marines, and in turn, the Marines of the 1st Division never doubted the firm courage and judgment of this general. It was these factors that played a major part in the conquest of the Solomons. Vandegrift departed the Pacific in late 1943 to become the eighteenth commandant of the Marine Corps.

Later, in *Memories*, Gen. Vandegrift wrote, "We struck at Guadalcanal to halt the advance of the Japanese. We did not know how strong he was, nor did we know his plans. We knew only that he was moving down the island chain and that he had to be stopped. We were as well trained and as well armed as time and our peacetime experience allowed us to be. We needed combat to tell us how effective our training, our doctrine, and our weapons had been. We tested them against the enemy, and we found that they worked. From that moment in 1942, the tide turned, and the Japanese never again advanced."

Another standout was Col. "Red Mike" Edson. I vividly remember my first encounter with Edson on Guadalcanal. He was commander of the Marine raiders at the time and was at the division command post when I arrived to give a report on enemy contact my patrol had made along the Lunga River.

I stood before him in awe and with a great deal of admiration as he asked me several questions about my report. "Red Mike" was, as his code name implied, a redhead. The colonel was a wiry man with a lean, hard face partially covered by a sparse, spiky growth of grayish beard. His light blue eyes were tired and red-rimmed, weary from long days of fighting. His red eyelashes were almost invisible, which highlighted the effect, and his eyes were as cold as steel. Even when he was being pleasant, they never smiled. He talked rapidly, spitting out his words like bullets, his hard-lipped mouth snapping shut like a trap. He was a first-class fighting man, one of the most aggressive Marine commanders in the Guadalcanal campaign. There were those who thought Col. Edson overzealous in leading his men into battle, too indifferent to casualties. But he did lead.

My last contact with Edson was at the 1st Marine Division reunion in 1951. He invited a number of Guadalcanal veterans up to his hotel suite for a drink and to talk about our experiences on the Canal. I was surprised but pleased that he remembered me. Needless to say, the visit made my day, and was the highlight of the reunion for me.

After Guadalcanal, Col. Edson was awarded the Congressional Medal of Honor for his actions during the Battle of Bloody Ridge. He was transferred to the 2nd Marine Division and served as its chief of staff at Tarawa, and he was assistant division commander at Saipan, where he served with distinction. He retired as a major general in 1947. Edson then served the State of Vermont as Commissioner of Public Safety. He died in 1955, at the age of fifty-eight, by his own hand.

Another great combat leader on Guadalcanal was Lt. Col. "Chesty" Puller. He shouted battle orders in a bellow that would have rattled the halls of Montezuma. He stalked about under enemy fire as though he was daring the enemy to hit him. Puller had an abiding love for the enlisted men who did the killing and dying and a sneering hatred for the stuffy officer who did the sitting and meddling. He thrived on combat and he became a legend to his troops.

Col. Puller was a born leader who went off into battle with his green eyes gleaming malevolently, a stubby pipe clenched in his crooked mouth, and a copy of Henderson's biography of Stonewall Jackson tucked into his duffel bag. Puller told one of his officers it was "the greatest book ever written" and treated the biography like a "professional Bible."

Puller stood out because he cultivated the image that his enlisted men were more important to him than his officers. Although he had shown a few indications of this approach to leadership in prior years, his attitude may have been shaped or redirected by the reading of Henderson's biography of Stonewall Jackson. Chesty had underlined passages in his copy that described a similar philosophy:

> It is manifest that Jackson's methods of discipline were well adapted
> to the peculiar constitution of the army in which he served. With the
> officers he was exceedingly strict. He looked to them to set an example
> of unhesitating obedience and the precise performance of duty. He
> demanded, too—and in this respect his own conduct was a model—
> that the rank and file should be treated with tact and consideration. . . .
> His men loved him . . . because he was one of themselves, with no
> interest apart from their interests; because he raised them to his own
> level, respecting them not mere as soldiers, but as comrades. . . . He
> was among the first to recognize the worth of the rank and file.[1]

Puller received two Navy Crosses fighting in the Caribbean. The third was awarded for heroic actions on Guadalcanal while commanding the 1st Battalion, 7th Marines. Then-Lt. Col. Puller, with several shrapnel holes in his body, led gallantly and tirelessly day and night, usually in the front lines alongside his beloved Marines. When he heard that one-third of the division soon would be rotated back to the United States, he requested that he be permitted to remain in a combat billet until the defeat of the Japanese. His request was approved. In the spring of 1944 he received his fourth Navy Cross for heroism on Cape Gloucester.

Puller became a larger-than-life legend. He served as executive officer with the 1st Marine Regiment on New Britain. Then he commanded that regiment in the incredible Battle of Peleliu. He again commanded the 1st Marines in Korea, at Inchon and the Chosin Reservoir, where he earned his fifth Navy Cross. Puller retired from the Corps as a lieutenant general, having enlisted in 1917 as a private and having held every rank in between. No U.S. Marine has ever won more combat decorations than "Chesty" Puller.

Gen. Puller's illustrious career reflects just about the entire history of the Marine Corps in the twentieth century. His gruff, give-em-hell attitude was admired throughout the Marine Corps, and his bravery and his nickname were known to the millions of Americans on the home front. Tough-as-leather "Chesty" Puller was a military hero and icon to generations of fighting men. He was truly a Marine's Marine.

To the fighting man, the history of battles in which he fought often makes the battlefield seem more neat and compact than he remembers it to have been at the moment he was fighting. Looking back at Guadalcanal, from August to December of 1942, it is easy to set up stakes at the turning points, marking the battles in which we threw back the four major counteroffensives the Japanese launched against us, once a month, from August through November. Yet, Guadalcanal was more than a campaign Marines fought in World War II. It was a place where a legion of leatherneck units fought under the name of the 1st Marine Division. All but abandoned by the ships that brought us there, reduced to eating moldy captured rice, kept on the line though stricken by malaria, dependent for food and ammunition on destroyers and fliers who broke through the enemy blockades and always at great risk, we fought the best soldiers Tokyo could send against us, killing more than 20,000 of them in the process. And we won.

In his author's note accompanying *The Thin Red Line*, his novel about Guadalcanal, James Jones wrote that, "What Guadalcanal stood for in 1942 and 1943 was a very special thing." He wanted his readers to remember the "special qualities that the name Guadalcanal evoked for my generation." He compared the fighting on the island to Valley

Forge and Shiloh. Morrison wrote, "Guadalcanal is not a name but an emotion, recalling desperate fights in the air, furious nights in naval battles, frantic efforts at supply and construction, savage fighting in the sodden jungle and nights broken by the screaming bombs and deadening explosions of naval shells."

In *Marlborough*, Winston Churchill wrote of great battles, which, "Won or lost, changed the entire course of events, created new standards of values, new moods, new atmospheres in Armies and in Nations, to which all must conform. . . . In the Pacific in World War II was the Battle of Guadalcanal." After studying the battle, Churchill simple wrote, "Long may the tale be told in the Great Republic." At the time, however, one wondered whether there would be anyone left to tell it.

All of our men who fought on Guadalcanal were heroes, and history has confirmed their valor. Society has a duty to them, to our children, and to the free world not to forget them. We must remember that war is a costly undertaking and the Marines paid the bill. The Duke of Wellington once said, "Nothing except a battle lost can be so melancholy as a battle won."

The total cost of the Guadalcanal campaign to the American ground combat forces was 1598 officers and men killed, 1152 of them Marines. The wounded totaled 4707, and 2799 of these were Marines. If the Marines had been better trained and equipped, our casualties undoubtedly would have been much lower. The Japanese, in turn, lost close to 25,000 men on Guadalcanal, about half of whom were killed in action. The rest succumbed to illness, wounds, suicide, and starvation.

President Roosevelt, reflecting the thanks of a grateful nation, awarded Gen. Vandegrift the Medal of Honor for "outstanding and heroic accomplishment" in his leadership of American Forces on Guadalcanal and awarded the Presidential Unit Citation to the men of the 1st Marine Division (Reinforced) for "outstanding gallantry" reflecting courage and determination of an inspiring order.

The Battle of Guadalcanal proved to be the Pacific War's true turning point. There were no successful Japanese offensives in the Pacific theater after Guadalcanal, and no more American retreats. The fall of Guadalcanal opened the gateway to Tokyo. Had the Japanese won this crucial round, there's no telling how much longer the war would have taken or how many more lives it would have cost.

Guadalcanal was also a deadly dress rehearsal for the island-hopping American offensive to come. Here the United States learned to fight a new kind of war, one that involved the complex coordination of ships, planes, and land troops in sometimes-nightmarish conditions. To the Marines fighting hand-to-hand in the steaming malarial jungle, this was definitely a bit of hell. It was made more hellish by the dreadful strategic mistakes and terrible tactical decisions on both sides.

The time had come for us to depart this place that the Japanese called the "Island of Death." Americans knew it as Guadalcanal, and the Marines that fought there just called it the "Canal." The nickname had an affectionate sound about it, but the Marines cursed and hated Guadalcanal, a pesthole that reeked with death, struggle, and disease.

On November 29, 1942, Gen. Vandegrift received a message from the Joint Chiefs of Staff. The crux of the message read: "1stMarDiv is to be relieved without delay . . . and will proceed to Australia for rehabilitation and employment." The word soon spread down through the chain of command that we were leaving for Australia, a place not yet cherished as it would be in the future. But any place was preferable to Guadalcanal.

[15] Departing for the Land Down Under

Finally, the time had come for us to leave. The day before we starting embarking, we had a memorial service at the cemetery situated among the tall coconut trees, the final resting place for those Marines who had sacrificed their lives in battle on that wretched island. As we bowed our heads in prayer, we felt the full meaning of the phrase "They died that we might live." At the memorial service, some 7000 war-weary Marines knelt beside the graves, each marked by handmade crosses and covered by palm fronds. We offered our prayers and paid our final respect to friends and comrades who would remain behind for all eternity.[1]

I remember my last day on Guadalcanal. It was December 20, 1942. We had been on the Canal without relief since August 7. For us, the battle for Guadalcanal was over. We had won. Now we were loading out on transports to sail to Australia for much desired rest and recuperation.

I wish I could describe the sight of the men as they ambled down to the beach in a slow gait and scrambled into the boats that would take them out to the troop transport anchored offshore. They were certainly a sad-looking outfit. Unshaven, with torn and tattered clothes, they were limping because they had jungle rot on their feet. "Ragged-ass Marines" was a fitting name for the weary, disease-ridden, bedraggled Marine pioneers who filed into the landing boats. We were dressed in frayed dungarees covered with Canal sweat and muck. Socks had become a luxury; many had long since rotted away. Boondockers were rundown

Some 7000 battle-weary Marines in full battle regalia stand at attention to pay their final respect to their comrades who were never to leave the island. Courtesy of the Marine Corps Historical Center.

Cemetery on Guadalcanal as it appears today. Courtesy of the Marine Corps Historical Center.

As he tells it, "Too Many, Too Close, Too Long," is Capt. Donald L. Dickson's portrait of one of the "little guys, just plain worn out. His stamina and his spirit stretched beyond human endurance. He has had no real sleep for a long time . . . and he probably hasn't stopped ducking and fighting long enough to discover that he has malaria. He is going to discover it now, however. He is through." Courtesy of the Marine Corps Historical Center.

at the heel, tied up with knotted laces or bits of string. Almost everyone had lost many pounds. Most had malaria. Surprisingly enough, almost everyone had his weapon, and these weapons were all in good condition. Even though everything else had gone to pot, a good Marine—and they were all excellent Marines—always takes good care of his arms.

As we stood at the gun rail on the Higgins boats, we took our last look through a misty rain at the rugged mountains and watched Guadalcanal and the shoreline fade into the distance. We left as we came, carrying only our packs and rifles. Everything else was left

War-fatigued Marines wait to board transports standing offshore. Courtesy of the Marine Corps Historical Center.

behind for use by the newly arrived Army and Marine reinforcements who would conduct the final mop-up operations on the island.

Our boat throttled back, bobbing up and down alongside the troop transport ship, the USS *Neville*. The command was, "Climb up them cargo nets!" The men were so weak that many of them didn't have the strength to make the climb and were assisted by nimble sailors. I was able to reach the top of the net unassisted, but I couldn't go any further. I just couldn't muster the strength to go over the top. I hung there, breathing heavily until the sailors grabbed me under the armpits and pulled me over the ship's rail. Once aboard, we would go below to the Marine's reward of a hot meal and a clean bunk, while the troop transport shuddered and made for the open sea.

Shortly after we got underway, we heard the announcement over the loud speaker: "This is the captain speaking. Welcome aboard

Marines climb up cargo nets to board ships off Guadalcanal. Courtesy of the Marine Corps Historical Center.

Marines, I just received the following message from Adm. Nimitz: 'Your successful fight against great odds will live as one of the most striking tales of Marine Corps history. The people of our country and those of us in the naval Service are gratified and proud of your outstanding performance of duty against the best the enemy had to offer. As long as our country has men with your heart, courage, skill, and strength, she need not fear for her future: To each and every one, a WELL DONE.'"

As the company acting first sergeant, I was afforded the privilege of the chief petty officer mess for a cup of hot coffee and conversation with the officers, who were eager to hear about our heroics on the Canal. I sensed they knew that I didn't want to talk about it. If only we could have sailed away from the memories. We were skeletons compared to the Marines who had landed on the island some five months before. Fatigue, sickness, and lack of nourishment had taken its toll.

After a few days on board, we were feeling much better. The food was good and we had plenty of it. There was a supply of fresh bandages and salve. The sea air was cooler and easier on those of us suffering from malaria and jungle rot. We enjoyed our salt water showers. It didn't matter that the salt water and soap tended to make you feel gummy, it was the best we'd had in a long, long time. There were no laundry facilities on board, but that didn't dampen our spirits. We had no change of clothes anyway. Our immediate concern was where we were headed and when would we get there. The glory was gone from it now, the valor, the doggedness. We were spent, fit only for the warm welcome that awaited our arrival in the "Land Down Under."

They took us first to Espiritu Santo in the New Hebrides, where we arrived on Christmas Eve. From the ship's deck offshore, Espiritu Santo looked like another South Seas island of enchantment. On shore, though, it was pure hell, a mass of mud shouldered by a rainforest and soaked by a torrent of rain. I never did find out why they dropped us off on this God-forsaken island. Conditions in Espiritu Santo were not much better than on the Canal. We spent the Christmas holidays in a hastily erected tent encampment among the mosquitoes and thousands of crawling insects.

Having endured the hardships of Guadalcanal, I was not surprised by the thunderous rains and the humid, sweltering heat that drenched our clothing and skin. I already knew the omnipresent mosquitoes lusting for my blood, that scrub typhus lurking under every bush leaf, and the crud (fungus) with a predilection for the toes, crotch, armpits, but that also thrived in the inner ear. The only thing different was there were no Japanese on the island.

[16] Australia Remembered

We were brought to Melbourne on a converted hospital ship, the USS *Tryon*, a naval vessel that served alternately as an evacuation hospital ship and as a troop carrier. We had been below decks since leaving Espiritu Santo, New Hebrides, six days earlier after having been driven below by a filthy storm in the Tasman Sea.

In the fierce winds and huge swells of the sea, the ship's bow would dip below the surface and the stern would come out of the water, causing the ship's propellers to turn faster than they were suppose to, causing the ship to shudder and vibrate as it rolled and pitched in the heavy seas. We grasped the bunk stanchions with both hands to keep from being slammed against a steel bulkhead. Many of us trapped below deck began to wonder if the small, converted troop transport was going to break up or capsize in the storm.

I was fortunate in seldom getting seasick. I did, however, feel queasiness enough at times to know about seasickness and to feel sorry for those affected by it. What bothered me most about this sea voyage aboard the *Tryon* was the copious quantity of vomit on the deck in the berthing compartment and the odor in the ship's head. The ship's berthing compartment smelled like a floating toilet.

Some people can sleep just about anywhere, but not me. In my entire six-day voyage aboard the *Tryon*, I doubt if I slept more than an hour—maybe two hours—each night on a throbbing canvas bunk in the berthing area. If you don't know what I mean by "a throbbing bunk" in a ship, it's because your shipboard domicile wasn't far enough below decks and to the stern to feel every pound of a tired diesel engine's piston.

A happy, blaring band played as we disembarked at Melbourne on January 12, 1943. Grins broke out as the band struck up the rollicking tune "Waltzing Matilda." Suddenly, every one of us knew it was going to be all right. With quiet but genuine relief and happiness, we assumed formation on the docks, where we boarded trains and crowded up to the windows. Then everyone began to whoop and shout, for the most astonishing thing was happening: the route was lined with young women, cheering, hugging themselves and each other, dancing up and down, blowing kisses, extending to the U.S. 1st Marine Division the fairest of all welcomes.

Most of the Australian men our age were off serving the British king, fighting in a war going on in faraway places like North Africa, Burma, and in New Guinea. Consequently, there were lonely, bored, unattached women everywhere. That's when more than 10,000 young American Marines landed at Melbourne. We were not only welcomed as heroes and given the run of the city, we were welcomed as healthy young men. We hadn't seen women who looked like us since leaving Wellington six months earlier.

I got a seat by the window. All the windows were open and the train was pulling out very slowly. There were girls along the sides of the railroad tracks. We did not expect this, but we quickly seized the opportunity that presented itself. I grabbed as many of the pieces of paper that the girls were holding out as I could, passing them out among the men in my rail car. The pieces of paper contained the girls' names and addresses. We were taken aback and amazed by all the attention we were receiving. We looked so terrible, still in the same rags we had worn on the Canal. We were just a train full of raggedy-ass Marines.

The train halted at Frankston, a suburb of the city, and we were herded into a fenced compound reminiscent of a cattle pen. On the other side of the fence were more girls, squealing, giggling, waving their handkerchiefs, thrusting their hands through the fence to touch us. We were beside ourselves.

Some elements of the division had the good fortune of being quartered in the cricket grounds, in the heart of the city. Others, like my battalion, sulked in a hastily erected tent encampment in the rural countryside. Shortly after arriving at Mount Martha, our new campsite, about thirty miles from Melbourne, I went down with malaria. While my fellow Marines and conquering heroes were prowling the streets of Melbourne for girls, I lay flat on my back in a hospital bed.

I spent more time in Australia in the hospital than outside of it because of treatment for a particularly virulent strain of malaria contracted on Guadalcanal. I felt like I had been burned with acid. One minute I shook with fever, and the next I shivered with chills. My bones ached. I couldn't eat or even drink water. I was fed intravenously. The fever caused my ears to ring so loudly that I felt like my eardrums were about to explode. At the time I thought, "This is what the furnace of hell must be like." All I wanted was a trickle of sweat to burst from my body. Only then would it be over. The only relief I had was the touch of the nurses, cooling my body with rubbing alcohol. Then my fever broke, and finally the sweat came in torrents. I felt like singing, shouting, and dancing a jig. But, of course, I couldn't. I didn't even have the strength to move my hands. I was drenched, the nurses moved me to another bed and I soaked that one too. Even though it was warm outside, I shivered with chills that seemed to last forever. They piled blankets over me. Nothing seemed to work, but I knew the worst was over.

Several more days passed before I could sit up and take any food. At first, the smell of food made me sick. The only thing I could hold down was tea and slices of dry toast. Finally, I was able to eat with the rest of the patients. Once I was well enough, I underwent eye surgery to remove scar tissue caused by flash burns when an enemy bomb had exploded nearby.

A week later, I left the hospital to find that arrangements were being made for me and other Marines battling the lasting effects of malaria to spend a period of convalescent leave in the Australian outback. First, we had to take care of some administrative details.

We received part of our six-month arrearage of pay in Australian pounds and were outfitted with our new uniforms, including those green jackets that we wore eighteen months before they gained the "Eisenhower" name. It was with a great deal of pride that I stitched the newly approved 1st Marine Divi-

Kerry Lane, as photographed by the Marine Corps in 1943, while he was a sergeant in B Company, 1st Pioneer Battalion, 1st Marine Division in Melbourne, Australia.

sion shoulder patch to my jacket.[1] The patch was authorized for wear to specifically commemorate the division's sacrifices and victory in the battle for Guadalcanal. The word Guadalcanal was etched into the red numeral on the division patch to commemorate in perpetuity that epic struggle.

We were instructed on the code of conduct expected of us because we would be guests of small rural towns, or "stations" as they were called in Australia. Many of us would be the guests of individual families. To make sure there was no breach of protocol, an escort officer

The 1st Marine Division shoulder patch was originally authorized for wear by members of units who served with or were attached to the division in the Pacific in World War II. It was the first patch to be approved in that war and specifically commemorated the division's sacrifices and victory in the battle for Guadalcanal. It features the national colors—red, white, and blue—in its diamond-shaped background with red numeral "1" inscribed with white lettering, "GUADALCANAL." The white stars featured on the night-sky blue background is in the arrangement of the Southern Cross constellation, under which the Guadalcanal fighting took place.

was being assigned to us with the necessary medical personnel to handle any medical problems we had and to give us our daily doses of atabrine pills.

The train trip from Victoria Station in Melbourne is somewhat vague in my memory, but I do remember that we were aboard many hours and passed the time by singing songs. One of the favorites was "Waltzing Matilda," and I can still remember most of the words: "Once a jolly swagman camped by a billabong, under the shade of a coolabah tree. And he sang as he watched and waited till his billy boiled. 'Who'll come a-waltzing Matilda with me?' " It was a great tune to march to and a rollicking tune to bellow at the top of our voices while rolling through the peaceful countryside.

The Australian outback, fertile farms and stretches of hot plains dotted with cattle and sheep reminded me of home. Something that didn't remind me of home and was unique to the outback was the thousands of kangaroos hopping around like grasshoppers— a picturesque sight I'll never forget.

When we arrived at the outback station of Boort we were at once clasped into the hearts of its people. We were looked upon as the conquering heroes and the saviors of Australia. We had preserved their way of life and their lifeline to America. Needlessly to say, we were overwhelmed by the huge crowd that turned out to greet us. The station residents were joined by sheep and cattle ranchers from many miles out who had come in from the bush with their families just for this occasion. I recall much of what the welcoming committee spokesman said to us: "We are happy to have you here with us. We give you great honor, not only because you fought for us, but for our children and grandchildren and for our people. You have shed your blood for us and you have defended our soil from the Japanese."

Some of us were selected by individual families to be guests of theirs, while others would stay in the local inn or in the dorm set up at the station's school. The method of selection came as a surprise to most of us. Individual family members simply approached a certain Marine and invited him to stay with them as their guest. And off we went.

I think Dawn, the daughter of my host family, was responsible for my selection. We made eye contact early on, and when the time came she made sure her father and mother headed in my direction. We rode in an open touring automobile powered by something that looked like a stove mounted on the rear bumper. I never understood how it worked, but it burned charcoal and somehow powered the car. We steadily moved through the outback, with smoke pouring from the stack atop the stove.

When we arrived at the ranch, I was given the choice of a room in the house or the outlying cottage. Actually, the cottage may have been a stable at one time, because Dawn called it "our paddock." A walkway connected it with the house, a short distance away. I chose the paddock. The mattress on the bed was kind of bumpy, but the sheets were cool and clean and I quickly drifted off to sleep.

I awoke the next morning to a soft rapping at my door. I looked up to see Dawn coming through the door, saying, "Hello, Yank." She smiled and asked me how I liked the paddock. I propped myself up on my elbow and told her I had slept like a log. She asked if I would like to be served breakfast in bed. I thanked her, and said I really preferred to eat with the family.

It felt great to be with a family again and to take part in their daily life. I picked grapes, pitched hay, and helped herd sheep and cattle. It seemed natural, since I was raised on a farm. My stay at their ranch was very special, and I will always be grateful to them for their hospitality. I remember the horseback rides every evening with Dawn and the many picnics we had together by the lake. Dawn and I corresponded during the war. Regretfully, we lost contact after it was all over. More than six decades later, I still have vivid and happy memories of my stay in the Australian outback. The joyful association with the Australian people made it easier to erase the awful memories of the war.

As our departure date arrived, virtually the whole town came down to see us off. They chatted about how much healthier we looked and how much they enjoyed having us visit them. As the train pulled out, I looked back. This was a small slice of Australia inhabited by the most generous, caring, patriotic, wonderful people on the face of the earth: a typical Australian town caught in the throes of war.

Upon reporting back to my unit at Camp Mount Martha, I was hit with a double whammy. First, I was to learn that my company commander, Capt. Stephens, had been sent home. Second, 1st Sgt. Avery, a newly arrived replacement from the States, had been assigned to fill the vacant billet in B Company Pioneers. To say I was astounded is to put it mildly. I was devastated. I never had the slightest doubt that I would be promoted to the rank of first sergeant. Capt. Stephens had assured me before I departed for R&R in the Australian outback that

I would get my promotion as soon as the paperwork could be processed. I never did find out if the paperwork went forward. However, I decided not to let this adversity get me down. As they say in the Corps, it was time to "suck it up" and carry on.

I did get a recommendation to appear before a warrant-officer selection board. While members of the board seemed to be very impressed with my combat record and performance as acting first sergeant on the Canal, some of the old World War I colonels serving on the board thought, at eighteen, I was too young to be promoted to warrant-officer rank of Marine gunner. The selection board did recommend that I be sent back to the States to attend officer candidate school. I declined this offer for two reasons: I didn't want to leave my unit at a time when it was preparing to go on another campaign, and I didn't have the prerequisite formal education for officer candidate school at that time.[2]

In an effort to establish a better relationship between Marines and Australians, baseball games were played every weekend at the Melbourne cricket grounds. Capt. Warren Sivertsen, who was assigned additional duties as the camp recreation officer at the time, organized the Camp Mount Martha team. I was a player and our coach. Most of the players on the team were from B Company Pioneers.

By the time I returned from my stay in the outback, many of the men in my company had chosen their favorite local girls and some had begun to go steady. One sure way to spend weekends with the young ladies of Melbourne was to be a member of the Camp Mount Martha baseball team. We played a scheduled game every Saturday afternoon. The Aussies would fill the bleacher seats, despite the strangeness of the game. When at bat, we were encouraged to get a hit by such strange yells as "Give it a bloody go, Yank." When we scored a run, the Aussies would let out a yell "Good-o, Yank! You made it." After the game, we would shower, change into our uniform, and go for a walk in the park or visit the St. Kilda's Esplanade.

Romance was inevitable, especially for young Marines who were half a world away from home. The engagement rate soared, and there were a number of marriages in our company. Some of us who didn't have steady girlfriends waiting for us after the game found dancing establishments where we could enjoy the popular music of the time. The girls there were eager to learn the American ways, including jitterbug dance steps. Most of the men could really cut a rug and were able to handle the fast-tempo jitterbug. I had two left feet when it came to dancing. I would only attempt the slow ones, like the two-step or shuffle. Some of the dances were different than what we had back home, but the Australian girls were willing to teach us. It was a lot of fun.

Several things about Melbourne stand out in my memory, but it was the attitude of the Aussies that impressed me most. After years of war and the enemy just over the horizon, the people were buoyant, living for the day. Compared to the little isolated part of the world I was born in, Australia was the most advanced nation on earth. Another thing I remember was the delicious food. Most Marines ate steak and eggs, or, as the Aussies would say, "styke 'n ayggs." Melbourne steaks were large, tender, and delicious, and the Marines consumed them by the thousands.

I was also struck by the warmness of the people. They were like folks from home. It was common for them to walk up to small groups of Marines and offer to buy them meals or drinks. We were taken into their homes as overnight or weekend guests. No formal introductions were needed. The fact that the guest wore a Marine uniform was enough. We were treated with unfailing hospitality, respect, and love. Often the host and hostess at these affairs had sons in uniform or had lost sons in battle. They felt drawn to troops far from home and on the way to meet the enemy. Overlooking the sometimes careless attitude of most Marines, they smiled and took us into their hearts. The thoughtfulness of the people of Melbourne was impressive, and the memories of their many kindnesses are still fresh in my mind.

Things were not always tranquil between the Yanks and the Aussies during our nine-month stay in Melbourne. When the 9th Australian Division (the rats of Tobruk) returned to Melbourne, they quickly became upset with the 1st Marine Division. They soon issued an ultimatum that every member of the 1st Marine Division was to stay away from Melbourne the following Saturday night. Maj. Gen. Vandegrift called every regimental commander personally with instructions that "Every member of the division, with the exception of those on guard duty, is to be on liberty next Saturday night. Do not, repeat, do not start any fights and do not lose any." Fire-hoses broke it up at the Flinders Street Station in the wee hours of that Sunday morning. From then on, we were the best of friends—most of the time.

Our stay in Melbourne was not all fun and games or full of romance. As the division regained its collective strength, we started the well-known tough Marine Corps training. This began simply with disciplinary drills and small-unit exercises, intensifying and expanding as the weeks went on and the troops' physical condition improved. From April until June 1943, tactical training was progressive, and it culminated in large-scale landing exercises using live ammunition for all weapons.

I missed much of this training as the result of hospitalization for malaria treatment and subsequent convalescent leave. Before the time for departing Australia arrived, I was able to go through range qualification with the new M-1 rifle issued to replace the familiar '03 Springfield. The M-1 Garand semi-automatic was not popular when it was first issued. The Marines had fought with the bolt-action, five-shot Springfield on Guadalcanal. This was the famous '03 that had made the Marines the sharpest shooters in the world. They hated to exchange it for the less accurate M-1, even though the Garand fired an eight-round clip as fast as a man could pull the trigger. Burning powder operated the M-1 loading mechanism, thus providing the greater firepower to which the Marines reluctantly yielded. For many of the NCOs, the new M-1 Carbine was the weapon of choice. It was a light, semi-automatic weapon capable of firing a fifteen-round clip of .30-caliber bullets. It provided firepower, but it was not tough enough to withstand the corrosion of the jungle—it would break down when fired too long.

I got to test fire my 12-gauge military pump shotgun, which I had obtained as my weapon of choice for the upcoming campaign, thanks to the brass oo buckshot shell episode involving Col. Chesty Puller and the Army quartermaster general. As the time for our departure drew near, Col. Puller, who was commander of Camp Mount Martha, drove his staff to complete the last detail in preparation. He warned the regimental supply officer that an Army quartermaster general was to check his requisitions. "Notify me at once when he arrives," Puller said. "I want to explain things in person."

The Army general arrived when Puller was out, and the lieutenant took the inspector to the supply dump. The general said, "Lieutenant, your requisitions are excessive."

He answered, "I'm sure Col. Puller would never have signed for more than we need, Sir."

"But he's asked for ten thousand brass oo buck shot shells. What the devil does he need with those?"

"To kill Japanese, Sir," the lieutenant replied.

"Doesn't Col. Puller know that buckshot is prohibited by the Geneva Convention?" the general continued.

Exasperated, the lieutenant replied, "Sir, Col. Puller doesn't give a damn about the Geneva Convention, any more than the Japanese did when they bombed Pearl Harbor."

When I heard the story about the shotgun shells, I went to the battalion armory and checked out a shotgun. I knew there wouldn't be a shortage of buckshot shells where we were going.

Our days in Melbourne were drawing to a close. "When are you leaving?" the girls asked. "They say you lads will be leaving soon," said the people who had invited us into their homes. They knew. They always seemed to know before we did. We Marines couldn't get enough pleasure. There weren't enough girls and we couldn't drink enough at our favorite pub on Collins Street. Eventually, the time came when we had to say good-bye: "Farewell women of the West. We, who are about to die, salute you."

The following article appeared in a leading Melbourne newspaper and highlighted the strong bond of friendship that existed between Marines and the Australian people:

American Marines who were part of the life of Melbourne only a little while ago are now working out their destiny in the heat of battle at Cape Gloucester, where they have made another successful landing.

The thoughts of many people must be with them in their present ordeal. When these lean-limbed young men swarmed into Melbourne after Guadalcanal people took them to their hearths and hearts. The Marines warmed to the welcome and wholeheartedly reciprocated the friendship. Often they became part of the family circle and even part of the family, for some of them more closely linked Australia with America by marrying Australian girls.

The Marines might be said to have taken possession of Melbourne. In the streets they were distinguished by their smart appearance, by the proud little metal spheres [the Marine Corps emblem] which they wore on their caps . . . it suggested that the Marines were ready to fight in any part of the world . . . and their custom of wearing their ties out-side their shirts, and also by their civility and courtesy.

The Marines were, indeed, part of the life of Melbourne. They took possession of the Melbourne Cricket Ground, and where Australian voices once yelled in the excitement of the football match or hummed to the more sedate tempo of cricket, strange new voices and accents from over the sea were heard. The Marine band of eighty players was heard on many public occasions. For their leisure, the officers had their club in Admiralty House in Collins-place, and there—unlike the Australian custom regarding clubs—they could take their lady friends for a little social jollity.

Then, all of a sudden, it seemed the Marines vanished. The neatly uniformed men disappeared from the streets, and Bill and Tom and Dick no longer visited the homes of their Melbourne friends. It wasn't long before the reason became apparent. Newspaper headlines revealed the secret: The Marines were fighting.[3]

[17] Going Back to War

On August 19, 1943, the first contingent of Marines sailed toward Goodenough Island and Oro Bay, some 2000 miles to the north. Here in the remote jungle boondocks of New Guinea, the men would put the finishing touches to training for their role in Operation Cartwheel. One week later, my unit, the 2nd Pioneer Battalion of the 17th Marines, moved by train to Brisbane, and then departed for Goodenough Island on September 11.

I was allowed to remain behind in order to complete a course of instruction at the Royal Australian Bomb Disposal School at Wagga Wagga, New South Wales. Here I would learn the deadly art of defusing unexploded (dud-fired) ordnance including bombs, rockets, projectiles, and land mines. Some of our instructors had been trained in London and others were veterans of the North Africa campaign. All were highly skilled in the procedures of defusing enemy ordnance with an antidisturbing or antiwithdrawal fusing mechanism.[1] I rejoined my unit approximately two months later. By October 23, the last contingent of our division had departed from Melbourne.

Once again, the 1st Marine Division was shoving off to make history. Only the most senior officers in the command knew we would invade Cape Gloucester, an island twice the size of Guadalcanal on the western tip of enemy-held New Britain. The landing beaches were at a point just over the horizon from New Guinea, where powerful Japanese forces were still being assembled.

American strategists targeted New Britain to provide protection for Gen. Douglas MacArthur's flank in New Guinea. They also hoped to swing control of the important waters between New Guinea and New Britain to the United States. The plan was to seize the strategic Japanese-held airfield at Cape Gloucester on the island's northwestern tip overlooking the waterway through which MacArthur's troops heading for the Philippines would have to pass.

The Japanese didn't give much thought to the western end of New Britain until the Allies started marching up the eastern coast of New Guinea, a hundred miles away across the channel. Only then did the Japanese set about fortifying western New Britain. They built a bomber strip at the remote village of Cape Gloucester.

The Allies were advancing up the New Guinea mainland because Gen. MacArthur had vowed to return to the Philippines and he wanted help on his flank. He wanted it from the 1st Marine Division, and he got it. On December 24, 1943, MacArthur dispatched the 1st Marine Division, the veterans of Guadalcanal, to capture the strategic Japanese-held airfield at Cape Gloucester, secure the western end of the island, and spearhead his island-hopping campaign across the Pacific.

Getting to the staging area was an ordeal. We embarked aboard converted Merchant Marine liberty ships for a miserable five-day trip to Goodenough Island, off the southeastern tip of New Guinea. We were packed in like sardines aboard dark, uncomfortable, and plodding ships. I remember looking out in disgust at the crowded decks, wondering why these ships, originally designed to transport cargo, were being loaded with Marines going off to war. No wonder we ended up calling them "rust bucket tubs."

The conversion of the liberty ships consisted of constructing a galley and heads on deck. (It was hard to tell which was which.) In strong winds, we fought to keep food in our mess kits and down in our stomachs. We weren't too happy to find out the only meat we had aboard was frozen sides of Australian mutton, which we classified immediately as "dead goat." The meat was uniformly disliked by all hands. We resumed taking our atabrine pills. As we arrived at the end of the mess line with our canteen cup in one hand and our mess kit in the other, the routine was to open up as a medical corpsman flicked a little yellow pill in your mouth.

We made our way up the Australian coast sailing the Great Barrier Reef. The reef was a natural protective barrier as we sailed at night. We had no idea where we might be going, certain only that we were headed north and back into the war. By that time, the Japanese had been cleared out of the Solomon Islands and most of New Guinea. We had launched our northward island-hopping progress across the Pacific. Conjecture about our destination kept our tongues wagging and our minds occupied during the days of inactivity, when we would sit gossiping on the greasy canvas covering the hatches.

We were permitted on deck at night, although we were told not to smoke once we left the protection of the Great Barrier Reef. We sailed through narrow seas lined by lush green jungles with steep banks. Suddenly, we were in a harbor, docked and unloading. One of the other transports in our convoy ran aground about half a mile to our starboard. The crew swung the landing crafts free and lowered them into the water. At the command, we clambered over the side, down the cargo nets, and into the Higgins boats.

We quickly saw that this was not an uninhabited island. There were no buildings, but there was a harbormaster on the beach bellowing through his megaphone to direct the unloading. Lines of olive-green trucks waited to carry us to a staging area some distance inland. Not until we arrived at the pioneer battalion staging area did I even think to inquire where we were. "Goodenough Island," one of the officers explained. I laughed and said, "I guess its good enough for Marines."

I was very pleased with my new assignment as platoon sergeant of the 2nd Platoon, E Company Pioneers, commanded by Capt. Olin H. Palmer from Blythe, Georgia. I respected Capt. Palmer, who was one of the finest young officers who ever pulled on a pair of Marine combat boots.

Training continued in the advance staging area on Goodenough Island, becoming increasingly realistic with the use of terrain closely resembling the target. That was something impossible to simulate convincingly in the temperate climate around Melbourne, Australia. Emphasis was laid on ship-to-shore operations, employing the new or improved equipment now beginning to reach the Pacific in quantity. Few 1st Division Marines until then had seen a landing ship tank (LST), landing craft infantry (LCI), landing craft vehicles and personnel (LCVPs), or amphibious trucks (DUKWs).

While on Goodenough Island, much of my time was spent giving lectures and demonstrating a new plastic military explosive, Composition C2, and a new land bangalore torpedo cylinder packed with TNT. The latter could be ignited and shoved into a cave or breach barbed wire entanglements. Emphasis was also placed on the use of a Composition C2 explosive satchel charge, and the new napalm flame-thrower designed for use during an assault on enemy fortified positions.

It was back to the jungle for us after several weeks of advance training and final preparation at our staging area. This time it was a place called Cape Gloucester, but once again we were going in after an airfield. Our destination did not come as any surprise, as the enemy also had word of the coming assault upon Cape Gloucester. Radio Tokyo blared the following message for days: "The 1st American Marine Division, assorted cut-throats, degenerates, and jailbirds, have been chased out of Melbourne, Australia, and are encamped in New Guinea. They will try to invade the Japanese-held island of New Britain. I am pleased to report that our soldiers are fully prepared to repulse this insolent attempt. The jungle will run red with the blood of the Guadalcanal butchers."

The initial concept of operations called for the conquest of western New Britain preliminary to storming Cape Gloucester. The plan split the 1st Marine Division, sending Combat Team A (the 5th Marines, reinforced) against Gasmata on the southern coast of the island, while Combat Team C (the 7th Marines, reinforced) would seize a beachhead near the principal objective, the airfield on Cape Gloucester. The Army's 503rd Parachute Infantry would exploit the Cape Gloucester beachhead, while Combat Team B (the 1st Marines, reinforced) provided a reserve for the operation.

Fortunately, Gen. Douglas MacArthur made a visit to Goodenough Island in late November 1943. Unfortunately for Gen. Walter Krueger, commander of the 6th Army, who accompanied him for a final briefing prior to the invasion, Col. Edwin A. Pollock, the assistant chief of staff of the 1st Marine Division at the time, advised Gen. MacArthur of the Marine's opposition to a complex scheme of maneuver involving Army airborne troops, "Division did not care for the plan, and there is no way we can support it, Sir." Krueger was unable to stare him down. Gen. Rupertus had backed Pollock.

The Marines' position was that it would be better to strengthen the amphibious forces than to try an aerial envelopment that might fail or be delayed by the weather. Although he made no comment at the time, MacArthur may well have heeded what Pollock said. Whatever the reason, Krueger's staff eliminated the airborne portion and directed the two battalions of the 1st Marines still with Combat Team B to land immediately after the assault waves, sustaining the momentum of their attack. He alerted the division reserve to provide further reinforcement

On December 24, three regiments of the 1st Marine Division, commanded by Maj. Gen. William Rupertus, embarked on troop transports and amphibious landing craft from New Guinea for the quick journey across the Dampier Strait. It was a hell of a way to celebrate Christmas Eve.

The word was passed to break camp and move out. We slipped into our packs, slung our weapons, and marched down the dusty road to the harbor at Cape Sudest. The harbor was choked with amphibious ships, and many of them were drawing up on the beach, their ramps down and their jaws yawing while troops, vehicles, and guns walked, rode, and bumped into their dark and spacious bellies.

We entered our LST. The ramp came up behind us, the jaws creaked shut, and we sailed away. The ship would have been all right if there had been about one-third fewer troops aboard. As it was, we could hardly move. Many of the Marines aboard were punchy from lack of sleep and seasickness before we reached our destination. Despite the miserable shipboard conditions, Navy and Marine cooks managed to serve us a wonderful Christmas dinner. There was turkey, mashed potatoes, bread, and even ice cream. We marveled to think that we could eat so regally.

Below deck, the chaplain was preparing to hold Midnight Mass. He reminded us that not all of us would live to see another Christmas, that perhaps some of us might die this very day. He told us to be sorry for our sins and to ask the forgiveness of God, to forgive those who had wronged us, to prepare our souls for death. We sang "Silent Night" and "Hark the Herald Angels Sing."

Part II   **Cape Gloucester**

[18]   Cape Gloucester, the Green Inferno

It was Christmas Day in the States, but out on the damp waters of Dampier Straights it was the morning of December 26, and once again the men of the 1st Marine Division were preparing to storm the beaches of a Japanese-held island. This time it was on the sunless shores of Cape Gloucester, New Britain, where thick swamp forests ran down to the sea.

At 0600 hours, the thundering of naval gunfire began. Cruisers and destroyers sailed back and forth blazing at the shoreline with orange-yellow bursts of naval gunfire. Rocket-firing LCI daintily picked their way through the opening in the barrier reef. They took up positions on either end of the landing beaches. Soon the, *swoosh-swoosh* sounds of missiles were audible beneath the booming sound of the naval gunfire.

At 0745 the 7th Marine Regiment, led by Col. Julian N. Frisbie, poured onto Cape Gloucester's battered beaches against token resistance. Maj. Gen. Iwao Matsuda, commander of the Japanese forces ashore, had not expected the landing to occur where it did because of vast swamps and heavy foliage in the area, so he had placed his men on either side of the morass.

The Cape Gloucester campaign was the only one of the four major landings made by the 1st Marine Division during which things happened when they are suppose to happen, as nearly as can be expected in war. The landing went according to plan. When the 7th Marines

*In December 1943, the 1st Marine Division was back in action. Here rifle-
men wade ashore at Cape Gloucester on New Britain. Courtesy of the
Marine Corps Historical Center.*

rushed ashore, they barged straight through a huge gap separating the
Japanese contingents and drove a wedge between them. However, they
advanced directly into the first of two natural obstacles to harass them
in inhospitable New Britain—jungle. After advancing a short distance,
Marine units became mired in swamps and mud so thick that they
sank to their armpits. Members of the column fell into waist-high sink
holes and had to be pulled out. A slip meant a broken or wrenched leg.

This was a form of opposition that had not been expected, one for which the men had made no preparation. The area was labeled on the maps as "Damp Flat," and some Marines said laughingly, "It's damp, alright. It's damp clear up to your ass!" Fighting in the "green inferno" would cover a great deal of that kind of terrain.

An hour after the 7th was ashore, the 1st Marines arrived, turned toward the airfield, and walked into a well-laid Japanese ambush. Tanks were called forward to clear the enemy from their hidden bunkers, and by nightfall the 1st Marines were was well on their way to the airfield, but not before they had encountered atrocious conditions along the way. Tanks became mired in swampy terrain. Bazooka rockets failed to detonate in the mud. Howitzers disappeared. Teeming rains forced troops to remove waterlogged canvas leggings and constantly check weapons and equipment for rust. The ground became a sea of mud. Amphibious tractors were the only vehicles able to transport ammunition and food to troops in the forward areas.

By the end of the first day, however, a beachhead had been secured. The reinforced 7th Marines landed near Silimatic Point and wheeled southward toward Borgen Bay. The 1st Marines, also reinforced but without its 2nd battalion, passed through the 7th to head west toward the airfield. Marines did not halt until they reached the Japanese outposts, some 1500 yards inland.

A second landing was made by the 2nd Battalion, 1st Marines, reinforced and designated Landing Team 21. That battalion landed at Tauali, seven miles southwest of Cape Gloucester. They were to block any Japanese attempt to retire or reinforce the airfield. The 5th Marines served as division reserve, ready for employment as needed.

The sound of naval gunfire and diving airplanes had already been stilled when a command post was established about fifty yards in front of the beach by Col. Robert G. Ballance, our newly promoted battalion commander, 2nd Battalion, 17th Marines, the division pioneers. Only one thing was needed for the security of the beachhead—a perimeter, a line of positions to oppose counterattacks. My unit, E Company, 2nd Battalion, would hold one of these positions to provide defense in depth in rear of the 2nd Battalion, 7th Marines' lines as its forces moved inland. Each company of the battalion moved forward to take up positions that formed a defense perimeter, a half-moon with our main force. We were its straight edge running along the beach. It couldn't have been more than 400 yards across its widest point.

It was the jungle and the rain that made Cape Gloucester so different from Guadalcanal. I knew it was going to be different the moment I led my platoon down the ramp and across the narrow black beach, then up a small, steep bank. We burst into the gloom of the jungle. That was when the rains began to fall and to receive us in a wet and dripping embrace. As we readied foxholes for our first night on the island, New Britain unleashed one of its terrifying storms. Over the next thirty days, torrential rains inundated the troops and transformed soggy areas into virtually impassable bogs.

The first night especially stunned the Marines. As we battled a Japanese counterattack, spectacular lightning illuminated our perimeter and booming thunder rivaled the sound of gunfire. The wind roared in from the Bismarck Sea at hurricane velocity, bringing splintering crashes. Almost blinded by the tempest, the wet and weary Marines shot wildly at where they hoped the enemy would be, and eventually drove them off.

On the second night ashore my platoon was fired upon by a Japanese probing force. I shouted, "Let 'em have it," and using my newly acquired Old Betsy 12-gauge pump shotgun, I poured a barrage of oo buckshot into the enemy trying to penetrate our position. There were about five minutes in which everybody on the perimeter was blasting away at the enemy as they made a hasty withdrawal into the jungle.

The wet, weary Marines encountered stiff resistance when they closed to within 1000 yards of the airfield in the early afternoon of

Marine riflemen follow a medium Sherman Tank through the New Britain jungle as they advance toward the vital Japanese-held airfield on Cape Gloucester. Official U.S. Marine Photo.

December 28. Twelve bunkers, each holding twenty or more Japanese soldiers armed with antitank guns and 75-mm fieldpieces, delayed the advance four hours until fire from American tanks forced the Japanese into the open. There they became easy targets for waiting Marine riflemen and tank commanders. This action, at a spot aptly named "Hell's Point," ended by late afternoon.

The next day, Col. John T. Seldon's 5th Marine Regiment, which had been held in division reserve at Cape Sudest, came ashore and joined the drive on the airfield. While the 1st Regiment attacked from the east, Seldon's men charged in from the south, scampered through a network of empty bunkers, and entrenched on the airfield and along a nearby ridge. On December 30, they had cleared the enemy

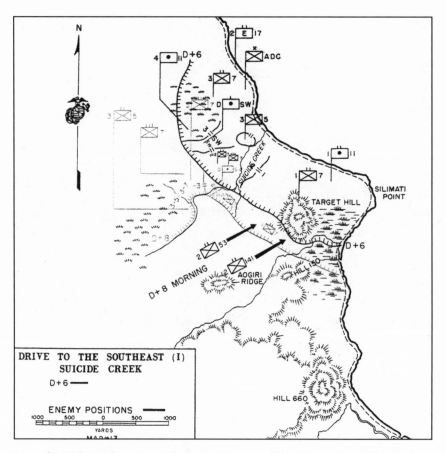

Map of Suicide Creek on Cape Gloucester. Courtesy of the Marine Corps Historical Center.

off two overlooking hills and the 1st and 5th Marines had secured the airfield.

Maj. Gen. Rupertus, commanding general of the 1st Marine Division, sent a triumphant dispatch to Gen. Krueger, commanding general of the 6th Army, offering the airfield as an early New Year's gift. The following day, December 31, Rupertus raised the American flag over Cape Gloucester. Gen. MacArthur, first to send congratulations, said: "Your gallant division has maintained the immortal record of the Marine Corps and covered itself with glory."

Nothing else was quite so easy as seizure of the airfield. The force now turned to secure its hold on the island by driving into the jumbled, ravine-cut country around Borgen Bay. The toll mounted rapidly. B. Gen. Lemuel C. Shepherd, the assistant division commander, directed the assault to clear the enemy from this area in order to extend the perimeter, a line of positions to oppose counterattacks.

B. Gen. Shepherd issued the operation order on January 1. The attack jumped off at 1000 hours the following morning when the 7th Marines and the 3rd Battalion of the 5th Marines began its advance through the swamp toward Aogiri Ridge. The 2nd Battalion of the 17th Marines followed in the wake of the infantry. We squished through the mud. The tracks left where the infantry trod were at least ankle-deep and many times were nearly knee-deep. We had walked miles, during which we had to strain to pull our feet out of the sucking mud to make the next step.

B. Gen. Shepherd employed an unusual and interesting scheme of maneuver in which one writer, Fletcher Pratt, has likened to that employed by Gen. Sherman against the fortified approaches to Atlanta during the Civil War in 1864. Briefly, Shepherd proposed to hold fast on the left and center on the beachhead perimeter, while the right of that line redeployed and attacked generally to the southeast on a front of 1000 yards. Because of the orientation of the old perimeter, such a move would cause the line of advance to lie straight across the front of 2nd Battalion, 7th Marines, which for several days had been holding the center along the shore of a small stream across which the Japanese had been industriously digging in.

To effect this movement, the 3rd Battalion, 7th Marines, which had been holding the right of the perimeter, moved deeper into the jungle and deployed to face southeast with companies in line. The 3rd Battalion, 5th Marines came up and extended still farther to the right with companies in line. The plan called for the two battalions to advance abreast across the entire front of 2nd Battalion, 7th Marines to a designated phase line, thereby pinching out that unit and tying in the left of 3rd Battalion, 7th Marines with the right of 1st Battalion, 7th Marines.

No one discounted the difficulties imposed by both the terrain and the enemy. The men of 3rd Battalion, 7th Marines laboriously hacked their way through the jungle for about 300 yards. There they came up against the prepared positions that the Japanese had been constructing for the past week in front of 2nd Battalion, 7th Marines. The 3rd Battalion had their forward progress rudely halted by a heavy volume of rifle and automatic weapons fire.

The 3rd Battalion, 5th Marines, with a greater distance to travel, encountered less resistance during the early phases. Patrols working well off to the right were encouraged to discover no signs of the enemy in that direction. But when they attempted an encircling movement from the west, the assault troops soon encountered the face of the same Japanese pocket that was holding up the 7th Marines. The 5th Marines were halted in turn. As a result, the attacking lines on the night of January 2 and throughout January 3, resembled a huge U, with the enemy strong points contained on three sides.

The 2nd Battalion of the 17th Marines reported difficulty negotiating the marshy ground and the dense jungle growth as they pushed forward. Fighting in the Borgen Bay area would cover a great deal of that kind of terrain. We stumbled through swamps, sometimes armpit-deep, and were tripped at every turn by tangle roots and creepers. We were ravaged as we went by swarms of mosquitoes and other blood-sucking insects that bit every inch of exposed flesh.

Rain and mud, rain and mud—that was it. The men in my pioneer platoon ceased to look like men. They looked like slimy frogs working in some prehistoric ooze. That first day the men kept on the move for eleven hours. Every foot was a struggle as we went about the difficult

"Ghost Trail, Cape Gloucester," by Kerr Eby, The Abbot Collection. Courtesy of the U.S. Naval Historical Center.

task of building a causeway through a stretch of jungle and mangrove swamp. At the end of the day, crouching under ponchos, we ate cold beans and beef stew from C-ration cans. A few minutes later I was asleep. I was dead tired, and I didn't give a damn about any Japanese attack. I lay under a tall mangrove tree trunk protruding two or three feet above the water level; the tree was supported by a dense tangle of stout prop roots. I kept my entrenching shovel nearby to kill snakes that might slither up to my dry perch during the night.

The second day was even tougher. It took several hours for the Marine pioneers to complete the corduroy causeway that would enable tanks to move forward in this hellish place. Slogging through the mud, the men cursed the jungle in hoarse whispers. Profanity seemed little enough to hurl against the snaking roots that reached out to trip us, the damnable muck that sucked us down, the million and one vines and creepers that clawed at the men and threw us off balance. Time and time again, Marine pioneers lugging eight-foot timbers for the causeway fell into deep sink holes up to their armpits and have to be pulled out by the stacking swivel.

For two days the assault battalions fought what amounted to a stale-mate, paying a high price in casualties for negligible gains. At the same time, pioneers of the 17th Marines labored mightily under atrocious weather and sniper fire to build a corduroy causeway across the coastal swamp to enable tanks to reach the scene of action. A betting man might have obtained good odds that it could not be done.[1] But during the afternoon of January 3, three Gen. Sherman medium tanks lumbered up to the near bank of Suicide Creek, looking reassuringly large and formidable to the hitherto unsupported infantrymen.

The Battle of Suicide Creek

Marines who fought at Guadalcanal thought they had seen every imaginable horror of war. But we watched the Battle of Suicide Creek unfold with disbelieving eyes. More men fell in one day's fighting at Suicide Creek than on any single day of fighting on Guadalcanal or Cape Gloucester. The fierce battle at Suicide Creek might have decided the Battle of Cape Gloucester. Blood flowed as copiously as the rain, turning the jungle floor into slimy mud littered with the bodies of the dead and wounded Marines, who were trampled by men fighting for their lives.

The distinguished writer and war correspondent Asa Bordages was attached to the 3rd Battalion, 5th Marines. He gave wartime readers of the *Saturday Evening Post* the following grim story of the swamp battle:

They came to "Suicide Creek." It had no name and it was not on the map, but that is what the Marines called it after they had fought in vain to win a crossing. The creek was swift, two or three feet deep, perhaps twenty feet across at the widest point, twisting between steep banks. The banks rose steeply from ten to twenty feet, up the little ridges into the jungle of Cape Gloucester.

The Marines didn't know that the creek was a moat before an enemy stronghold. The deadly defense could not be seen, they couldn't see that the heavy growth across the creek was salted with pillboxes, machine-gun emplacements armored with dirt and logs, some of them several stories deep, all carefully spotted so they could sweep the slopes of both banks of the creek with interfacing fire.

Only snipers shot at the Marine scouts who crossed the creek. Those Marines felt their way through the thickets. More Marines followed, down into the creek, up a steep bank, on into the jungle. Then they got it. The jungle exploded in their face. They hit the deck, trying to deploy into the bullet-lashed brush and strike back. Marines died there, firing blindly, cursing because they couldn't see the enemy soldiers who were killing them, or not saying anything—just dying. The others could only hug the ground as bullets cut the brush above their heads, like a sweeping blade of fire. They couldn't even help the wounded.

Snipers picked off some Marines as they lay there. It is a perfect situation for snipers when machine guns are firing. Nobody can hear the single pop of a rifle above the heavier fire. You don't know you're a target until you are hit.

From the American side of Suicide Creek, Marines gave the trapped platoon overhead fire. The idea was to fling such a volume of fire at the enemy's positions that the enemy must hug cover and slacken his fire. The overhead fire spread an umbrella of bullets above the pinned-down platoon, enabling those Marines to crawl back across the creek, pulling their wounded along with them.

That's how it went all day as Marine detachments felt for a gap or a soft spot in the enemy's positions along the creek. Marines would get hit and pull back. Detachments would push across the creek at other points, then blasted by invisible machine guns. Each time a few more dead Marines were left in the brush as the unscathed Marines fell back across the creek. Then they'd do it all over again.

There was nothing else they could do. There is no other way to fight a jungle battle. Not in such terrain, where the enemy digs in and the Marines orders are to advance. You don't know where the enemy is. His pillboxes are so camouflaged that you can usually find them only when they fire on you. So you push out scouts and small patrols until they're

Marine fire team wades across Suicide Creek on Cape Gloucester. Courtesy of the Marine Corps Historical Center.

fired on. Then you push out patrols from different directions until they, too, draw fire. Thus you locate the enemy. Then you have to take the emplacements, the pillboxes, one by one, in desperate little battles.

Japanese snipers had infiltrated the line and killed Marines at short range. One unit was broken when it tried to wade the stream. Its survivors were driven to hide in the weeds at the edge of the creek. At midstream a Marine who failed to make it hung over a log, his body riddled by scores of bullet holes. For half an hour or more he called to his mates, before he died, "Here I am! Here I am!"

The attack stalled. The line became U-shaped; with a pocket holding back the center. Gen. Rupertus, from Division, relieved the commander of the 3rd Battalion, 7th Marines, and sent Col. Puller forward to assume command, with orders to reorganize and drive forward.

Puller's orders were clear, "Now, we'll go forward. We have enough power to drive, and we're going to drive. Blow your way through, and think of nothing else."

The half-track, a bulldozer, and tanks were ready by dawn. At 0800, the push began. The tanks finally reached the penned down 3rd Battalion, but found that the banks of the creek too steep for crossing. The gully formed a natural tank trap. So a Marine bulldozer was called forward to cut down the banks of the creek and make a fill in the stream so that the tanks could cross against the enemy.

The Japanese saw the danger suddenly confronting them. They concentrated fire on the bulldozer. Man after man was shot from the driver's seat. Some killed, some wounded. But there was always a Marine to jump into the seat. One Marine who jumped into the seat was S. Sgt. Kerry Lane. He had no shield, no protection at all. He sat up in the open like a shooting gallery, a target for all the enemy fire. Although wounded in the shoulder by a sniper's bullet, Lane kept on operating the bulldozer until the fill was made and the tanks were rolling across the creek.[1]

In the heat of battle, I hardly realized that I was wounded. I heard no noise, felt no pain, not at the moment. I was a little woozy after being hit in the left shoulder, and I was somewhat unsteady on my feet after crawling down from the bulldozer. My first reaction was to rally my platoon, which was hunkered down in the weeds at the edge of the creek so we could assist in directing the tanks across the fill.

The tank drivers had limited vision because they were buttoned up. The only way we could communicate with tank drivers was by using the telephone in a box attached to the rear of each tank. I told Capt. Palmer, my platoon commander, who was crouched down by me, "I've got to get on that phone and direct them tanks across the fill. If I don't get them moving, we are all going to die in this damn creek."

He said, "You will never make it. The machine-gun fire is too much, and besides you're bleeding." I glanced down at my tattered utility shirt and saw that it was soaked in blood. I realized that I needed medical attention, but at that point I figured this might be my last battle, so I did what I had to do and hoped that I'd make it across the creek. When you're young you don't fear things. You respond automatically. You just go and do it.

I said, "I ain't got time to worry about bleeding," and yelled to the pinned-down Marine pioneers to give me cover as I staggered and crawled across the fill to the lead tank on the opposite side of the creek under heavy enemy fire. I raised the lid on the box and picked up the hand phone. I told the guys inside to move forward and I would guide them across the newly cut fill in the creek bed. The lead tank commander responded and directed the two tanks in the rear to crank-up and follow him.

Directing the tanks across the fill proved to be an extremely difficult and hazardous task. The enemy was just as determined to prevent us from crossing as we were to cross. Once again, I was proud of the way my pioneer platoon performed under heavy enemy fire. The lead Sherman tank commenced a gingerly negotiation of the improvised ramp, wallowed through the shallow water, and successfully mounted the opposite bank. Infantrymen following in close support cut down two Japanese sappers trying to detonate magnetic mines against the tank's sides.[2] Other medium tanks followed, also accompanied by infantry. These tanks shattered the enemy's heavily reinforced log-and-earthen bunkers that barred the way.

The advance of the tanks made untenable the position of the enemy opposing the 3rd Battalion. When the Japanese tried to hold against the frontal attack by the Marines, tanks and infantry from the flanks hit them. They had to retreat or be crushed, and they retreated.

Once across Suicide Creek, the Marines grouped for Aogiri Ridge. The 3rd Battalion, 7th Marines and the 3rd Battalion, 5th Marines

The first tank across Suicide Creek. The author's platoon assisted in this operation. Courtesy of the U.S. National Archives.

surged onward past the creek, squeezing out the 2nd Battalion, 7th Marines, which crossed in the wake of those two units and come abreast of them on the far right of the line that closed in on the jungle concealing Aogiri Ridge. The 1st Battalion, 7th Marines joined the southward advance, tying in with the 3rd Battalion, 5th Marines, to present a four-battalion front that included the 2nd Battalion and 3rd Battalions, 7th Marines.

The battle for Suicide Creek was over for me. I collapsed from exhaustion and loss of blood. One of the infantrymen who was crouched nearby helped me to a sitting position, called for a medical corpsman, and tried to reassure me that I would be all right. The corpsman applied a field dressing to my wound and gave me a shot of morphine and a plasma injection. Then I was tagged, placed on a stretcher, and moved to the beach for medical evacuation off the island.

Stretcher bearers remove a wounded Marine from the battle scene during the Cape Gloucester campaign. Courtesy of Marine Corps Historical Center.

Col. Puller spoke to me briefly before the stretcher barriers removed me from the scene of battle. His parting words to the corpsman treating me were, "Take good care of this sergeant. He's one hell of a Marine!"

When the landing ship with its cargo well modified to transport wounded Marines docked at Cape Sudest, New Guinea, there were a number of khaki-colored ambulances waiting for us. We were transported inland to an Army field hospital and dropped off at a battle clearing station. My dog tags were checked by an Army nurse.

The clothes I had on were the ones that I had worn since the start of the ill-fated Suicide Creek battle. They were filthy with mud and blood and had holes in them. After our clothes were discarded in a cluttered pile, the ward medics came with warm pans of water and cleaned us up, but made no attempt to clean the wound in my shoulder, where the old blood had caked, dried, and plastered the bandages to my body.

A short time later the nurse returned with a pair of clean hospital pajamas and instructed the ward medics to move me to a nearby operating room, where she carefully started removing my bandages. Drainage from the wound caused it to stick to my skin. As she worked, she spoke in a soft, reassuring voice that everything would be all right. Her voice was so honeyed that all distractions faded for a moment. Just the sound of her voice made my brain register instant images of things soft and feminine. I hadn't realized how much I had missed female companionship.

While lying on the operating table, I tried to recall the details of how I was wounded. But somehow I couldn't get everything straight. The turmoil of the previous few days was like a distant, bad dream. I winced with apprehension as she removed the bandages with scissors, gently pulling it with her hands. When the bandages came off, she checked the wound for signs of infection and continued to prep me for surgery.

The Army surgeon who performed the operation told me that I was one lucky Marine and that I must have had a guardian angel riding with me. The doctor said if the bullet was a fraction of an inch in one direction would have been fatal. The bullet fragment was most likely a 6.5-mm round fired from a Japanese Arisaka sniper's rifle. The surgeon assured me that, barring any complications from infection, my prognosis for complete recovery was very good.

After a short stay in the recovery room, the nurse had me moved to a large ward that held several patients. I enjoyed her soft, feminine warmth and touch as she helped me into bed and pulled the covers up over me. She then ran a soothing hand across my forehead as if she were checking for a fever. It had been several months since I had slept in a bed with clean white sheets. I felt safe for the first time since we waded ashore on Cape Gloucester.

The next morning I asked for a pencil, writing paper, and envelope. Within a few minutes, a Red Cross lady appeared. Gently, she helped me get into a comfortable sitting position, and I wrote a letter to my parents. It was standard Marine Corps procedure to send a telegram telling them I had been wounded in action. They would be worried about me when it arrived. I wanted them to know the actual extent of my injury as soon as possible, so they would not be so concerned. Later, I learned that they had been informed by telegram that I was seriously wounded in action and had been evacuated to a field hospital in New Guinea.

After two weeks in the hospital, my ward nurse informed me that arrangements were being made for me to go on a two-week convalescence leave to Australia. I told her that, as much as I would like to revisit that wonderful country, I felt I should return to my unit. She said, "You can't go back yet. You lost a lot of blood, and the wound area in your shoulder needs additional time to mend."

I looked straight into the eyes of that Army nurse and said, "You tell the doctor that if I'm well enough to go to Australia, I'm sure as hell well enough to return to combat."

Shaking her head she said, "I doubt you are well enough for that, but I will inform him of your desire to return to duty."

The next morning, my doctor came to the ward and pronounced that I was well enough to rejoin my unit. I looked up at him. The nurse was standing nearby and laughing. I said, "It doesn't look like you two can't wait to get rid of me." They both smiled, and he said, "We discussed your desire to return to duty and decided the best thing for us to do was to let you go back and take care of the rest of those Japanese soldiers on Cape Gloucester so we all can go home early."

They both shook my hand and gave me a few parting words of encouragement. I couldn't have received better treatment during my stay in the Army hospital. There were daily sponge baths, back rubs, reading, eating three fine meals a day, and movies at night. The nurses were charming, very knowledgeable, and they provided medical care far above and beyond the call of duty.

Then it was good-bye to the hospital and back to Cape Gloucester. As I prepared to travel by plane, I had mixed emotions about leaving, but my desire to be with my command was overriding. The big transport plane rose with a roar from the airstrip at Cape Sudest. This was my first airplane flight. I settled down into my bucket seat, with my left arm in a shoulder sling while the plane leveled out to fly low over the Dampier Straight. We gained altitude over New Guinea, where the jungle had the appearance of row upon row of tightly sown brussels sprouts. An hour or so later, our transport plane came down with a rush at the captured Cape Gloucester airstrip. We landed on a narrow runway covered with a type of corrugated steel called "Marston mat" that made the plane vibrate and sound like it was falling apart. This was a terrifying experience.

As the plane hit the tarmac and taxied to the field operation terminal, I tried to imagine how the tactical situation might have changed since I was evacuated off the island two weeks earlier. Once we went through the process of checking in at field operations, we got aboard waiting jeeps and trucks for our ride back to rejoin our units.

During my two weeks of hospitalization, my platoon of pioneers from E Company, 2nd Battalion, 17th Marines participated in the attack, capture, and defense of Aogiri Ridge, renamed "Walt's Ridge" in honor of Lt. Col. Lewis W. Walt, who led the attack. The fight for the strategic ridge typified the Cape Gloucester campaign—a struggle of brave men against the enemy and the elements. My platoon also became part of a task force led by Capt. Joseph Buckley, Weapons Company, 7th Marines, to bypass Hill 660 and block the coastal trail beyond the objective.

With a bulldozer and one of the Army's rocket-firing DUKWs, they pushed through the mud and set up a roadblock athwart the line of retreat from Hill 660. The task force encountered fierce resistance as the Japanese directed long-range plunging fire against Buckley's command as it advanced past Hill 660 and cut the line of retreat for the Japanese defenders.

The Marines spent all of January 12 resting and reorganizing in preparation for an assault on what had been designated the final objective, the conspicuous landmark Hill 660. Securing that hill would deprive the Japanese of their last vantage point from which to interfere with operations on the landing beaches. The enemy occupied the position with one reinforced company supported by a number of weapons of the 30th Machine Cannon Company and one 75-mm gun.

To make the assault, Gen. Shepherd selected the 3rd Battalion, 7th Marines. The battalion had a new commanding officer, Lt. Col. Henry W. Buse Jr., formerly the assistant division operations officer. He had relieved Col. Puller, who returned to his position of regimental executive officer on January 9. The 3rd Battalion had been in reserve for several days, so those Marines were in comparatively fresh condition. The plan called for the 3rd Battalion, 5th Marines to continue mopping up Aogiri Ridge and consolidate that position. Meanwhile the 2nd Battalion, 7th Marines were on the right, occupying what was called the Force Beachhead Line. The 1st Battalion's mission was to extend the perimeter southward by maintaining contact with the right of the 3rd Battalion.

At 0800 on January 13, after artillery, mortars, and support aircraft had given the target area thorough preparation, Col. Buse moved his unit out from the 0–4 phase line in column of companies. They arrived in assaulting position an hour and a half later without encountering any resistance, although the terrain was especially difficult. The rising ground of the approach dropped sharply to the northern base of the hill proper, thus forming a deep gulch. Both slopes were cluttered with trees and jungle undergrowth and strewn with boulders. Buse set up his command post on the rear lip of the ravine. His assault elements descended the first slope and started up the second.

In covering the Hill 660 battle, Marine combat correspondent and *Washington Post* writer Sam Stavisky wrote:

> Foot by foot, man by man, the hostilities persisted without letup throughout the afternoon. By 4 o'clock, we could see that the

prospects of gaining the crest were dubious. Right then, Lt. Col. Buse had to make another decision: either abandon the plan to capture the hill that day and swing around the south base to form a junction with the weapons company on the beach, or take the bolder, more danger-ous course of trying to seize the hill before darkness fell. Lt. Col. Buse chose the audacious alternative . . . but to do so, the Marines had to overcome a number of obstacles. The angle of the slope was very high. The Japanese had machine guns cunningly placed all over the ridgeline. And the leathernecks were dead tired after fighting for eighteen days. They had been pushed to their limits; they were going on raw nerves. At that critical stage, the Marines rose spontaneously and, shouting defiance, charged up the near-vertical face of Hill 660 at 0600 hours, one hour before darkness. The defenders ran before they could be completely encircled.[3]

A few Japanese evidently escaped to the safety of the swamp at the hill's southeastern base. One group estimated at upward of thirty fled down the northeastern slope into the pocket formed by the weapons company's roadblock. Those Japanese made things lively for Buckley's people during the night by trying to break through or around the posi-tion. A rain-soaked dawn revealed many of them dodging through the jungle beyond the cleared field of fire, attempting to reach the same swamp by skirting the perimeter.

The 3rd Battalion gained the crest of Hill 660 at about 1830 hours on January 14. That was just in time to signal their achievement to the weapons company below before a furious rainstorm broke and acceler-ated the onrush of dusk and eliminated visibility. The exhausted men dug in as best they could among the dead Japanese. The storm lasted all night. No counterattacks occurred, which was just as well, because the Marines were in no condition to give the best of themselves.

The weather cleared the following day, bringing some rest to the weary, as well as additional automatic weapons to consolidate the captured position. Continued mopping-up operations netted a few stragglers, but revealed no formidable enemy forces.

Not until 0530 on the morning of January 16 did the Japanese make any real effort to dispute possession of Hill 660. That took the form of a banzai assault in the traditional manner. There were approximately two companies of howling fanatics swarming up the southern slope. For a while the fighting was close and vicious, but as soon as he could obtain sufficient space, Col. Buse devised an ingenious and lethal method of destroying those of the enemy who had survived to that point. He blanketed their front with 60-mm mortar fire and their rear with 81-mm and artillery. Ranges closed gradually on each other with devastating effect.

Somewhat earlier the same morning, a Japanese platoon of thirty men and one officer made an infiltration attempt against the lines of the 1st Battalion, 7th Marines. These attacks were the last gasp of the Japanese in that area. After daylight, mopping-up patrols on Hill 660 found 110 dead in the area. Simultaneously, Capt. Buckley's group repulsed a weaker attack on the coastal flat without much difficulty, killing 48 more Japanese. For all tactical purposes, the Cape Gloucester operation was over and the southern perimeter secured.

Extensive reorganization became the order of the day after accomplishment of this phase of Gen. Shepherd's ADC Group mission. The 7th Marines as a regiment, together with the 3rd Battalion, 5th Marines and their various supporting elements, had carried the burden of the campaign's heaviest fighting. The mission consisted of a sustained drive of two weeks, moving through some of the most difficult jungle territory in the world, and enduring some of the worst weather in which troops were ever required to operate.

When I rejoined my unit, I was surprised to find that we were in reserve. We no longer had a front to defend. But we had a new enemy—the trees. We lost several Marines at Cape Gloucester to huge falling kanaris trees. Aerial bombs and artillery shells had weakened the roots. Our new position was in woods so grim, so stark, and so scarred by battle that it might have been a forest on the moon. The Japanese had defended the site, and a fierce artillery barrage had been laid down along with a pounding from the air. Scores of coconut trees, pounded by bombs and shells, collapsed, smashing fighting positions and tents.

While casualties as the result of enemy action had subsided during this period, more and more men lay awake at night with malaria attacks, alternating between being bathed in sweat or shaking from a chill. Those with dengue, also called "break bone fever," groaned with pain. Some men's eyes turned yellow. Weakness set in upon those with jaundice. All of the Marine units suffered a great deal of sickness from malaria carried by anopheles mosquitoes that attack at night, dengue fever that developed from the bite of daytime mosquitoes, and jaundice from unsanitary eating conditions. Fungus grew quickly in the hot, moist climate, and was aggravated by sweat. Everyone had the crud.

In February, Gen. Shepherd instituted search-and-destroy patrols on the western side of New Britain. The essential purpose of those patrols was to locate the headquarters of the most senior Japanese officer, Gen. Matsuda, and to learn where his forces were withdrawing. At that time, a vigorous pursuit along the coast and on the inland trails had failed to snare the retreating Japanese. The Marines captured Gen. Matsuda's abandoned headquarters in the shadow of Mount Talawe. They found there a buried cache of documents. But the Japanese general and his troops escaped.

Once it was determined that Matsuda was withdrawing toward Rabaul, small amphibious parties leap-frogged ahead to cut him off. Because a trail led from the vicinity of Mount Talawe to the south, Gen. Shepherd concluded that Matsuda was headed in that direction. The assistant division commander organized a composite battalion of six reinforced rifle companies and elements of the 17th Marines, some 3900 officers and men in all, which Gen. Rupertus entrusted to Col. Puller.

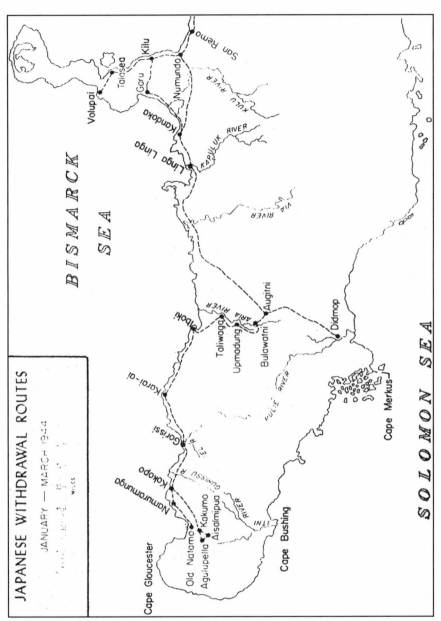

Map of the Japanese withdrawal routes, New Britain, January–March 1944. Courtesy of the Marine Corps Historical Center.

These patrols were to advance from Agulupella on the east-west track, down the Government Trail all the way to Gilnit, a village on the Itni River, inland of Cape Bushing on New Britain's southern coast. Before Puller could set out, translated information discovered at Matsuda's former headquarters revealed that the enemy actually was retreating to the northeast. As a result, Gen. Rupertus detached the recently arrived 1st Battalion, 5th Marines and reduced Puller's force from almost 4000 to fewer than 400. That was still too many to be supported by the 150 native bearers assigned to the column for the march through the jungle to Gilnit.

During the trek, Puller's Marines depended heavily on supplies dropped from airplanes. Piper Cubs capable, at best, of carrying two cases of rations in addition to the pilot and observer, deposited their loads at villages along the way. The 5th Air Force B-17s dropped cargo by the tons. Supplies delivered from the sky made the patrol possible, but did little to ameliorate the discomfort of the Marines slogging through the mud.

Despite this assistance from the air, the march to Gilnit taxed the ingenuity of the Marines involved and hardened them for future action. This toughening-up seemed especially desirable to Puller, who had led many a patrol during the American intervention in Nicaragua from 1927 to 1933. The division's supply clerks, aware of Puller's disdain for creature comforts, were startled by requisitions from the patrol for hundreds of bottles of insect repellent. Puller had his reasons, however. According to one veteran of the Gilnit operation, "We were always soaked, and everything we owned was likewise. That lotion made the best damned stuff to start a fire with that you ever saw."

As Puller's Marines pushed toward Gilnit on the Itni River, they killed perhaps seventy-five Japanese and captured one wounded straggler. The Marines also captured some weapons and odds and ends of equipment. Also taken back was an American flag, probably captured by the soldiers of the 141st Infantry during Japan's conquest of the Philippines.

After reaching Gilnit, the patrol fanned out but encountered no further opposition as they advanced toward the southern coast. Although some of the Japanese got through, for all intents and purposes, the search-and-destroy patrols were deemed successful.

[20] Cape Gloucester in Perspective

The brutal struggle for the island of New Britain, lying 400 miles south of the equator off the eastern New Guinea coast, offered its own unique brand of torment to both Japanese and American combatants who fought there in late 1943 and early 1944. Steamy jungles, torrential rains, and dogged Japanese resistance confronted U.S. forces with a test worthy of the world's best fighting men. Gen. MacArthur declared that: "This war has shown no finer victory."

Here, apparently, military teamwork came near to perfection. Here, it would seem, that components of the Amphibious Task Force—air, naval and ground—cooperated so smoothly as to make the results easy. Frank Hough, a Marine historian with a strong distaste for overstatement, called the invasion of western New Britain "the most nearly perfect amphibious assault in World War II."

The truth is that nothing was easy on Cape Gloucester. Jungle, swamp, and mountain combined with atrocious weather to multiply our problems. The Japanese held an inestimable advantage because of their familiarity with the terrain, one that they exploited with great skill. It took maneuvers on our part to cope with this array of difficulties. Before the fighting ended, it had sprawled over more ground than any other Marine campaign of the war.[1]

Each side lost hundreds of others—dead or incapacitated because of accidents or tropical diseases ranging from malaria to jungle rot, a fungus that readily developed into disabling sores. Mosquito-borne

malaria threatened the health of the Marines, who also had to contend with other insects, little black ants, little red ants, and big red
ants on an island where even the caterpillars bite. Although Marine
veterans of the fighting might argue otherwise, the Japanese probably
suffered more grievously from disease. Even before the battle began,
the defenders had run short of food and medicine, a result of air
strikes that sank Japanese barges carrying supplies along the coast.

Sometimes the weather was worse than the enemy. At Cape
Gloucester, sixty-four inches of rain fell in a single day and bulldozers
vanished in the spongy, bottomless swamps. On the first day of the
invasion, December 26, the first storm struck: a solid wall of water that
lasted for hours. The wind roared in from the Bismark Sea at hurricane
velocity, bringing down giant trees with splitting crashes. The Marines
liked to say of Cape Gloucester that in the wet season it rained all day,
every day, whereas in the dry season it only rained every day.

To some who fought there, it seemed the campaign was planed to
coincide with the onset of the monsoon season, for torrential rain
began falling early in the afternoon of D-Day. During the early
morning hours of December 27, 1943, a terrific storm struck the Cape
Gloucester area. Rains continued for the next five days. Water backed
up in the swamps in rear of the shoreline, making them impassable for
wheeled and tracked vehicles. The many streams that emptied into the
sea in the beachhead area became raging torrents.

Troops were soaked to the skin, and their clothes never dried out
during the entire operation. Most of the men not in front-line foxholes slept in the newly issued jungle hammocks, undoubtedly one of
the most complicated methods of sleeping ever devised for use by
troops in a combat environment. A Marine entered his hammock
through an opening in a mosquito net, lay down on a length of rubberized cloth, and zipped the net shut. Above him, also enclosed in the
netting, stretched a rubberized cover designed to shelter him from the
rain. Unfortunately, gales as fierce as the ones we experienced on Cape

Gloucester set the cover to flapping like a loose sail and drove the rain inside the hammock. In the darkness, a gust of wind might uproot a tree, weakened by flooding or the effect of the preparatory bombardment, and send it crashing down. A falling tree could topple into a hammock occupied by one of the Marines, who would drown if someone did not slash through the covering with a knife and set him free. (B Company Pioneers lost several Marines, including one of our most capable and respected officers, because of a falling tree. Some fifty Marines were killed of suffered injury during the campaign from trees brought down by wind or shellfire.) Despite these shortcomings, a majority of men in the division found the hammocks more comfortable than curling up on a poncho in the mud. Rain filled up our foxholes, so we were forced to lie on top of the ground if we didn't use a hammock. In some cases it was a choice of drowning or getting shot.

The island's swamps and jungles were an ordeal even without the wind, rain, and disease. At times, we could see no more than a few feet ahead of us. Movement verged on the impossible, especially where the rains had flooded the land or turned the volcanic soil into slippery mud. No wonder that the assistant division commander, Gen. Shepherd, compared the New Britain campaign to "Grant's fight through the Wilderness in the Civil War."

The battle at Suicide Creek, Aogiri Ridge, and the fight for Hill 660 typify the Cape Gloucester campaign. It was a struggle of brave men against the enemy, the elements, and the unknown. The men of the 1st Marine Division had plunged into that unknown and emerged triumphant. After a final action on April 22 that completed the destruction of the retreating Japanese, Marines occupied the village of Talasea midway up the Willaumez Peninsula, which effectively cut off any Japanese remnants still on western or southern New Britain. Marine units advancing into Talasea were surprised to find a luscious plantation, ringed with tempting fruit trees and stunning tropical flowers

Tanks found it rough going on Cape Gloucester, New Britain. Courtesy of the Marine Corps Historical Center.

and bordered by a peaceful harbor. One Marine who was there said it was "like finding heaven in hell."

After a massive bombardment of Rabaul, a major naval and air base had been isolated and left to wither on the vine. In the New Britain area, 50,000 Japanese troops were pinched off and left to starve when Rabaul was bypassed. Capture of the air base on New Britain enabled us to bomb and harass the Japanese at will.

The 1st Marine Division was jungle-wise and combat-ready when it landed on New Britain. When we left, four months later, our mission accomplished, we were an even more effective team. Ahead for the division would be months of intensive training for the newly arrival replacements and then combat again, this time at Peleliu, one more bloody step closer to Japan.

Sgt. Kerry Lane in a bivouac on Cape Gloucester. The author is carrying his weapon of choice, the Winchester 12-gauge Model 97 shotgun. Courtesy of the author.

One of the new weapons in the division's arsenal during the Cape Gloucester campaign was the M4 medium tank, nicknamed the "Sherman" in honor of William Tecumseh Sherman, whose Union troops marched from Atlanta to the sea. The M4A1 model used by the Marines weighed 34 tons, mounted a 75-mm gun, and had frontal armor some three inches thick. Although a more formidable weapon than the 16-ton light tank, with a 37-mm gun used at Guadalcanal, the medium tank had certain shortcomings. A high silhouette made it a comparatively easy target for Japanese gunners, who fortunately did not have a truly deadly antitank weapon. Also, narrow treads provided poor traction in the mud of New Britain.[2]

Though the struggle at Cape Gloucester did not inspire long chronicles written for posterity, what was accomplished there was as important as the results of other campaigns. As always, the men never ignored an opportunity to attack. They risked their lives, not for some fantasy or slogan, but for the buddies at their side. Guadalcanal stopped the enemy's progress. Cape Gloucester would prompt the evacuation of Rabaul, because the enemy began to realize that the United States was determined to dictate the terms of peace in Tokyo.

In early May 1944, the division was relieved by the Army and there was a good deal of conjecture and discussion on the possible employment of the division. Many hoped that instead of moving to a staging area on another island, the convoy would proceed directly to Melbourne, Australia. Both officers and enlisted men could not visualize the employment of the division in the near future. They felt that rest, reorganization, and rehabilitation were an absolute necessity. Regardless of the speculation about returning to Melbourne, as everyone had hoped, we watched the shore of Cape Gloucester recede as our ship pushed through the Pacific and away from New Britain and bound for Pavuvu, Russell Island. The day was May 4, 1944, four months since the 1st Marine Division had attacked and won the Japanese stronghold.

I remember the struggles, tragedies, and even a few good times. The highlight of the campaign for me came when the late B. Gen. Francis I. Fenton, on behalf of the president of the United States, presented me with the Silver Star, awarded for valor during the Battle of Suicide Creek for my actions in bulldozing a path and guiding the tanks across the creek, and the Purple Heart, awarded to those wounded in combat. I've been asked many times about being a recipient of the

B. Gen. Francis I. Fenton, in the name of the President of the United States, presents the Silver Star to S. Sgt. Kerry Lane (second from left, first row) for conspicuous gallantry during the battle of Suicide Creek at Cape Gloucester, New Britain. Courtesy of the author.

Silver Star, a medal awarded for conspicuous gallantry in action, while serving with the 1st Marine Division in World War II. I don't know what other men say, but I know in my heart that it's just like being on a ball team. No one man wins these things. I had thirty-three men in my platoon. A piece of that Silver Star belongs to each and every one of them.[3]

Since Guadalcanal days, I've said that probably the greatest heroes were the ones nobody ever heard of. They died out there somewhere, saving their buddies, probably performing an act that was well beyond the call of duty, and nobody would ever know about it. Those heroes probably outnumber all the Silver Star medal holders we've ever had in our country. Yet, none of them have ever been recognized. They are the real heroes.

In a campaign lasting four months, the 1st Marine Division had plunged into the unforgiving jungle and overwhelmed a determined and resolute enemy. Those Marines captured the Cape Gloucester airfields and drove the Japanese from western New Britain. A number of factors helped the Marines defeat nature and the Japanese. Unlike the Guadalcanal campaign, control of the air and the sea provided mobility and disrupted the coastal barge traffic upon which the enemy had to depend for the movement of troops, large quantities of supplies, especially badly needed medicines, during the retreat to Rabaul.

[21]   Pavuvu

The 1st Marine Division departed Cape Gloucester in two echelons on April 6 and May 4, 1944. My unit, the 17th Marines, sailed in the second echelon. Left behind was the 12th Defense Battalion, which continued to provide anti-aircraft defense for the Cape Gloucester airfield until relieved by an Army unit in late May.

If nightmares are a special kind of dream, then Pavuvu was a dream. When we entered Macquitti Bay we never imagined that we would stage on the largest of the Russell Islands, ten miles wide and 1500 feet at it's highest point, located sixty miles from Guadalcanal. The coconut trees swayed in the breeze. It wasn't Melbourne, but it was beautiful.

That is until night set in and the rats took over and the land crabs assaulted far beyond the beaches. There were so many hordes of rats that flame throwers were used to kill them. Twice as many would return the next night. If you didn't shake out your boondockers in the morning, you might just stick your foot into two or three land crabs.

On Pavuvu we were expected to prepare for the next battle in an atmosphere of undernourishment, malaria, jungle rot, dysentery, and almost unbearable boredom. The ground was like Cape Gloucester, ankle deep in mud. Coral, brought in helmet load by helmet load, had to serve as tent decks. For some time there were no electric lights, no mess hall, no slopchutes. God always seemed to provide water for afternoon showers, but you had to gauge your lathering as best as you could. Some of the men suffered severe concussions from being beaned by coconuts, but I doubt any Marine was ever awarded the Purple Heart for being hit on the head by a falling coconut unless he had evidence to convince the awarding authority that the enemy did it while that Marine was engaged in mortal combat.

I recall hearing the following story while attending one of the "Old Breed" Marine Reunions: One Sunday night on Pavuvu, our chaplain told us during one of the few times we were able to have service that we were going to have a collection. He told us about the missionaries who had saved our downed fliers and seamen; they had taught the natives that we were there to help them regain their freedom. He gave a very short sermon in which he said, "Now look here! You have money in your pockets and you can't do anything with it except gamble. So I want you to help these people get started again. All right now, we'll pass the hat!" Incredibly, he collected over $20,000.

To this day, aging survivors of the old breed continue to seek an answer to a decades-old nagging question: "Why the hell did we end up in Pavuvu?" Enlisted men who volunteered only for wartime duty and career officers, now retired, still harbor deep feelings of bitterness and resentment about the time they spent there. Several explanations have surfaced through the years of why Pavuvu was selected as the 1st Marine Division's base camp to prepare for the invasion of Peleliu. Some are from little-known official documents. Others reflect the personal instincts and wisdom of salty career Marines, from sergeants to generals.

Regardless of the reasons, Pavuvu was nothing short of unmitigated agony and privation during most of the four months the division was there. It was a terrible place, and it would remain a nightmarish memory for many years to follow. In Melbourne there were enough good things to go around, and around they went. At Pavuva nothing was good, and everyone shared the bad.

Things were looking up by the end of July. First and foremost was the arrival of 4860 replacements. This meant that slightly more than half of the division's veterans, with two or more years of overseas combat duty, might be going home. This was cheering news to those actually returning to the States, but it did little to raise the spirits of those left behind.

Despite my request to remain with my unit for the upcoming Peleliu campaign, I was ordered home for extensive treatment at the chronic malaria treatment center being established at Klamath Falls, Oregon. While this treatment was helpful at the time, I never lost my malaria. It will most likely revisit me the rest of my life and send me again and again into a darkened room where, beneath layers of blankets, I'll shiver with the fever.

I departed with great pride in my outfit and my fellow Marines who accomplished so much. I had witnessed innumerable instances of cool courage, bold bravery, and unselfish heroism blended with faith, friendship, and self-sacrifice.

[22] Homeward Bound

Almost everyone came down to the pier to see us off, including the division band. As we went aboard ship they played "Mairzy Doats," "The Moori Song," and a tune appropriate for the occasion, "California, Here I Come." The band repeated the last verse over and over again until the troop transport USS *General Howze* was out into Macquitti Bay. Then the band broke into the pride-inspiring Marine hymn "From the Halls of Montezuma." The band played the last stanza over and over until we cleared the bay and put out to the open sea.

On the first day at sea, nature threw its own brand of terror— a typhoon—into the ship's path. For two days we experienced terrifying seas, and it was almost impossible to go up on deck. But for the remainder of our voyage it was one of calmness both at sea and on board. Typhoon warnings were issued on several occasions, but they generally ended in a driving rain that forced us only temporally below deck.

Other than the first two days of rough seas, our trip home was a pleasant journey. Our ship the *General Howze* had such high speed it didn't bother with escorts or a zigzag course. And of course, the faster it moved, the better we liked it. It was a welcome relief to be on a clean ship, with good food and freshwater showers, that was not crowded on deck or below. The ship's captain and crew made every effort to attend to our needs and to make our voyage home a pleasant one.

The shipboard conversation was largely about what we were going to do once ashore. Most spoke of such things as a good meal, a decent bed, a private bathroom, or driving a car. Some of the big spenders spoke of such things as a lobster dinner at Fisherman's Wharf and spending a night in a suite at the Mark Hopkins Hotel overlooking the waterfront and the Golden Gate Bridge. Others talked of kissing the ground of "the good old USA," and a few threatened to kiss the first American girl they saw. All were anxious to get home, but we had learned to wait. We passed the hours talking, sleeping, and standing at the ship's rail looking at the rolling horizon. Very few spent time writing; what they had to say would soon be delivered in person.

Each day, along with the "Now hear this" announcements made throughout the ship, would come the information about the ship being on schedule. Finally, the time came when the ship's captain announced that on the following day, about noon, we should be able to see the Golden Gate Bridge. The information was met with great excitement. It was both a cheer of joy and a tribute to us for having survived the ravages of war.

By midmorning the following day, the ship's rail was crowded with those waiting to get a first glimpse of California. We had all been packed and ready to go since daybreak. We stood at the rail as the ship moved along the California coast. The ship slowed, as ships do near port, and seemed to creep through the waves. Then, finally, there stretched before us was the glistening Golden Gate Bridge, magnificent, graceful, and strong. As we passed under it, we looked up. We moved slowly by Alcatraz, where a slight mist purpled the elegant landmark. The flickering hues of the clouds mingled with the swirling blues of the russet brown surrounding hills.

Passing under the Golden Gate that August day in 1944 was like a fresh start at life. We made it. After two years in the Pacific, I had earned five combat stars, a Silver Star, a Purple Heart, a presidential citation for outstanding gallantry, and promotion to the rank of staff sergeant.

That's about as good a life as you can get. For most of us, the terror of combat had faded from our psyche. We could look forward to pretty girls, good food, and cold beer.

If I could relive any year of my life, it would be the year that started in mid-July of 1944. There had been the jovial speculation that the war would end in 1948, and one could hear the phrase, "The Golden Gate in '48." Were it not for the atomic bomb, that date would have been a good guess.

I doubt if any of us expected a big welcome ceremony—I know I didn't. We had received the greatest gifts of all: we were alive and we were home. Among us there were those who wept, and we were not ashamed. When we docked in San Francisco, all of us were yelling and waving. We got no more than smiles from the few deck hands and female bus drivers. I don't recall seeing anyone kissing the ground or displaying any inordinate acts of patriotism when we got off the ship. We felt relief. I'd say we were about as happy and free of ill will as mortals could be. By the luck of the draw, we had survived. No one questioned why we had survived while others had not. For myself, it's always what's ahead that counts, not what's behind.

Shortly after our arrival in San Francisco, we were bused for several hours to Camp Pendleton, the big Marine Corps base north of San Diego, where we were processed. After a general orientation and a complete physical examination, I was granted a thirty-day leave to visit my family in North Carolina. In addition, I received thirty extra days for convalescence and travel. After that I would report to the chronic malaria treatment center established at the Marine Barracks in Klamath Falls, Oregon.

Homecomings are always something special. Mine, in September 1944, was no exception. It was great to be with my family again after two years of fighting in the war. One thing that stands out in my memory was the reaction of my father, who was very stern and seldom showed any emotion. That was the first time in my life I ever saw him cry. He just stood there in the driveway to the farm with tears streaming down his cheeks as we embraced. He said, "I'm glad you are home, son."

The years of World War II were hard years for many. Even the ones who stayed home knew that a war was going on. Almost everything was rationed. Farmers like my family were allowed three gallons of gasoline per week, and they did not ask for more except if there was an emergency. I was very thankful that my family saved several gasoline coupons for my use while I was home on leave.

The evening after dinner on my first day at home, my father and I started our conservation as we usually did. I asked him how the farming was going. He replied that he could not complain. At that time many people were complaining about the low price of tobacco, cotton, peanuts, and other farm commodities. I asked him, "How on earth could you feed and clothe the family during a depression period when prices for all farm products were so low?" He said, "Well, I'll tell you son. When I went to town, I didn't buy what I wanted, and I didn't buy what I needed. I just bought what I couldn't get along without."

Nothing much had changed in regards to clothing and modern conveniences while I was away fighting in the war. My younger brother and sisters were still wearing hand-me-down clothing Mama made. The farmhouse was still not electrified. My mother didn't have a washing machine or clothes dryer, and the little house out back was still the place where one tiptoed lightly to in the dark whenever nature called. (Some outhouses had toilet paper, but more commonly an old Sears and Roebuck catalog lay there to be used as needed. In case of a dire necessity, one could always rely on a basket of corncobs in the corner.)

There still was no farm mechanization. Most farmers, like my Dad, still used the mule, the perennial beast of burden, to plant, cultivate, and harvest everything they grew. Farmers had the mule or workhorse to thank for every sweet potato, ear of corn, bushel of soybeans, and bale of cotton they grew. The few farmers who could afford a tractor were unable to use it exclusively because of the severe gasoline rationing during the war.

By the time of my arrival, there was a new slogan sweeping the countryside: "Gardening for Victory." With wartime food supplies dangerously dwindling, the American people showed their patriotic spirit by planting, harvesting, preserving, and sharing. A victory garden on every farm and in every backyard, where possible, afforded the answer to part of the problem of feeding the nation.

American farmers, as they traditionally do in time of crises, stepped up to the challenge. Despite the critical shortage of farm labor, farm families like mine in rural eastern North Carolina were eager to help out by increasing the food supply. They planted a variety of popular basics vegetables like sweet corn, snap beans, cabbage, and potatoes and sold at roadside stands what they didn't need for their own consumption. My parents charged a nominal fee from those who could afford to pay. Those who could not were allowed to pick their own vegetables free of charge.

The long train trips across country and the time spent with my family while on convalescence leave provided me with the opportunity to evaluate the effect of war on the home front. During that time I never heard one person express any doubt that we could win the war. There was no job too hard and no sacrifice too great for Americans. The United States of America became truly great and reached her zenith during those hard years of sacrifice and austerity from 1941 to 1945. Her sons and daughters were proud to have served her, and they were proud of themselves and their country for giving their best.

Other than the visit with my family, the one thing that stands out in my memory is how the town people and neighbors treated the skinny kid who came home a decorated Marine. Everywhere I went people embraced me with respect and kindness. Although, most of them had read all about my heroic action during the war in the local and area newspapers, they still wanted to greet me personally and to talk about the war.

Ben Gibbs, the manager of the local movie theater, asked me to appear on stage before the main feature. I was introduced to the audience, which gave me a standing ovation. Needless to say, this was a very emotional event for me. I felt very humble, but very proud.

A good part of my time was spent visiting my hometown of Hertford, North Carolina. Downtown Main Street was the place to be, for it encompassed one entire block where all the major activities were located. On one side of Main Street were a bank on one corner and a hardware store on the other. Situated between them were the movie theater, the scenic town square, and the early-eighteenth-century Federal-style Perquimans County Courthouse. A family drug store on one corner and a Trailways bus station on the other corner anchored the other side of the street. Both had a soda fountain, snack bar, and booths. Sandwiched in between the two were the U.S. Post Office and the Hertford Café. This is where the townspeople gathered for their morning coffee and conversation. The proprietor, Sam "the Greek" Hourmouzer, also referred to as "King of the River," was a warm man with a great sense of humor. He loved to sit and talk, he was friendly, and he would be the first to help anyone. Sam was very patriotic. No serviceman or woman in uniform ever paid for a cup of coffee in his café.

A visitor to downtown Hertford today could easily be transported back to 1944, when I came home from the war. Most of the storefronts along either side of Main Street are still there. And while some of the names and faces have changed, the foundation remains the same. Sure, there has been a major effort in recent years to make Hertford's downtown historic district look more quaint and picturesque, but it's not the looks that makes this friendly rural community special—it's the people.

[23]　　**The Last Post**

　　　　　　　After I returned from the Pacific, the 1st Marine
Division went on to participate in the Peleliu and Okinawa campaigns.
Most of the officers and men had been in the South Pacific more than
twenty-four months before the assault on Peleliu. The Marines had
achieved the first victory by American ground forces in World War II,
at Guadalcanal. It was an epic event, considered by many historians to
be the turning point of the conflict against Japan. They had also conquered Cape Gloucester, New Britain, a success that was a major, if not
determining, factor enabling Gen. Douglas MacArthur to begin his
northward drive to recapture the Philippines, with the ultimate objective of forcing the unconditional surrender of the enemy.

　　All six Marine divisions during World War II had organic pioneer
battalions. True to their moniker, the Marine pioneers were innova-
tors. Pioneers performed shore party, demolitions, explosive ordnance
disposal, and provisional infantry tasks. Our flexibility also allowed us
to do more with less. "Every Marine is a rifleman" is more than just a
slogan. Combat support units like the Marine pioneers were fully
capable of defending themselves on the battlefield.

　　Ernest Hemingway, who knew something of men and war, wrote,
"I would rather have a good Marine by my side than anything in the
world when the chips are down." Most of the Marines I served with
during the Battle of Guadalcanal and the swamp battle known as
"Suicide Creek" believed it was better to die than to let one's comrades

down in combat. The ultimate payoff of this *esprit de corps* was a head-long aggressiveness that won battles. If it were not for the old breed taking the first step at Guadalcanal and the follow-up campaign of Cape Gloucester, which allowed island after island to be taken from these bases, I wonder where the Pacific campaign would have gone. Have they been forgotten already? For my many buddies left on the islands of Guadalcanal and Cape Gloucester, I hope not.

The young men of my generation who joined the Marine Corps and fought in World War II were among the best this nation ever had to offer. They were full of patriotism and had a gung-ho spirit. The greatest privilege of my life has been to wear the uniform of a U.S. Marine, to serve with a special group of men during war that shared my belief that as long as there is a nation, there will be a Marine Corps, and as long as there is a Marine Corps, there will be a nation.

My last military assignment was as commanding officer of the Ordnance School, Marine Corps Development and Education Command, at Quantico, Virginia, where I was also the base ordnance officer. I retired from the Marine Corps on June 30, 1971, at the age of forty-eight. At my change-of-command and retirement ceremony, I was awarded the Meritorious Service Medal for outstanding service.

Today, I live in a white Victorian-style farmhouse with white columns and a wrap-around porch by the side of the road. I raise Black Angus breeding stock and strive to be a friend to my fellow man. The hardships I have undergone only make the good part of my life that much more enjoyable. Much of my effort today is directed toward making my grandchildren, and the other young people of America, understand that if they are to have freedom, they must be prepared to fight for it. Because I have paid the price of sacrifice, I appreciate freedom all the more. In that respect, perhaps, what I have suffered is a godsend.

My main mission in writing this book is to memorialize and honor the veterans of World War II. My secondary mission is to educate the public, particularly the younger generation, on what people went through in World War II, what the war was about, and what we fought for. Often I am invited to speak at local schools on Veterans' Day. I relish the chance to remind the students of the men and women who gave their lives for the America that many of us take for granted. I want to leave our children with the knowledge that in order to do what they enjoy today—the freedom to do what they want to and to express themselves as they want—somebody, somewhere gave up their life. Freedom is not free, and we must remain strong and be prepared to defend our freedom and way of life.

So much of my journey since my retirement from the Marine Corps in 1971 has been gratifying to me. I have watched my children and grandchildren grow up and work the land. In the evenings my wife, Connie, and I often sit in the porch swing or rocking chairs, watching our herd of Angus cattle grazing on the lush, green pastureland nearby. It is so peaceful, especially in the twilight of the evening. But I feel a tinge of sadness for the young men at Guadalcanal and Cape Gloucester who were denied the blessings that have marked my life so far.

You can say, how much is life worth? I look at mine here, what I've had, and all the benefits of a good life. I think about those who died, left behind in battles in which I fought. I have awakened in the middle of the night many times thinking of the men I served with that never had a chance to come home, never had a family, never got to go to school. They made the ultimate sacrifice.

Our nation's colors fly from a tall flagpole in the corner of my front yard every day, and that flag is well lighted at night. The flag is there so that I don't forget the great sacrifices that were made to allow me the simple freedom of running up the colors. It is there to honor those who gave of themselves so that the rest of us might enjoy the freedom we take for granted. I fly the flag everyday so I don't forget those men I served with during World War II, the Korean War, and Vietnam. They are the men who didn't come home—a sergeant, a commanding

*The flag flying in the front yard of Lt. Col. Kerry Lane's Post
Oak Farm in Spotsylvania, Virginia. Courtesy of Bill Blevins
of the* Free Lance-Star. *Copyright © The Free Lance-Star,
616 Amelia St., Fredericksburg, Va. 22401. All rights reserved.
This photo may not be reproduced in any form or by any
means without written permission of the publisher.*

officer, and a friend—men I'll never forget. I fly it in memory of the
ones who returned, but in flag-draped coffins. And for the one's who
still remain behind somewhere, forgotten by their countrymen.

Each year surviving veterans of the 1st Marine Division who
fought in the epic Battle of Guadalcanal and at Suicide Creek on

In his book, Kerry L. Lane has allowed us to participate in his World War II experiences. He is now a gentleman farmer in the beautiful rolling farmland in historic Spot-sylvania, Virginia, a far cry perhaps from his never-to-be-forgotten days as a fighting Marine. Courtesy of the author.

Cape Gloucester, New Britain, gather for a reunion on August 7. We laugh and talk of friends who are gone. It is a special time because we share a bond that's hard for those who did not fight there to under-stand. As the Marine hymn plays and voices join in, there are tears. Standing tall is the author of this book, one of the few and the proud.

Years have passed and my memory isn't what it once was. Like many of my fellow Marines, I didn't keep records or diaries of all the incidents I was involved in during my thirty-two years of service in the Corps. I may have erred in some of the dates and times of events, but someone may contact me to refresh my memory. As I continue the journey into the sunset of my life, I know that as long as we have men and women in our armed forces who are willing to give us their last full measure of devotion on distant battlefields, there will always be a bright dawn ahead for America.

I was a callow youth when I joined the Marine Corps, but I came out of it with more confidence and the feeling that I was going to do the right thing. Not long from now I will be eighty years old. World War II ended fifty-eight years ago, and as I write this, the number of us who fought in that war grows smaller by the day. When the Lord calls me home, whenever that may be, I will leave with the greatest love for this country of ours and eternal optimism for its future. *Semper Fidelis.*

Glossary

American terms

Asiatic a Marine who had served in the Pacific too long
beating their gums bitching or complaining
boondockers Marine field shoes or boots
boondocks rough terrain; also called the "boonies"
cold cock to punch someone, knock him flying
cruise one tour of duty; an enlistment period
deck floor or ground
dogface (doggie) any soldier, no matter what branch
earbanger one who fawns on another for personal gains
galley swabbie Navy cook or messman
gear Marine equipment
gung ho motto meaning "work together"
gunny gunny sergeant
hard charger tough fighter who is always out front
head any form of toilet
K-bar Marine fighting knife that was great for opening cans
mustang officer who advanced up through the enlisted ranks
piece weapon a Marine's rifle, but never his gun
pogey bait an old naval term for candy, sweets, any snack
sack where Marines sleep, a bed or substitute thereof
scuttlebutt unfounded rumor; also a drinking fountain
sea bag Marine khaki barracks bag
shavetail lieutenant young inexperienced officer
skipper company commander
skivvies underwear
slopchute any place that serves beer or other alcoholic beverage
snow job deception
stand-down cease all operations for a period of time
stacking swivel nape of the neck

SOS shit on a shingle, dried beef on toast
swab jockey (swabby) slang for sailor of any rank
top, top soldier first sergeant, very important rank
under hack under arrest, restricted to quarters in case of officers
the word confirmed information

Australian terms

Aussie Australian
bloke a fellow or man
cobber a friend
digger Aussie soldier
fair dinkum honest to goodness
good-O, Yank good for you, you made it
Shelia a girl

Japanese terms

banzai charge
bushido way of the warrior, code of the samurai
hari-kari to commit suicide with a sword
rikusentai diehard; the Japanese special naval landing forces
sake alcoholic beverage made from fermented rice
tabis soft clover, hoof-type, two-toed, rubber-soled shoes
zenmetsu annihilated

Notes

Chapter 1

1. The eleven General Orders are: (1) To take charge of this post and all Government property in view; (2) to walk my post in a military manner, keeping always on alerts, and observing everything that takes place within sight or hearing; (3) to report all violations of orders I am instructed to enforce; (4) to repeat all calls from posts more distant from the guardhouse than my own; (5) to quit my post only when properly relieved; (6) to receive, obey, and pass on to the sentinel who relieves me all orders from the commanding officers (field officer of the day), officer of the day, and officers and noncommissioned officers of the guard only; (7) to talk to no one except in the line of duty; (8) to give the alarm in case of fire or disorder; (9) to call the corporal of the guard in any case not covered by instructions; (10) to salute all officers, and all colors and standards not cased; and (11) to be especially watchful at night, and during the hours of challenging, and to challenge all persons on or near my post, and allow no one to pass without proper authority.

Chapter 2

1. A fourragère is a military decoration awarded to an entire unit of troops, consisting of a colored and braided cord to be worn on the left shoulder by every member of the unit. To this day Marines who serve in the 5th and 6th Marine regiments continue to proudly wear the mark of distinction bestowed upon those Marines who went before them.
2. Today, some sixty years later, Marines still ride "tall in the saddle" at Guantanamo Bay, Cuba. Marines of Rifle Security Company Windward, U.S. Naval Station, use horses to patrol the fence lines separating the Naval Station from Communist Cuba.
3. McMillan, George. 1949. *The Old Breed: A History of the 1st Marine Division in World War II*. Washington, D.C.: Infantry Journal Press.

Chapter 3

1. A mustang officer is a former enlisted Marine who advanced up through the ranks or who received a battlefield promotion.

Chapter 4

1. Labor difficulties with the highly unionized stevedores resulted in the entire task being undertaken and carried through by Marines. Because of security regulations, no appeal to patriotism could be made to the regular dockworkers—care was taken to have civilians believe that the entire flurry was merely preparation for a training exercise.

Chapter 5

1. "Enemy troops strength is overwhelming. We will defend to the last man."—25th AirFlot Diary. Minutes after Tulagi radioed its last defiant message, shells from the cruiser USS *San Juan* smashed the radio shack with a broadside salvo. Tulagi was never heard from again.

2. In the first combat operation of an American parachute unit, the losses were twenty-eight killed and about fifty wounded; nearly all of the latter required evacuation. The dead included four officers and eleven NCOs. The casualty rate of just over 20 percent was by far the highest of any unit in the fighting to secure the initial lodgement of the Guadalcanal area.

3. Adm. Nimitz in a later review of all reports of the Battle of Savo decided not to censure any individual commander but did describe Fletchers withdrawal as "most unfortunate." Potter, E. B., *The Great Sea War: The Story of Naval Action in World War II.* But later, others could and did. In *History of United States Naval Operations in World War II: The Struggle for Guadalcanal* R. Adm. Samuel E. Morison categorically refutes Fletcher's statement that his ships were short on fuel.

4. "Appreciate the courageous and hard fighting of every man in your organization. I expect you to expand your exploits and you will make every effort to support the land forces of the Imperial Army that are now engaged in a desperate struggle." —Adm. Yamamoto

Chapter 6

1. McMillan, George. 1949. *The Old Breed: A History of the 1st Marine Division in World War II.* Washington, D.C.: Infantry Journal Press.

2. The celebrated American adventure novelist Jack London, who visited the Solomons in 1908, wrote: "If I were a King, the worse punishment I could inflict on my enemies would be to banish them to the Solomons. On second thought: King or no King, I don't think I'd have the heart to do it!"

3. The phrase "the whole nine yards" came from World War II fighter pilots in the South Pacific. When arming their airplanes on the ground, the .50-caliber machine-gun ammunition belts measured exactly twenty-seven feet before being loaded into the fuselage. If the pilots fired all their ammo at a target, it got "the whole nine yards."

Chapter 7

1. Because it was mismarked on the Americans' maps as the Tenaru, the savage confrontation that took place there was to go down in Marine annuals as the Battle of the Tenaru River.

Chapter 8

1. Apparently this was the shout that has passed into Guadalcanal lore as "Gas attack! Gas attack!" I regard with skepticism attributions of English phrases to Japanese infantrymen, although I am guilty of having perpetuated some myself (including this particular one) in wartime writings. *Totsugeki* means "Charge!"
2. Tregaskis, Richard. 1943. *Guadalcanal Diary*. New York: Random House.

Chapter 9

1. Familiar but unaffectionate names by which Guadalcanal defenders identified the nuisance raiders that droned around almost nightly. Technically, "Charlie" was a twin-engine night bomber from Rabaul, "Louie" was a cruiser float plane that signaled to the bombardment ships. But the harassed Marines used the names interchangeably. "Washing-Machine Charlie" was so called because the distinctive clanking rhythm of its engine sounded similar to a clothes washer.
2. During the retreat from Yorktown, Confederate forces planted several "land torpedoes" in way of the Federals, and thereby delayed somewhat the pursuit. Employed as booby-traps and placed at key points along the withdrawal route to Richmond, these "torpedoes" would burst with awful noise, scattering their death-dealing fragments among the pursuing Federal forces. Magruder, Maj. Gen. John B. 1862. *Lee's Lieutenants*. New York: Charles Scribner's Sons.
3. The USS *North Carolina* saw action in every major naval offensive in the Pacific. Hers is a history of daring-do and close calls, battling the worst that the Japanese military and nature could throw at her. Along the way she became the most decorated American battleship of the war.
4. "To the victors go the spoils: The spoils of war are as much a part of a warrior's right as his willingness to fight. It has always been that way and probably always will be." *Guadalcanal Echoes*

Chapter 10

1. The "ippon" ("log") bridge, as it was called on captured Japanese maps, was what the name implies: forest logs thrown across a narrow point in the gorge. But "Nippon" was a more familiar word to Americans than "ippon." The crude span became known in operations orders and reports, and later in Guadalcanal lore, as the "Nip" or "Jap" bridge.
2. *Guadalcanal Echoes*

Chapter 11

1. Shaw, Henry I. 1992. *First Offensive: The Marine Campaign for Guadalcanal*. Marines in World War II Commemorative Series. Washington, D.C.: Marine Corp Historical Center. The scheme of attack used during the Third Battle of the Matanikau was very much like a plan Gen. Robert E. Lee used at the Chickahominy during the Civil War, when he had Magruder make a demonstration south of the river and sent D. H. Hill and Longstreet across at successive bridges, with Jackson closing the trap at the rear.
2. The Americal Division, named for Americans in New Caledonia, was formed in 1942. It was the only division in the history of the U.S. Army to have a name rather than a number. It never served in the continental United States, except to discharge its soldiers to the Reserve List, during World War II. *Guadalcanal Echoes* 2002, no. 5, p. 4.

Chapter 12

1. Hoffman, Jon T. 2002. Guadalcanal: Chesty Puller's Defense of Henderson Field. *World War II Magazine* November, p. 34.

Chapter 13

1. The heroics of that day were recalled several years later by Maj. Warren S. Sivertsen during the 1st Marine Division Reunion, held in New York City. His account appeared in *The New York Herald-Tribune* in August 1947:

> Dawn, November 13, found the Cruiser *Atlanta* dead in the water, slightly down by the bow, listing to port, drifting toward Guadalcanal. She has sustained at least fifty hits. Fires were burning forward, and it was very quiet. *Atlanta's* crew put up a courageous but losing battle to save their ship. All wounded and surviving crewmembers were transferred to a fleet tug, out from Tulagi and landing boats from Kukum. As the burning *Atlanta* continued to drift toward enemy-held Point Cruz, concern about Japanese boarders continued to mount. An urgent message from the Navy Task Force Commander was received requesting every effort be made to deny Japanese boarders access to the highly classified and sensitive documents aboard the flagship.
>
> Fortunately, the Pioneers had a demolitions section headed by Kerry Lane, a Marine Sergeant, who loved to blow up anything. To Lane's ears an explosion was the sweetest music conceivable. He and his crew spent the afternoon improvising a large time bomb to be placed aboard the *Atlanta* as a scuttling charge. Marines ashore heard a loud explosion and watched as the *Atlanta* sank three miles off Lunga Point at sunset. Rear Adm. Scott's flagship came to rest in a body of water off Guadalcanal often referred to as Iron Bottom Sound.

Chapter 14

1. Davis, Burke. 1962. *Marine! The Life of Lt. Gen. Lewis B. (Chesty) Puller, USMA (Ret.)*. Boston: Little, Brown & Co.

Chapter 15

1. The chaplain read this poem during the memorial service:

   "The Chaplain wore no helmet and his head was bowed in prayer.
   His face was seamed with sorrow but a trace of hope was there.
   Our ranks were hushed and silent and diminished by our loss.
   At our feet, the rows of crosses told how much the battle cost.
   Rows of neat white crosses and the Stars of David too
   marked the gravesites of our brothers whose fighting days were through.
   Friends of mine were lying there
   Jim, Bill, Ski, Dusty and other's whose names I now forget.
   Each had a simple marker, but the one closest to me
   was a plain white wooden cross marked "Unknown USMC."
   In this final camp of comrades it was somehow strange and odd
   that a man should lie among them known only to his God."
   —Author unknown

   "And when he gets to heaven
   to St. Peter he will tell:
   'One more Marine reporting, Sir,
   I've served my time in Hell.'"
   —Epitaph in a cemetery at Lunga Point on Guadalcanal

Chapter 16

1. The patch was issued to the men after the Guadalcanal campaign. It was the first patch of the Pacific war. It shows a red numeral "1" on a field of blue, surrounded by five white stars that signified the Southern Cross, at which the Marines would gaze as they waited in their foxholes for the bombs or bayonet charge.
2. I eventually advanced through the ranks of the Marine Corps to become a commissioned warrant officer and received a field commission as second lieutenant some eight years later, during the Korean War. I was promoted to the rank of lieutenant colonel during the Vietnam War.
3. *The Sun News Pictorial*, Melbourne, Australia, December 29, 1943 (as provided by Thomas F. Shields, Kendall Park, New Jersey).

Chapter 17

1. This specialized training at the Australian Bomb Disposal School would prove to be invaluable in future assignments as a bomb disposal technician in World War II and as an explosive ordnance disposal officer during the Korean War, and later as the commanding officer of the 1st Explosive Ordnance Disposal Company, Force Troops, Fleet Marine Force, Pacific from 1957 to 1961.

Chapter 18

1. "The ingenuity and perseverance displayed throughout the Cape Gloucester campaign to bring tanks into action through terrain in which they were never designed to operate proved a source of wonder to many people." *VI Army Observer's Report.*

Chapter 19

1. Shaw, Henry I. 1992. *First Offensive: The Marine Campaign for Guadalcanal.* Marines in World War II Commemorative Series. Washington, D.C.: Marine Corp Historical Center.
2. Magnetic land mines carried by Japanese sappers who detonated them against the sides of vehicle could immobilize even the Sherman M4 medium tank.
3. Shaw, *First Offensive.*

Chapter 20

1. When the 1st Marine Division, reinforced, added up the costs of its four-month campaign on New Britain, the casualties totaled 310 men killed or died of wounds and 1083 wounded in action. When Gen. Rupertus relinquished command of Backhander Force to Gen. Brush, the toll of enemy killed and captured stood at 4288 and 420, respectively (1st Marine Division, April 1944 War D, entry of April 28, 1944).
2. A Sherman tank and Marine infantrymen, some using the M-1 for the first time in combat, formed a deadly team in the comparatively open country near the Cape Gloucester airfield during the early phase of the campaign. The M-1 rifle, a semi-automatic, gas-operated weapon, weighing 9.5 pounds and using an eight-round clip. Although less accurate at longer range than the venerable '03 Springfield, the M-1 could lay down a deadly volume of fire at the comparatively short ranges of jungle warfare. Another small-arms weapon that proved to be a deadly fighting instrument in short-range jungle warfare was the Winchester Model 97 military shotgun. Its awesome firepower and target saturation capability were unmatched by other military small arms. Only the shotgun fires a single round that launches a swarm of submissiles toward an intended target, and each missile processes a hit-and-kill probability.
3. I learned later that Puller told Capt. Palmer, my platoon commander, that he was going to recommend me for the Navy Cross. He did, but the Navy screwed up. V. Adm. Thomas C. Kinkaid, the overall Amphibious Task Force commander, retained awards authority. All recommendation for medals, including those recommended by Marine commanders ashore, had to be reviewed by his staff before being forward to the Secretary of the Navy for final approval. Somewhere in the process Puller's recommendation that I be awarded the Navy Cross was changed to the Silver Star Medal. I'm quite certain "Chesty" Puller would not take it lightly had he known that someone who never stepped ashore on Cape Gloucester changed his recommendation. I still get letters from Marines who feel very strongly that my bulldozer heroics at Suicide Creek was a Navy Cross effort and that I should request a review. I appreciate their support, especially from those Marines who were there. But Marines don't ask for awards, others make that decision.

Bibliography

Berry, Henry. 1983. *Semper Fi, Mac.* New York: Berkley Books.

Davis, Burke. 1962. *Marine! The Life of Lt. Gen. Lewis B. (Chesty) Puller, USMA (Ret.).* Boston: Little, Brown & Co.

Gallant, T. Grady. 1980. *On Valor's Side.* New York: Zebra Books.

Griffith, Samuel B. 1966. *The Battle for Guadalcanal.* New York: Ballantine Books.

Guadalcanal Echoes. Irvine, Calif.: Guadalcanal Campaign Veterans.

Hammel, Eric. 1987. *Guadalcanal: Starvation Island.* New York: Crown.

Hough, Frank. 1958. *The Island War.* U.S. Marine Manugram. Washington, D.C.: Washington Historical Branch, Headquarters Marine Corp.

Leatherneck Magazine. Quantico, Va.: Maj. Gen. Leslie M. Palm Marine Corp Association.

Leckie, Robert. 1979. *Helmet for My Pillow.* New York: Bantam.

Manchester, William. 1980. *Goodbye, Darkness: A Memoir of the Pacific War.* Boston: Little, Brown & Co.

Marine Corps Gazette. Quantico, Va.: Maj. Gen. Leslie M. Palm Marine Corp Association.

McMillan, George. 1949. *The Old Breed: A History of the 1st Marine Division in World War II.* Washington, D.C.: Infantry Journal Press.

Merillat, Herbert C. 1982. *Guadalcanal Remembered.* New York: Dodd Mead & Co.

Morison, R. Adm. Samuel E. 1966. *History of United States Naval Operations in World War II: The Struggle for Guadalcanal.* Boston: Little, Brown & Co.

Nalty, Bernard C. 1994. *Cape Gloucester: The Green Inferno.* Marines in World War II Commemorative Series. Washington, D.C.: Marine Corp Historical Center.

Pratt, Fletcher. 1948. *The Marine's War.* New York: William Sloan Associates.

Shaw, Henry I. 1992. *First Offensive: The Marine Campaign for Guadalcanal.* Marines in World War II Commemorative Series. Washington, D.C.: Marine Corp Historical Center.

Sledge, Eugene B. 1981. *With the Old Breed.* Navato, Calif.: Presidio Press.

Swearengen, Thomas F. 1978. *The World's Fighting Shotguns.* Alexandria, Va.: Chesa Ltd.

Tregaskis, Richard. 1943. *Guadalcanal Diary.* New York: Random House.

Index